PERSONAL CONSTRUCT
PSYCHOLOGY 1977

PERSONAL CONSTRUCT PSYCHOLOGY 1977

Edited by

FAY FRANSELLA

Academic Department of Psychiatry,
Royal Free Hospital School of Medicine,
London, U.K.

1978

ACADEMIC PRESS

London · New York · San Francisco

A Subsidiary of Harcourt Brace Jovanovich, Publishers

ACADEMIC PRESS INC. (LONDON) LTD.
24/28 Oval Road,
London NW1

United States Edition published by
ACADEMIC PRESS INC.
111 Fifth Avenue
New York, New York 10003

Library of Congress Catolog Card Number: 77-93494
ISBN: 0-12-265460-9

Printed in Great Britain

CONTRIBUTORS

BEARD, R.F. *Centre for the Study of Human Learning, Brunel University, Kingston Lane, Uxbridge, Middlesex, U.K.*

BOLTON, D.E. *Department of Psychology, Institute of Psychiatry, de Crespigny Road, London, S.E.5., U.K.*

DAVISSON, A. *Department of Psychology, College of Saint Benedict, St. Joseph, Minnesota 56374, U.S.A.*

FRANSELLA, F. *Department of Psychiatry, Royal Free Hospital, Pond Street, Hampstead, London, N.W.3, U.K.*

GIORGI, A. *Department of Psychology, Duquesne University, Pittsburgh, Pennsylvania 15219, U.S.A.*

HARRI-AUGSTEIN, S. *Centre for the Study of Human Learning, Brunel University, Kingston Lane, Uxbridge, Middlesex, U.K.*

KELLY, G.A.*

KERRICK-MACK, J. *Department of Anthropology, University of Washington; Counselor, Division of Adolescent Medicine, School of Medicine, University of Washington.*

MENDELSOH, M.B. *Department of Psychology, George Mason University, 4400 University Drive, Fairfax, Virginia 22030, U.S.A.*

MESHOULAM, U. *Department of Psychology, Merrimack College, North Andover, Massachusetts 01845, U.S.A.*

MURPHY, A. *Centre for the Study of Organizational Change and Development, University of Bath, Claverton Down, Bath BA2 7AY, U.K.*

PARRY, G. *MRC Social and Applied Psychology Unit, The University, Sheffield S10 2TN, U.K.*

PERRY, W.R. *Division of Mental Health, State of Hawaii Department of Health, Honolulu, Hawaii 96813, U.S.A.*

POPE, M. *Centre for the Study of Human Learning, Brunel University, Kingston Lane, Uxbridge, Middlesex, U.K.*

PROCTER, H. *Tone Vale Hospital, Norton Fitzwarren, Taunton, Somerset, U.K.*

RADLEY, A. *Department of Social Sciences, University of Loughborough, Loughborough, Leicestershire LE11 3TU, U.K.*

SALMON, P. *Institute of Education, University of London, 25 Woburn Square, London, W.C.1., U.K.*

SHAW, M.L.G. *Centre for the Study of Human Learning, Brunel University, Kingston Lane, Uxbridge, Middlesex, U.K.*

SIVERTSEN, N. *Rødbratbakken 5, Oslo 8, Norway.*

THOMAS, L.F. *Centre for the Study of Human Learning, Brunel University, Kingston Lane, Uxbridge, Middlesex, U.K.*

*deceased

PREFACE

This volume is not simply a selection of papers in the usual 'proceedings' sense although the contents are indeed based on talks given by the authors at the *Second International Congress on Personal Construct Theory* held in Oxford, England in July 1977. The Congress itself was unusual in having no selection procedure determining what should and should not be in the programme. Anyone could present a paper, guide a discussion group, run an experiential session or just talk.

But for this volume some selection had to occur. Over one essay there was no problem. We are delighted that Mrs. Gladys Kelly has given permission for us to include what must be one of George Kelly's few remaining unpublished papers. 'Confusion and the Clock' was written for a book he never completed, a book to be on and entitled 'The Human Feeling'.

Apart from this, we selected papers to show the diversity of ideas that George Kelly's original work is stimulating and the many-faceted nature of its appeal. In line with this, papers were further selected to represent the ideas of those whose work along similar lines has not recently been or is soon to be published - the New Faces criterion. To further illustrate the ramifications of George Kelly's ideas, abstracts of all talks, papers, work-shops and the like are included. The final result will, it is hoped, show what can and is being done with ideas stemming from the personal construct psychology approach.

ACKNOWLEDGEMENTS

The Editor is grateful to Mrs. Gladys Kelly for agreeing to the publication of the late George Kelly's paper 'Confusion and the Clock'.

The Editor also wishes to thank Don Bannister and Miller Mair for their constant encouragement, advice and practical help, which made the production of this volume possible.

CONTENTS

PERSONAL CONSTRUCT THEORY OR PSYCHOLOGY?

FAY FRANSELLA

*Department of Psychiatry, Royal Free Hospital,
Pond Street, Hampstead, London NW3*

The seeds of this Congress on personal construct theory
were sown during the results of that magnificent achievement of Al Landfield's in selling the theory to the Powers-
that-Be in Nebraska for the 1975 symposium. Not least of
the effects of that Nebraska meeting was to bring together,
for the first time, a group of people from all parts of the
world with one sole interest - the ideas of George A. Kelly.

That Nebraska Symposium in 1975 showed, by the number
of people attending, the speakers and the diversity of subject matter, that the time was right for the world to be
publically informed that Personal Construct Theory was a
force in psychology to be reckoned with. That a second
international gathering can number over two hundred people
is further evidence of increasing interest.

But what do we ourselves and others make of this evidence of our deep and enduring concern with the psychology
of personal constructs? What is the significance of this
act in which we are engaging? This behavioural experiment?

It clearly *has* significance for each one of us who is
here publically professing interest, as well as for others
who are not. But, first and foremost, what would have been
its significance for George Kelly himself? How would *Kelly*
have construed such an event - a man who was reluctant to
teach his own theory in his own University - a man who is
recorded as having said that if he found he was attracting
followers, he would write another theory? I wish I could
know his answer. On the face of it, his is a very grandiose
statement indeed. But it is, of course, a grandiose theory.
In fact it is a *total* psychology. So even more strange why
he should not want followers.

Perhaps, if he were here he would be threatened in some
way. If so, where might lie the threat, for Kelly, in having followers? His psychology of personal constructs has
lain relatively dormant for nearly 20 years and is only
now suddenly finding a collective voice. Perhaps the threat
is only in my construing of his constructions. Perhaps he
could have remained detached and would have waited to see

what we, the followers, were going to make of it and what
we were thinking of doing with it in the future. But for
a man who lived through, and with, and by, the psychology
of personal constructs - I think not. I believe that he
would have been very ambivalent about this Congress and
the previous gathering of interested parties, particularly
with many members seeing his psychology of personal constructs as an alternative psychology.

Perhaps, for him, followers would have meant disciples -
people who would want to keep the theory 'pure' and un-
sullied. Such people would then divide themselves into
factions, each vieing with the other to prove who has the
'best' interpretation of the Master.

He would be right to feel threatened for there is grave
danger to any theory when constructs are used in a pre-
emptive manner, but especially to the psychology of personal constructs - this and nothing but this is construct
theory. For such thinking is death to experimentation,
death to hypothesis making, death to reconstruction and,
perhaps because of its reflexive nature - death to personal construct psychology itself. Thus, perhaps Kelly
did see followers in this light and so would have had to
develop another theory because the followers would have
killed off the first one.

I submit that this Congress is threatening in a variety
of ways to many others besides Kelly. I can only speculate
privately as to the possible threats to individuals here.
But I suspect that for some the threat will lie in becoming publically associated with an alternative psychology.
It is one thing to privately rant and rave about the
iniquities of establishment psychology, to go about one's
business working within a personal construct psychology
framework in one's own field, and struggling to get the
odd journal paper published. It is quite another to publically stand up and be counted. By stating what you
stand for you are also making a statement about what you
are rejecting.

Let me speculate now about the significance that these
public statements of identity may have for the rest of
psychology. For many years, personal construct theory was,
by and large, seen as something that possibly academics
should know about, something to joke lightly about, to
even be vaguely pleased about since there are very few
theories of any calibre in psychology. Since for many it
clearly need not be taken seriously, it posed no real
threat. Yet there must have been *some* niggling doubts in
some minds surely. For instance, was it not odd that
students often demanded to be taught it? Just a few people
on the side-lines must surely have been keeping a weather-
eye open 'just in case'. In case of what? In case it found
a public voice and started to hold such things as International Congresses. I truly believe that this 1977 Con-

gress is indisputable evidence to other psychologists that
Personal Construct Psychology can no longer be ignored.
This must threaten and thus place the approach in very
real danger.

But these other psychologists, who may now be threatened
by the awareness of the coming-of-age of Kelly's ideas,
will see other evidence that personal construct psychology
has arrived on the public scene and so can no longer be
ignored. Almost any new book on personality you like to
pick up includes Kelly as one of the theorists to be discussed. I was at first pleased by this discovery - surprised but pleased. But this pleasant surprise soon became
tinged with disquiet. For how come it is being categorised
as a personality theory instead of the total psychology
that it is? I think that one of the reasons for the insid-
uous and so almost unnoticed development of interest in
this alternative psychology has been the inability of the
psychological world to agree on the constructions to be
placed upon it. While construed as unimportant, the element 'personal construct theory' did not have to be fitted
into psychologists' existing construct sub-systems to do
with their discipline, thus arousing no anxiety and posing
no threat. However, the gradually mounting evidence that
it must be taken seriously has meant that it can no longer
be left out in a psychological no-man's land. This must
lead to personal as well as professional threat since for
many, the professional sub-system has lines of implication
to core constructs.

One reaction to threat is to show hostility. So some
are saying, 'let us not construe it as an alternative
psychology, let us squeeze it into our existing psychological framework'. What better way is there to reduce
its importance than to categorise it as just another theory
of personality? That cuts it down to size! After all, if
academics are not teaching courses on personality, there
is no need to mention personal construct psychology at all.

Premature categorisation is bad enough, yet there is
more to the problem. Look at the majority of these personality texts. Even if the exposition of the theory is
good (and this is not always the case by any means) virtually no reference is made to *any* research work stemming
from it, or to *any* extensions of the theory, or to *any* of
its practical applications. A theory or a psychology can
only live by being knocked around, extended and, above
all, used.

If we take the psychology of personal constructs seriously, we must make sure that psychology does *not* compress
Kelly's work so that it can be slotted into a single
category and left for the dust to gather on it! People
should *not* be allowed to tuck it neatly away in a dusty
personality theory cupboard.

But such attempts to categorise and explain away or to

ignore the implications of the theory are relatively easy
to spot. There is an even greater threat, more hidden and
potentially much more dangerous. At the same time that
personal construct psychology is becoming seen as something that can no longer be ignored, many psychologists,
in many psychological walks of life, have elaborated their
own professional construct systems and 'incorporated' the
essential ideas of personal construct psychology and made
them their own. Jim Mancuso (1974) has already pointed to
this danger by giving examples of those using Kelly's
ideas and then calling them something else. Many are using
these ideas to prop up existing mini-theories rather than
using them to better understand those individuals the mini-
theories seek to describe. If this move continues, it will
effectively emasculate the theory. Personal construct psychology will become redundant and will be relegated to
the history books.

I am just going to take one concrete example to demonstrate this point. In a 1974 module on cognitive behaviour
modification, Donald Meichenbaum reviews the recent literature on the role of cognitive variables in stress and
emotional reactions. He starts by quoting from Epictetus
(1st century A.D.), 'Men are disturbed not by things, but
by the views they take of them'. Meichenbaum takes as his
example two people who are to give a public lecture, one
has high- and one has low-speech anxiety. During their
lectures, some members of the audience walk out. The high-
anxiety individual says to himself, 'I must be boring'
and so forth, the low-anxiety individual says, 'they must
have another appointment, too bad they have to leave and
miss a good talk'. This, in 1974, inidcates, to a behaviour
therapist, that those 'pesky' cognitive variables he always
suspected were lurking around the corner are indeed really
there. So, he says, if we cannot sweep them under the car-
pet, let us have them out and see how we can best deal
with them. Few would deny that that is a reasonable way
to behave.

Meichenbaum then cites one research strategy which is
designed to assess the role of these pesky cognitive variables in stress reactions. This is to directly influence
'the subject's appraisal system' (p.3). How does one do
this? One either provides the subjects with a particular
'interpretations framework' or 'the environmental circumstances may be manipulated so as to influence the subject's
sense of self-control and competence ..... presumably, an
individual will appraise a potentially aversive situation
as less threatening if he perceives himself as having some
control over the aversive stimulus' (p.3). Meichenbaum
summarises existing research as indicating 'that how one
responds to stress in large part is influenced by how he
appraises the stressor, to what he attributes the arousal
he feels, and how he assesses his ability to cope' (p.4.).

This, twenty years after Kelly's work was published!

Meichenbaum, not unreasonably, goes on to describe the division he sees between the semantic therapies (which include Kelly's) and behaviour therapy as 'becoming more fuzzy all the time and indeed may be indistinguishable' (p.12). His answer? *Cognitive behaviour modification* which is 'designed to influence the nature of the client's internal dialogue' (p.17).

Should we be concerned about these events which I choose to construe as placing Kelly's ideas in jeopardy? It will surely depend in part on how much we ourselves have invested in personal construct psychology up to now - which in turn determines the degree of our own threat at the possibility of its being subsumed within other psychological systems. It will also depend on how strongly we feel about Kelly's basic ideas on what psychology should be about.

One of Kelly's great concerns was to provide a way of thinking about, and coming to understand, human beings which necessitated the use of no constructs 'foreign' to the theory. Hence his rejection of the constructs of learning and motivation. He did not deny a person's right to use these constructs, but if 'learning' or 'motivation' are considered within a personal construct psychology framework, they just look different or are seen to be redundant. Whether a construct in another theory is seen as useful or redundant will largely depend on its lines of implication. Kelly looked at the construct 'transference', elaborated it and used it. But if we take the construct 'oral fixation' we see it has lines of implication suggesting something 'fixed', 'occurring in very early childhood' and related to another construct, that of 'psychic energy'. Many individuals working within construct theory will have no difficulty in using, and finding useful, the notion that construing takes place at a very early age and can affect our present behaviour. But they may find it necessary to reject the notion of a psychological energy system, and so will need to alter Freud's notion of 'oral fixation' beyond his recognition or else will find it not useful. This must surely be one of construct theory's greatest strengths. It allows us to consider any of the many important ideas in other approaches and to incorporate those we consider useful within our single theoretical system.

If we wish to preserve Kelly's theory intact until such time as we have examined its full potential as a total psychological system, how do we prevent it being taken over by, for instance, the behavioural modifiers? I believe we must come down from our Mount Olympus and mix with the common herd - *we must get our hands dirty!!* For too long we have fostered our personal pleasure in the theory, showing how, by asking different questions, it can make psychology look different. But I do not think we can any

longer hope to succeed by following that strategy alone.
The psychology of personal constructs will have ceased to
exist before that happens - the threats we are posing for
the rest of psychology are too great. We must be prepared
to enter the territory of the behaviour therapists and
show them that their search for a framework within which
cognitive variables and behaviour can be studied together
is available. *If behaviour therapy is up for grabs - we
must be in there doing the grabbing!* We must enter any
field in which there is at present no theory or philosophy
of the person to demonstrate the potential usefulness of
this alternative approach. This would include most of
those areas so beloved of the textbook authors, called
memory, perception, emotion, psychopharmacology, psycholinguistics and psychophysiology. Kelly did not look upon
his ideas as adding up to just another theoretical statement - for him the psychology of personal constructs was
something that lived - it was something that was relevant
to all psychological aspects of all creatures - it was
a *total* psychology with the person as its focus. So let
all prefixes of 'psycho' refer to Personal Construct
Psychology.

I can see no way of minimizing the dangers that now
confront Kelly's psychology. We can be our own worst
enemies and kill this alternative psychology stone dead
by tightening our construing prematurely; we can allow it
to be prematurely classified and tucked neatly away in
some psychological hideyhole; or we can allow it to be
subsumed and so made redundant. If any of these things
are allowed to happen, we are here attending a funeral
rather than a Christening.

I believe we should make it clear that we think the
alternative psychology of personal constructs is, potentially, more productive, more useful and more personal than
any existing approach. *We are making a take-over bid for
the discipline of psychology.* We must not allow it to be
incorporated within existing psychological frameworks -
if we have to we must do the incorporating. It is up to
each one of us to see that it is kept alive and active,
constantly being elaborated by being open to ideas in
other frameworks, thus constantly changing and constantly
threatening!

PROBLEMS ENCOUNTERED IN DEVELOPING A PHENOMENOLOGICAL APPROACH TO RESEARCH IN PSYCHOLOGY

AMEDEO GIORGI

Department of Psychology, Duquesne University, Pittsburgh, Pennsylvania 15219, U.S.A.

I would like to begin with two quotes from two respected scholars, whose names you will instantly recognise, but first I would like to present to you the relevant quotes. The first is as follows:

The chief characteristic distinguishing the (New Psychology) from the old psychology is undoubtedly the rejection of a formal logic as its model and test. The old psychologists almost without exception held to a nominalistic logic. This of itself was a matter of no great importance, were it not for the inevitable tendency and attempt to make living concrete facts of experience square with two supposed norms of an abstract, lifeless thought, and to interpret them in accordance with its formal conceptions. This tendency has nowhere been stronger than in those who claimed that 'experience' was the sole source of all knowledge. They emasculated experience till their logical conceptions could deal with it; they sheared it down till it would fit their logical boxes; they pruned it till it presented a trimmed tameness which would shock none of their laws; they preyed upon its vitality till it would go into the coffin of their abstractions..... The New Psychology is content to get its logic from (this) experience, and not do violence to the sanctity and integrity of the latter by forcing it to conform to certain preconceived ideas. It wants the logic of fact, of process, of life..... For this reason, it abandons all legal fiction of logical and mathematical analysis and rules; and is willing to throw itself upon experience, believing that the mother which has borne it will not betray it. But it makes no attempts to dictate to this experience, and tell it what it *must* be in order to square with a scholastic logic..... (Dewey 1884, pp.287-288).

The second, briefer, quote is as follows:

I have raised the question as to whether psychology

will remain a narrow technological fragment of a
science, tied to an outdated philosophical conception of itself, clinging to a security blanket of
observable behaviours only; or whether it can possibly become a truly broad and creative science,
rooted in subjective vision, open to all aspects of
the human conditions, worthy of the name of a mature
science (Rogers 1973, p.387).

The first quote is by John Dewey, in 1884, and the
second is by Carl Rogers in 1973. Both argue against outdated philosophy and abstractions in psychology. Dewey
expressed more of an optimism about what the 'New Psychology' could achieve, probably because he was nearer to
its beginning. One hundred years later, Rogers is much
more sober and resigned in making his plea. But then, he
has a century of experience behind him that Dewey did not
have. It would have been nice to have been able to make
the quotes perfectly symmetrical by quoting from a psychologist writing in 1984 - but we are not quite there yet.
But if we continue on the same course, I am sure there will
be some lonely, despairing, isolated psychologist in 1984
who is finally becoming fed-up with the way psychology is
developing, will take pen in hand, and begin a long sustained polemic about the problems with psychology.

I have begun my presentation with two quotations out of
hundreds that could be chosen, concerning promises and
pleas for a better psychology because, without ever con-
sciously choosing it, I have found that I have spent most
of my professional career engaged in the same task.

Indeed, my initial impulse, when I agreed to speak to
this conference, was to present to you my own version of
a constructive alternative to psychology, which is based
upon, but not limited by, phenomenological philosophy, and
more specifically upon the thought of Merleau-Ponty. Of
course, I could not give you the whole picture, but I
could give you a quick critique of traditional psychology,
a theoretical justification of why I adopt a phenomenological approach, a survey of some examples of this approach, and then end up with the usual strong plea that
more psychologists should be doing more of the same. However, I began to feel uneasy about this particular organization of the paper and an interrogation of my feelings
revealed that I was uneasy because here I was once again
making a plea for changes in psychology rather than presenting a full fledged example of the new psychology that
would be self-evident, self-sufficient and beyond all
criticism. How many times in the course of my career had
I made such a plea! How many times have I heard others
make such a plea! How many times have I seen in the recent
and older literature a call for a change in psychology.
How often have I read about the dawning of a new day in
psychology like Dewey's! Moreover, was I not speaking to

a group, whose members had organized, presumably, precisely
in order to implement a constructive alternative to psychology? Certainly the pleas are by now loud and clear.
Why add another voice to the chorus - especially to a
group that might already be in agreement with the major
thrust of the paper and is more interested in hearing
some solutions rather than another paper promising more
than it can deliver.

Thus my thoughts began to turn to the whole issue of
constructive alternatives in psychology and to why the
discrepancy between the perceived need for a change in
psychology and the actual achievement of a constructive
alternative was so great. The pleas for change are legion
the actual achievements miniscule in comparison. Even
discounting the excessive idealism that the fantasy of a
'criticism-free paper' held out for me, in cooler moments,
I was *also* aware that the demand that I had to produce an
entire counter-system in order to satisy my own criterion
of an acceptable paper was really an unreasonable imposit-
ion that I ought not have succumbed to - but I did. Why,
when anticipating a public presentation, do I get entangled
in the hopeless tension between defensive and cautious
expressions, on one hand, and unrealistic expectations,
on the other, when privately I know that both logic and
experience has convinced me that I am absolutely right
about the main point - viz. the practice and self-understanding of psychology has to change. What expectations
of what audience am I 'internalizing' to such an extent
that my truer conviction wavers? I am not at all sure
that I have answers to these questions, but these are the
issues I would like to bring to your attention today for
obviously I think they have a value beyond my own case.

I shall do this in the following way: I will first
sketch briefly the project to which I am committed, then
present an example of what I consider to be a sound approach and the beginning of a method for research in a
phenomenologically grounded psychology, and then give you
some idea of the difficulties I have encountered in attempting to communicate this project to colleagues of more
traditional persuasion.

A Phenomenological Approach to Psychology

First, the project. My training was in experimental
psychology, and more specifically psychophysics. I was
always impressed by the rigor of the scientific method as
such, but I was not sure why experiments had to be limited
to either animals or part-processes of humans. I kept
wondering why the whole person, or at least integral
human phenomena, could not be submitted to rigorous research. My first attempts were to try to apply the same
approach and method to such human phenomena and I came
to the conclusion that it could not be done. A better way

of understanding such phenomena was necessary and this
necessitated a change in method, and ultimately, a change
in approach. Any study of a concrete human phenomenon
requires that one considers the approach, method and content in relationship to each other (Giorgi 1970). In other
words, in order to achieve the same rigor with human phenomena I had to do different things because the phenomena
differed, and to make a long story short, my project is to
try to initiate a manner of doing rigorous research with
concrete human psychological phenomena as they are lived
(i.e. behaved and experienced) by human beings. Hence the
community to which I wish to speak most directly is the
scientific academic establishment, who, more often than
not, are quite content to continue along the well-worn
path of natural scientific psychology - sometimes more
liberally, sometimes more conservatively - rather than
turn to any constructive alternative. They have confidence
that the self-corrective process of science is sufficient
and nothing more is called for than 'normal science'. I,
on the contrary, do not share that optimism and I am convinced that a wholly new approach is necessary, although
certainly many findings of the traditional approach could
be integrated into what I call the human scientific approach - sometimes directly, but mostly with modification.
I have argued this point more thoroughly elsewhere,
(Giorgi 1976) and on a number of occasions, and I present
it here primarily for purposes of communication. If you
are interested, by the way, the response on the part of the
psychological community I am speaking to has been one of
almost total indifference. In any event, my project is to
attempt to replace the natural scientifically based research practice in psychology with a human scientifically
based one.

I would now like to present an example of a type of
concrete research within the framework of my own constructive alternative to give you some feel for what I am trying
to do. Let me say, by way of introduction, that I am using
the phenomenon of learning as an example, that my approach
is descriptive and my analysis qualitative thus far, and
that I want to study the phenomenon of learning precisely
as it is lived in the everyday world by ordinary people
before any psychological distinctions are introduced. My
claim is that the procedure about to be described follows
both phenomenological and human scientific criteria. First
I simply ask subjects the following open-ended questions:
'Please describe for me a situation in which you have
learned'. Sometimes answers are written, sometimes they
are taped in an interview. I have an example of each.

Example One

In a health food store in downtown Pittsburgh a friend
and I asked the clerk if she knew how to make yogurt. She

said 'yes' and proceeded to give us the recipe. This is
what I thought she said: 'To a half-gallon of milk, add
$\frac{1}{4}$ cup of plain Dannon yogurt, to serve as the culture.
Keep this mixture at a temperature between 90 and 110° for
five hours. Then chill the yogurt in order to make it
firmer'. Because of its simplicity, I did not write down
the recipe but assumed that I could remember it. I tried
the recipe about 10 days later. I added the $\frac{1}{4}$ cup of plain
Dannon yogurt to a half-gallon of milk. Then I put the
mixture in our oven at 110° and made a mental note as to
when five hours would be up. I checked the mixture four
or five times during the five hour period. I noted some
thickening in the beginning but it did not get past a
soupy consistency even after it had been in the oven for
five hours. Unsure as to whether it was progressing properly, but wishing to follow the directions and impatient
for the yogurt to be finished, I took the bowl out of
the oven and put it in the refrigerator thinking that perhaps it would firm when chilled. I checked it in the refrigerator once after two hours and again after four and
all that had occurred was the chilling of the soupy mixture. Then I decided that something had gone wrong and I
tried to think of what it was. I immediately considered
the period when I kept the mixture in the oven because I
was uncertain about it when I took it out. Perhaps I hadn't
given it enough time.. but the recipe said five hours ...
Aha! Although I had kept the bowl in the oven for five
hours, the recipe called for *keeping the mixture* at 90 to
110° for five hours and the mixture started out quite
cold. I added another $\frac{1}{4}$ cup of yogurt in case I had killed
the first yogurt culture by the temperature changes it
went through in the first unsuccessful run. I put the bowl
in the oven and left in in for 10 hours (overnight). When
I got up the next morning I checked it and the mixture had
become yogurt. I took it out of the oven and put it in
the refrigerator where it got thicker.
    The next day I described the experience to the friend
who had also heard the instructions given by the clerk in
the health food store. I described my mistake in keeping
the mixture in the oven for five hours where the instructions called for keeping the mixture at the high temperature
for five hours. I was at her apartment a few days later
when she was preparing to make yogurt. She had borrowed
a bowl from a neighbor to make the yogurt in because she
didn't have any large glass bowls. She took the bowl in
her hand and asked me if it would be big enough. I looked
at it had estimated that it was only $\frac{1}{2}$ the size of the
bowl that I had used, and my bowl could hold $\frac{1}{2}$ gallon of
milk. She looked at me in a puzzled way and told me that
the recipe called for a $\frac{1}{4}$ cup of yogurt per *quart* of
milk. On hearing this, I stopped for a moment and wondered
how mine could have worked since I had not followed those

instructions. Aha! I had added the extra $\frac{1}{4}$ cup of yogurt in case I had killed the first culture. Evidently I hadn't killed the first culture, and the two portions together were enough to turn the mixture into yogurt the second time around. So in spite of the fact that I had successfully made yogurt it was only after my friend had corrected my misconception that I knew how to make yogurt.

Example Two

Subject: You know I left my restaurant downtown to come here. All I wanted was a little delicatessen. Just what I needed for my restaurant and I thought I was rid of all the problems. Now, after last night I wonder if I can keep it up.
Researcher: What happened? I thought things were going well for you here.
Subject: They were. That is I thought they were until last night. I learned so much last night and now I don't know what I should do.
Researcher: What did you find out?
Subject: I learned about these girls (waitresses). Last night with the snow and all, the young crowd came here. This place was packed and business was great. Then I realized the girls were cheating. We must have cooked hundreds of hamburgers but when I went over the slips only a few people had paid for hamburgers. The girls gave their friends all this food and only wrote them a slip for a coke or a cup of coffee. This has been going on for months. Last night I caught them. I really didn't know what to do. I felt like I wanted to hit them; then I felt like crying because of all my hard work trying to make a go of it here. I learned that after all these months these girls don't have any respect for me. I also found out that they don't give a damn about their jobs. So I fire them, what do they care! All they are concerned about is getting a date for Friday night and giving away my food.

   In my restaurant downtown it was different. The girls wanted to work; they needed the jobs to keep their families. These kids today don't give a damn about anything. I don't know how much money I've lost. What a fool I have been! I've really been stupid! I learned last night what a foolish mistake it was to come here. I know now that I just can't handle young kids. I could hardly stand to come here today. I talked to them this morning and they just laughed and talked behind my back. Now that I know all of this, I don't know what to do. I guess I started out wrong. I think I need to get some new people and start all over again. This time in the beginning I'm going to be tough. Everyone will know from the start who is boss. We won't have the same problems. This time they are going to respect me. I learned last night that you sure can't run a restaurant unless you are respected.

Researcher: How was it that you learned all this last
night?
Subject: I don't know. I guess I was watching more than
usual and I knew we had sold lots of hamburgers. I watched
and listened to these kids. If I had stayed blind to this
whole thing much longer they would have walked off with the
store. I was just too trusting and I wanted to be their
friend. That does't work - you can't be the friend and
the boss. You can't run a restaurant without respect. No
sir, old Harry isn't going to be fooled any longer.

Confronted with data of this type, I had to come up
with an analysis that was penetrating, psychological and
potentially intersubjective. Condensing a more torturous
and sinuous process into an almost distorting schema, the
procedure that evolved is as follows: (1) I read the whole
description in order to get a sense of the whole; (2) then
I go back and read the description again, more slowly, and
delineate each time a translocation in meaning is perceived
with respect to the intention of discovering the meaning
of learning. This procedure results in a series of meaning
units. (3) I then clarify or elaborate the role of the
meaning units with respect to their revelatory power for
the phenomenon of learning by relating them to each other
and to the sense of the whole. (4) I then reflect in the
given meaning units, which are still expressed essentially
in the concrete language of the subject, and transform
those that are particularly revelatory of the learning
process into the language of the psychological science.
In other words, each meaning unit is systematically in-
terrogated for what it reveals about the learning process
in that situation for that subject, but it must be expressed more directly in psychological language rather
than remaining in the naive language of the subject.
(5) Next the insights that emerge from the analysis have
to be integrated into a coherent description that expresses the essential structure of learning for that situation. All meaning units have to be accounted for. (6)
The structure is then communicated to other researchers
for purposes of confirmation or criticism. (Another example is contained in Giorgi, Fischer and Murray 1975).
Thus, for the examples I used, the structures, described
at the highest level of psychological generality are as
follows: (*a*) First, learning is the extension of one's
ability to transform situations in the world beyond one's
current capabilities through the mediation of a significant other and is accompanied by the awareness that this
can be done on demand. (*b*) Second, learning consists in
the discovery of the fact that the life-project that the
subject thought he was realizing was not being realized
because the assumptions he held concerning the situation
were erroneous.

I want to make 3 general comments before moving in to

other aspects of my talk. First I want to speak about one
particular difficulty involved in communicating results
of this type of research in addition to the ones I shall
enumerate later. Unlike traditional research which has an
established community to speak to and which correctly or
incorrectly demands that the listener accommodate himself
to the mode of presentation of the researcher, in this
type of research the burden on the researcher to present
his findings according to the background and interests
of the listener is much more obvious. Thus, I presented
here the most general description of the structures, in
part because of time limitations and in part because I
am addressing a community of psychologists for whom the
description should make general sense, but it is clear to
me that a full appreciation of those structures is impossible without relating them to a discussion involving the
particulars of each situation whereby the general structures
would be clarified and elaborated, and presumably, supported by the details. However, to do that task adequately
would require a workshop setting rather than a talk and
thus I am limited to outlining a basic minimum.

Secondly, I want to mention that results from this type
of research lead to a typology of learning situations as
they occur in our present life-world - at least in the
West. Thus the first type is what I call 'behavioral
expansion', that is, the subject's repertoire of behavioral
possibilities has been extended as a consequence of the
learning, and the other type is what I call 'Breaking
Wrong Assumptions in a Situation' - and both these types
have appeared across many situations thus far in my research. A type, as I use the term, always implies the relation of a subject in a situation. There are many interesting problems associated both with the way in which
knowledge of such types leads back into the life-world
and difficulties concerning how best to express the types,
on one hand, and how they relate to psychological learning
theory, on the other. For example, with respect to life-
world feed-back, learning in the first case consisted in
being able to execute a process in correct sequential
order that led to a certain achievement and in general it
resulted in something better for the learner. In the second case, learning was, at least initially, costly for
the subject. He had to break out of his comfortable attitude and it was clear that the new demands placed upon
him by the discovery he had made would provide difficulties
for him since he obviously preferred to 'trust' people
and be their 'friend' rather than try to command respect
through authority or whatever. At a more theoretical level
it would be interesting to see how a view of learning
based on research such as this that more explicitly includes the subject's personal history and relations with
others as they relate to learning compares with more trad-

itional research based upon condition or verbal learning
paradigms. Unfortunately, most of that effort is still
before me.

My third point flows directly from my last comment.
It is painfully clear to me that I am just beginning this
research effort. I may even be willing to concede that I
am only on the threshold of genuine psychological research
as I would hope to understand it if I were at the end of
my project - assuming there is an end. But I am sure that
one must begin with descriptions of some sort, and come
to grips with the problems involved in trying to understand them in a psychological significant way, by doing,
either implicitly or explicitly, something similar to
what I have described. But I interpret this effort differently from many of my colleagues. I consider this phase,
the beginning and the search for adequate descriptions
and their interpretation, to be an important part of science itself. It is not something that is done once, historically speaking, and then assumed and forgotten - but
rather, something that has to be done again and again,
and we must keep confronting the problem of beginnings
with the more sophisticated achievements and try to cope
with the tension that such a confrontation produces.

Many of my colleagues assume that this kind of effort
was completed long ago and start researching at a more
sophisticated level without giving it further thought.

I mention these three points because I wanted to indicate that I am sensitive to some of the questions you may
have about the research I am doing, and also because I
wanted to provide at least a minimum of context for the
difficulties encountered in trying to communicate such
research.

Difficulties of Constructive Alternatives

External

Let me say at the outset that the most significant
problem I have experienced in trying to present findings
of the type I have just described as *both* what is really
necessary for studying genuinely psychological phenomena
as scientific is the understanding of science that is
accepted in our socio-cultural world - i.e. one which
implicitly or explicitly accepts the natural scientific
interpretation of science. I am most tempted to tell
colleagues that they should forget everything they learned
about being scientific and simply do any intelligent thing
they deem necessary to study a phenomenon adequately. But
then I would come back and call that science, because presumably, the procedure would have respected the nature
and mode of presentation of the phenomenon in question.
Why we are not all more suspicious of prescriptions that
tend to introduce tensions - not to say contradictions -
between human phenomena and the very access to them, is

indeed an interesting question. Be that as it may, the
interpretation of science is the major stumbling block and
it is my impression that all of the beliefs, opinions, confidence, values, etc., that we have in and concerning science today are such that it functions at the ultimate
arbiter of reality for our times as did theology and religion in the Middle Ages. Whatever we want to assert or
know must be checked against the body of discovered facts
and acceptable procedures of science - as though nothing
new could ever be created again outside that context -
just as all beliefs and opinions of the Middle Ages first
had to be checked against the body of revealed truths of
theology. The scientific world-view so encompasses our
perceptions, feelings and judgements that to challenge it
is to challenge reality itself. Yet, in my opinion, unless
this world-view can be relativized, psychology can never
become an authentic science. I shall now try to show in
a concrete way how the world-view of science functions,
and I shall do it in terms of psychology polarities.

Propaedeutic to Science vs. Real Science As alluded to
above, very often I hear that the descriptions and analyses
I have presented to you are all well and good, but they
are really just propaedeutic to science and what I have
to do now is to get on with the real task of science
which is - and then you can fill in the blank - to test
hypotheses about these learning situations, or else learn
to quantify them so that they can be made objective and
precise, or else to have them confirmed by others so that
we can go beyond my own subjective expressions, etc. In
my opinion, I can provide a reasonable response to all of
these objections and show how science itself participates
in the very thing it is objecting to in my presentation.
In other words, at the minimum, my position is defensible.
But the point I want to make here is simply that all objections of this type come from expectations concerning
a certain conceptualization of science; real science means
hypothesis testing, quantification, verification procedures,
etc. This type of objection is based upon the assumption
that one kind of science exhausts the general notion of
science or that the verification aspect of science and
science itself are one - and indeed those who hold this
review can find support for it in certain schools of philosophy of science. But there are other philosophies of
science and theorists of the practice of science (e.g.
Radnitzky (1970), Habermas (1973) that hold other views
and at the very minimum it must be admitted that the question is at least open, and that the reduction of the total
practice of science to one of its phases is at least debat-
able. But that dubiety and openness does not filter down
to practice. The burden is on those of us who want to express ourselves differently.

Face Validity vs. Real Validity There seems to be a strong
cultural bias against the very possibility that words or
meanings can be objective. Thus, to obtain descriptions
and analyze them qualitatively almost always has to be
accompanied by an 'apologia' that is usually twice as long
as the results themselves. Thus, although, again in my
opinion, an argument as tight as the one used for quantitative data can be made for the use of descriptive material,
a very real problem of 'face validity' exists, and if one
tends to ignore this question of 'face validity' then one
is literally unable to communicate what he or she had
found because the person experiencing this difficulty cannot hear the results as the researcher intends them. Thus,
one is forced to confront a huge communication problem,
that very soon becomes *the* major issue, rather than the
findings. The root of this difficulty is also the expectations that one has concerning science and the sense of
objectivity that science projects.

Dimensions of Science vs. Total Scientific World-View If
the problem were merely one of understanding objectivity
correctly, the precise role of measurement and quantification, or any other single aspect of science, then I think
the problem would at least be manageable. But it really
is a case of world-views that represent a system of inter-
connected dimensions that make it impossible to handle on
a one-by-one basis. Thus, some colleagues can accept that
approaches to psychology need not be atomistic, quantitative, from an external view-point, but will then insist
on a certain kind of objectivity that implies adhering to
the very features he was willing to concede. Or others,
may have no difficulty with any of the aspects I just
mentioned but then will insist on repeatability as the
sine qua non without realizing that the insistence of repeatability presupposes the very system that produced
atomizing, quantification or external viewpoints as criteria. In brief, it is the very system or world-view itself
that has to change and once one realizes this, one can
recognize that one is engaged in the enormous communication
problem that historians of science like Kuhn (1970) have
described as 'speaking across paradigms'. Thus, the communication function once again becomes as important as
the research findings themselves because no one can do research and not try to communicate them to someone, and
the audience to whom the research is directed influences
how one writes about it. Thus, one either ignores the
differences in world-views and basically does not communicate or one deliberately tries to speak across paradigms
or world-views, and in my experience, that means that the
forward-edge of one's own thought is truncated because one
implicitly begins to speak to the criteria of the listener's
world-view, and a side-effect is that one's own position
is weakened in the debate that ensues, because he has

couched his findings in language that will make it intell-
igible to the colleague from a different viewpoint, but
this also means more vulnerable to his arguments and critiques precisely because the results have been so languaged,
and thus, either communication breakdown occurs once again
because the differences in world-view have been camouflaged
by trying so hard to communicate or else the listener is
not convinced by the arguments because they have been com-
promised. But to have one's own development truncated in
such a fashion all the time also means that one's own
thought or research *actually does not develop* at least as
quickly as it should, and thus we are vulnerable to the
charge that while we often talk about changes in psychology
or real differences in viewpoint we don't really do anything about it. To overcome this difficulty one would
first have to have at the level of practice a more pluralistic conception of science - one that might admit that
there are many ways for science to be science. While
statements concerning pluralistic science are easy to find,
it does not seem to be an effective principle in practice.

*Priority to a Certain Conception of Science vs. Priority
to the Phenomenon Being Investigated* Very often many of
the factors, concepts, ideas, variables, etc. including
that social phenomenon known as 'the experiment' that
often misrepresent the phenomenon being researched are
introduced in the name of science - and it is in the name
of science that I want to introduce procedures and methods
that respect the integrity of the phenomenon. But the idea
of science that guides the two groups must differ since
at a concrete level, as I have tried to indicate, natural
scientific psychologists and human scientific psychologists do different things. For example, like the natural
sciences many psychologists still seek the universal laws
of behavior or mental life. Why? Because otherwise we do
not have science. But what if psychological phenomena do
not present themselves as fitting lawfulness as we understand it from the natural sciences? At least this question
should be raised. But if it were true, wouldn't it then
be incumbent upon science to use methods and concepts
that are adequate to the phenomenon? The natural sciences
manipulate objects and processes, so psychologists speak
of manipulating not only objects and aspects of the environment but even situations and experiences. Why? Manipulation
and control are the **way** science does things. But are we
using the term univocally when we speak of 'manipulating
feelings', for example. Or would it perhaps not be better
described as 'coercion' or 'socially determined behavior
for a given motivational level' or perhaps 'collusion
between researcher and subject'. Is not science interested
in precision? If any of the latter expressions really do
describe the research situation more adequately, would
not it be wise to use them? Examples can be multiplied

endlessly, but I think the point is clear. If there is a conflict, it is not one of science vs. non-science, but one of science against itself. (Or, perhaps better still, a conflict of an early phase of science against a later, more sophisticated phase. That is why the self-understanding of science that a psychologist adopts is so important: if one believes that psychology has arrived, and it looks like natural science, then one's whole outlook on how to do research is determined; if, on the other hand, one interprets psychology to be at a beginning phase, then different ways of doing research are still possible. What one *must not do* is simply assume that psychology, at a more sophisticated level of development, will look just like the natural sciences do now.) In any event, since I know that concrete differences exist between what I want to do to be scientific in psychology, and what others want to do, and since I claim my procedures are necessary in order to deal with human phenomena, I call what I find necessary to do 'human science' and I call the concept of science that guides the other activities natural scientific psychology since it is clear that that is its source of inspiration.

Intrinsic Difficulties

Everything I have said so far, I think, is true, and I think the problem of communication is a genuine one. However, I do not want to leave you with the impression that all of our difficulties with a constructive alternative in psychology are due to that alone. That would be too facile an explanation. There are certain intrinsic difficulties that we also face, and I would like now to mention some of them.

Lack of Unanimity Among Dissenters The fragmentation among those who would choose a constructive alternative for psychology is so great as to leave me without the hope for a solution. I was tempted to seek a loop-hole in time, but the quotes I presented at the beginning dissuaded me from doing so. From my own experience, I would guess that about 50% of the psychological community has some difficulties with the status of psychology, and would like to see some kind of alternative. But when it comes down to the positive articulation of the alternative, then it seems to me that no one articulation or expression commands more than 1 or 2% of the psychological community. What to do about this I am at a loss to say, but I do know that its existence hampers the development of the constructive alternative because you have numerous individuals working on similar problems without knowing each other, and the meeting of each other is not a simple solution either because the problems and proposed solutions are often expressed in such difficult theoretical terms that the similarities are masked. In addition, these communities are often characterized by the defensiveness that accompanies isolation and thus, there is a tendency to work on problems longer than necessary because of the anticipated negative critique that comes with publication, and that, too, slows down development.

Lack of Second Generation Development One of the major stumbling blocks to the development of a constructive alternative is the lack of what I term 'second generation' studies that develop a problem to its next logical step so that a historical continuity can be perceived. For example, Bartlett (1932, 1958) has done some very interesting beginning work on thinking and remembering, and he is everywhere respected, quoted, referred to as an example of a different type of research. But who has followed-up his research? Who as developed that line of thought and deepened or transformed his initial insights? Why have his studies not initiated a whole program of research like the Ebbinghaus or Pavlovian tradition? Why did it stop with its founder? Limiting myself merely to those who are sympathetic to my own particular constructive alternative I can cite the same phenomenon with respect to Buytendijk in Holland, D. Katz in Sweden, and E. Rubin in Denmark. In each case, a solid initial effort of research failed to develop beyond the founder in any significant sense. It could well be that this group is a genuine exception to the rule - but it will be so only to the extent that it operates within a Kellyian spirit rather than in a literal way and actually transforms problems beyond Kelly's way of expressing them - perhaps even beyond recognition. If it merely tries to preserve some literal Kellyian viewpoint, it cannot hope to succeed, for history usually deals harshly with such groups. Fortunately or unfortunately, as the case may be, I am not competent enough to make that decision, only you can.

In any event, why this lack of second generation development exists, I am not sure, but it certainly is a difficulty for those who want a constructive alternative in psychology. If you will, one could describe it as the problem of a lack of institutionalization for the constructive alternative. I would not tax your patience by actually doing it, but I could list a critique of traditional psychology for every decade of its existence from the 1870's to the 1970's that sounds essentially the same. The quotes with which I began this paper actually are a continuum. But it was always the voice of a lone dissenter, or small group at best, against the institutionalization of the discipline, and in each succeeding decade, a solitary individual started all over again because he either was not aware of the earlier effort, or did not know how to go beyond it. Of course, it was, and continues to be a mismatch; the institutionalized tradition rolls on using past achievements and the weight of history as evidence.

Thus, only the institutionalization of the critical view -
of the constructive alternative - can perhaps succeed in
not only resisting the tradition, but more importantly,
also in going beyond the initial effort of a founder and
start establishing 2nd and 3rd generation research efforts.
Clearly, a sense of history and theoretical developments
are implied if this effort is to succeed.

Premature Dialoguing and Totalizing   Another factor that
hinders the development of the constructive alternative is
that once one has started differently, instead of being
patient and developing the intrinsic logic of the new
approach, one compromises with the established criteria
due to an impatience to communicate or as a way of responding to critiques, or else, one prematurely extrapolates
from a solid, limited base to a whole systematic view and
too quickly tries to comprehend too much. Thus, what was
solid as a limited explanation or theory, becomes over-
extended and hence vulnerable. We should realize that
there is more strength in limiting our theoretical explanations to relevant contexts, and to move on from there
only with caution. No sooner do I say this, however, than
I hasten to confess that I find it increasingly difficult
not to speculate about where my researches will lead me
since I am constantly being asked if what I am doing will
lead to the hypothetical-deductive method, or if I am
willing to predict the number of types of learning, or
what kind of changes might I expect my learning-types to
undergo, etc. These questions all stem from known practices
of science, or from known findings from other traditions,
and while I can understand why these questions are asked,
trying to force the flow of my own research into that
direction denies it its intrinsic development. It may even
turn out that my research program will be no different
from other research, but at least I want to discover it
on my own and, because the unfolding logic of the phenomenon has led me to it, and not because the questions I
put to the phenomenon were determined by extreme concerns.

Ignorance of other Human Science   Lastly, I think we should
be more aware of the development of other human sciences.
Traditionally, psychology has been stronger in exposing
students to training in mathematics, statistics and the
natural and biological sciences. For a traditional conception of psychology, perhaps that makes sense - but
for psychology conceived as a human science at least, it
seems not to be the best background. Occasionally one
runs across individuals who happen to be knoledgeable in
psychology and other discipline - be it sociology or history or whatever, But what I have in mind is exposure to
methods and research problems across all the disciplines
that can be identified as a human science in order to see
just how concrete problems are tackled. Such an analysis

would reveal, I am sure, a very different picture of research than a philosophy of science or methodology derived
from the logic of the natural sciences. I think most of
us would find problems with which we could readily identify,
and for very sound reasons - there are basic structural
similarities. For example, one interest of sociologists
is the study of social institutions such as education,
and many sociologists are likewise educators, so they are
faced with the problem of studying a structure of which
they are a part - psychologists have the same problem when
studying e.g. perception; they live what they have to
study. Anthropologists often study primitive societies,
and face the problem of entering into a totally different
socio-cultural structure as they study it. Psychologists
face a similar problem when studying children since it is
clear that one cannot simply project the structure of
adult consciousness into the child. How should one enter
into the world of the child while studying it without
merely recording the effect of our own disturbance? Eco-
nomists try to study an abstract relation defined as exchange of commodities or goods on a rational or logical
basis when they know that such exchanges are radically
influenced by non-rational factors. Psychologists try to
understand emotions scientifically, (i.e. rationally)
when they are by definition non-rational. This is not a
new psychologism claiming that psychology has a special
priority. There is no privileged position for psychology.
All I am saying is that human phenomena share certain
fundamental characteristics that all of the separate human
sciences have to face in one way or another and that seeing
how others confront these fundamental problems can be of
value for us. For example, if when starting my learning
research I was fully aware that in anthropology, economics,
history, political science, linguistics and sociology
researchers all have had to make use of a typology, I may
have been more prepared to meet the kind of findings that
I did. Instead, I had as an attitudinal set the more
quantitative expressions of traditional learning research
and hence felt on the defensive in presenting 'merely' a
typology. I think this state of affairs is true beyond my
own case, but a better acquaintance with other human sciences would prepare us all more adequately.

By way of summary, I would like to say that in this
paper I have tried to concentrate in the general problem
of a constructive alternative in psychology rather than
on my particular version of it. There were two general
problems: (1) the problem of communication with colleagues
of other viewpoints; and (2) the difficulties involved
with institutionalizing a fragmented community whose only
unity is a negation - the critique of traditional psychology - so that historically continuous research can
ensure. The central difficulty for the first problem re-

volved around the concept of 'science'. Explicitly or
implicitly, the constructive alternativists want to en-
large, modify or ignore the natural scientific conception
of science whereas the larger community, again implicitly
or explicitly, uses that very understanding of science
as its primary frame of reference - thus communication
problems are inevitable. Overcoming the second difficulty
would involve genuine breakthroughs. One would have to
try to understand what the many existing constructive
alternatives had in common, and then be able to express
the commonalities in a genuinely psychological language
that would be acceptable to at least most of the separate
communities involved. If that were possible, although
highly unlikely, then I think the question of a sustained
research program would solve itself.

Can these aims be achieved? I am not sure, but I would
like to turn to the two authors I used earlier for a sense
of direction. In the same 1973 article, Rogers (p.379)
asks: 'Does our profession *dare* to develop the new conception of science which is so necessary if we are to
have a true, psychological science'. Thus, I submit we
have to be bolder about doing the different kinds of things
we think are necessary. And how do we do that? In the same
1884 article Dewey (p.289) said: 'We can conclude only by
saying that, following the logic of life, (psychology)
attempts to comprehend life'. Hence, only by better descriptions of and insights into human life as it is actually lived can we come to comprehend it better.

The sad part is that the promise held out by Dewey 100
years ago is still being answered today by Rogers' plea.
Even sadder to me is that I am ending another paper with
promises and pleas. Many things have been posited as the
sign or hallmark of psychology's coming of age - but to
me, it will be when the promise and pleas will have dis-
appeared from the literature.

Acknowledgement

This paper was written while the writer was a Fellow
at the Netherlands Institute for Advanced Study in the
Humanities and Social Sciences in Wassenaar, Holland and
grateful acknowledgement is hereby made to the Institute.

GEORGE KELLY AND THE AMERICAN MIND (OR WHY HAS HE BEEN OBSCURE FOR SO LONG IN THE U.S.A. AND WHENCE THE NEW INTEREST?)

ALLAN DAVISSON

Department of Psychology, College of Saint Benedict, St. Joseph, Minnesota 56374, U.S.A.

In 1965 J. C. J. Bonarius began his review of ten years of personal construct theory with the optimistic observation that the theory promised integration of the 'seemingly opposite views of humanistic and scientific psychology.' Today, well over twelve years later, George Kelly's work is showing a vitality and appeal that suggest that optimism about its insights is well-founded. But its reception in America, in particular, has been curiously slow and even yet Kelly and personal construct theory lack major status in American psychology.

If there were widespread agreement on major aspects of the contentual model for psychology in the United States, this lack of theoretical appeal might be more understandable. Or if it could be shown that psychology as an academic and research discipline has now splintered to such an extent that the major vitality in the field is in specialities and sub-specialties, then a broad-based philosophy of behavior such as that offered by Kelly would seem less relevant. But the prestigious Nebraska Symposium on Motivation devoted its 1974 sessions to the problem of psychology's conceptual system and suggests that widespread agreement is not present in psychology and that the vitality of the field is currently not to be found in diversity. The volume of papers begins with the suggestion that 'we have been guiding ourselves by a limited conception of science and, accordingly, by a restricted conception of the human being.' (Cole 1975) (Interestingly enough, the Nebraska Symposium in 1975 was devoted to Kelly and personal construct theory). A consequence of this restricted conception is that psychology is in a stage of transition or 'crisis' that echoes comments made by Robert Watson ten years ago. Watson (1967) pointed to the 'lack of universal agreement about the nature of our contentual model' and went on to add that 'an all too common dismissal of work in psychology in other countries as quaint, odd, or irrelevant' reflects a 'provincialism in psychology in the United States.'

The work of George Kelly has had long-standing prom-

inence in Great Britain - prominence that is only now beginning to spread substantially in the United States. Perhaps American provincialism about something popular in
Britain is part of the explanation for Kelly's obscurity
in his own country. But reasons more substantive than this
seem present, and an exploration of some of these reasons
provides an interesting commentary on the ways in which
theoretical insights are accepted and utilized in psychology. And an understanding of the growth of personal construct theory in the American psychological milieu should
also provide a better understanding of the directions in
which work with Kelly's viewpoints can be expected to go.

A more concrete picture of the extent of personal construct theory's acceptance - or non-acceptance - can be
seen in a bibliography issued by Landfield at the University of Nebraska in 1976 that provides a listing of references published in the 1970s relevant to personal construct theory. This bibliography lists 39 articles developed in Britain and/or by Britons and seven published in
the Commonwealth and/or by Commonwealth psychologists.
There are 36 citations of work by Americans, seven of which
are unpublished research. Only two of the British references are to unpublished research.

Out of 44 personality theory textbooks published since
1961 in the United States, 32 mention George Kelly either
in a bibliographic reference or somewhere in the text.
Of those 32, only twelve have major articles on Kelly
(i.e. ten pages or more), and ten of those twelve texts
have been published since 1970.

A survey of introductory psychology textbooks published
in the United States between 1960 and 1975 found that only
eight out of 52 mention Kelly and his work.

These bibliographic counts provide a tangible indication
of Kelly's place - or lack of place - in American psychology.

There are several possible reasons for this slow acceptance of personal construct theory in the United States.
Kelly's personality, the status of American psychology
over the past two decades, national readiness for his perspectives inside and outside professional psychology, and
other related issues in the history and sociology of
science provide perspective on those reasons. The summary
of issues in this paper is an effort to point out some of
the factors that have influenced acceptance and utilization of personal construct theory insights. Exploration
of the question provides an intriguing and sometimes
frustrating comment on the way in which science is 'done'
in psychology. An added problem in this analysis is that
Kelly is often misunderstood - Mancuso (Landfield 1977)
writes that Maddi's presentation of Kelly is his new personality text ignores the Choice Corollary and that 'one
cannot fathom Kelly's motivational position if he ignores

the Choice Corollary'.

Kelly's personality provides an interesting starting point in the list of factors. He has been described by people who knew him as a private and reserved individual who was not comfortable touting his own views. He had a reluctance for self-advertisement inside or outside of professional psychology circles. Contemporaries or near-contemporaries achieved far more personal prominence. B. F. Skinner has made major efforts to appeal to the general public, and Clark Hull's theories were spread extensively within experimental psychology.

Kelly did relatively little publishing and what writing he did sometimes showed a tendency toward an earthy 'down home' style prose. A pithy illustration of this is his rejection of push and pull theories of motivation with the comment 'in terms of a well-known metaphor, there are the pitchfork theories on the one hand and the carrot theories on the other. But our theory is neither of these. Since we prefer to look to the nature of the animal himself, ours is probably best called a jackass theory' (Kelly 1958 p.50).

Kelly's attitude toward the scientific establishment of his day seems to have been implicit in his language. Holland (1970) summed Kelly up as enthused about 'the good life of inventing and exploring different ways of seeing the world, and each other...(He) seems to celebrate and exemplify the scientific quest'. But Kelly's 'engaging modesty, his constant deflation of his own pretensions by the use of colloquialisms, promises a completely humane, fun-loving irreverence towards the established systems, structures, and orthodoxies of that dehumanized *Science* which he obviously despises and frequently attacks (Holland 1970, p.111).

Theoretical Reasons

The status of research and theory in the United States may provide more substantive insights into the role of personal construct theory than these personality-related reasons. A variety of terms are used to describe the psychological milieu at any given time. Watson (1967) uses the term 'prescriptions' to include the paradigms, or perspectives, or theories, or doctrines that guide psychology at any given time. Whatever the term, the state it describes provides a directive function for the discipline. Grants and research are influenced; graduate student commitments and interests are directed; and the prescriptions provide a ready system of classifying theoretical friends or enemies.

The dominant themes in American psychology might well be classified by the two categories Bonarius mentions: scientific and humanistic psychology. But the dominant content of either view varies over time. In 1955 the dom-

inant view or 'prescription' is perhaps best typified by
the term 'neo-neo-behaviorism' coined by Sigmund Koch
(1964). While the period saw a revival of interest in
such heretofore repressed areas as 'instinctive behavior,
perception, complex motivational processes, and thinking',
a dominant feature of the period was 'detailed retrospec-
tive analyses' of their earlier positions by 'influential
theorists'. 'The result', Koch suggests, 'is an extensive
sub-anthology on extensions of neobehaviorist theory to
the long-forbidden areas - a kind of massive study in the
return of the repressed' (Koch 1964, p.20). (It was still
possible as late as the 1969 APA Convention to mount a
discussion on the then current utility or non-utility of
drive theory.)

Against this context, George Kelly presented a view
of man and his behaviour that saw man as active, changing,
and self-directed. Each individual is his or her own scientist developing theories to see what is effective in
enabling one to cope with life's alternatives. He attacked
the more prevalent notions of motivation and made man an
agent long before mainline motivation got around to it in
any major way. Ten years later Hunt's Nebraska Symposium
(1965) article on intrinsic motivation presented a sub-
stantial effort to show the inadequacies of the drive
theory model of motivation and to provide a motivational
perspective that brought agenthood closer to the individual.

Personal construct theory also had an intensely idiosyncratic orientation - Kelly was interested in 'minds'
rather than 'mind'. And he was interested not only in
individual minds but in minds in motion. This perspective
may have had appeal for some clinicians, but for psychologists trained in the experimental tradition Kelly's approach was outside the usual pale of experience. Individual
variance was a scientific nuisance or a statistical challenge but it did not represent a desired element on the
reductionistic path. Beyond this individualistic orientation, Kelly suggested telic concerns - his Fundamental
Postulate bases a person's processes on the ways in which
'he anticipates events'. The general orientation was hol-
istic - the language of *persons* 'anticipating' and 'construing' was not the language of the behaviorally oriented.
Kelly's opening comments in his book (1955) differentiate
his view of man from those who take a 'man-the-biological-
organism' view on the one hand, or a 'man-the-lucky-guy'
viewpoint on the other. He is explicit about the inadequacy of stimulus-response theory to explain man, comment-
ing that 'stimulus-response theorises are particularly
convenient at the focal point of animal learning' (1955,
p.18) but suggesting that this is about their limit. In
his explanation of the Choice Corollary, he draws the
distinction between his view of man and that of S-R psy-

chology's substitution of a person's active anticipation for the assumptions that 'explain why certain responses become linked to certain stimuli' (1955 p.68).

Kelly's formulation of personal construct theory presented it as a relatively complete system with little room for additional development. Subsequent research has tended to focus on explication of consequences of aspects of his theory or on different applications of the repertory grid technique rather than on formal extension of the theory. A key aspect of drive theory was its concern with and ability to generate testable hypotheses that would expand the theory itself. The ability to inspire and direct research has been an important element in the history of theoretical acceptance in American psychology. The hypothetico-deductive method provides thesis topics far more readily than does personal construct theory. And Skinnerian psychology has an advantage over Kelly's perspectives - it takes far less time and energy for a neophyte graduate student to master the fundamentals of Skinnerian behaviorism than to master personal construct theory.

While Kelly's work did not fit well with the prevailing views of the segment of the psychological community that classified itself as scientific and behaviorally oriented, his work seemed to have little appeal either to those who saw themselves as humanistic and whole-person oriented. The language of the American humanistic perspective has been typified by Koch (1969) as diffuse enough that there is little common language across differing perspectives. But there are general elements of humanistic psychology that are found in one form or another in most of the perspectives.

Buhler (1971) lists some of these. Her emphasis on the study of whole persons has a ring of familiarity to those who have worked with Kelly's viewpoints. But Buhler adds that the basis for this study of the whole person is 'understanding as against the method of explaining' (italics hers). Kelly is explicit about his view of man-the-scientist and indicates that the ability to specify a construct system is basic to his theory.

Another major issue in the humanistic perspective is the emphasis on development. Buhler refers to the importance of considering the entire life-cycle. The neo-Freudians are even more explicit about tracing the impact of early development in subsequent personality development. George Kelly spends very little time dealing directly with early development.

The humanistic psychotherapist sees problems that are outside Kelly's consideration. Buhler suggests that the essential goal of the humanistic therapist is 'to help the person experience his existence as real'. Kelly's 'man-the-scientist' has little doubt about the reality of

his existence but has the goal of a scientist in a more
formal context - 'the scientist's ultimate aim is to predict and control' (Kelly italicizes this) (1955, p.5).

There seems to be a striking similarity between Kelly's
view that persons evolve construction systems that will
allow them to effectively cope with the world and the
humanistic focus on a healthy person's development toward
some kind of life goal. Concepts such as self-realization
(Horney, Fromm), self-actualization (Goldstein, Maslow)
or Rogers' growth process seem to point to a set of similar concerns. But there is a deterministic bent and vagaries of a long-term time frame in humanistic thought
that differentiate most humanistic thought from what
Kelly's perspective suggests. The humanistic life-goal is
a broader and less concrete concept than Kelly allows and
there is an element of motivational force that runs counter
to Kelly's insistence that the individual's own efforts
to effectively construe events are the basis for development of a personal system.

Kelly's view of man is not the open view of the humanistic perspective. Kelly as much as says this when he
excludes 'man-the-lucky-guy' from his definition and takes
the science model as his basis for understanding the person. He sought an objectification that is not typical of
the humanistic method of dealing with the individual. The
process of construing is a definite, definable, and testable process that is little related to the style of those
who speak of 'experience itself' as the principal data
source and main analytic framework.

Personal construct theory seems to have staked out a
territory that was neither scientific nor humanistic
enough in the 1955 sense of the terms for Kelly's views
to become a significant factor in American psychological
thinking. But Kelly's work did achieve prominence in
Great Britain. Brief consideration of reasons for the
British interest in personal construct theory helps provide additional insight into why Kelly finally seems to
be achieving more prominence in the United States.

There is a sense of 'psychology-in-use' that seems more
pervasive in the British approach to psychology than in
the American. An analysis of journal articles might provide more concrete support, but this impression comes
from an experience directing a month-long course for
American students in Britain examining the contrast between British and American psychology. This impression
also fits with the observations of various British psychologists such as Don Bannister who is credited by many
of his colleagues as a major factor in establishing the
prominence of Kelly's work in Britain.

Bannister, in discussion, observed that the British
were concerned with the importance of the person and a
systematic recognition of personal perspectives to a

greater extent than Americans were in the 1950s and 1960s.
British psychology has a strong empiricistic orientation,
including a strong concern with methodology, but it also
has been concerned with idiosyncratic description and
assessment while American psychology has emphasized nomothetic concerns. Kelly's repertory grid is an idiosyncratic
tool that depends for its measures entirely on information
provided by the individual being tested. And the Rep Test,
as it has come to be called, provides highly systematic
information in a framework that not only provides a sophisticated presentation of individual construct systems, but
has also proven to be open to sophisticated statistical
analysis.

The British university system may also have been a factor in the dissemination of Kelly's views. British psychologists have suggested that the British university system has relatively open communication channels across
institutions, and that frequent and open communication
between the institutions is common. The American university
system, in contrast, for reasons of geographical as well
as theoretical distance, is not as open to easy exchange
in a regular and informal manner. Even today there is a
tendency for various psychology departments to establish
themselves in a special and somewhat unique orientation
or perspective, and this proclivity has the effect of
insulating them from other institutions. In some of the
larger universities, this insularity may even be found
between different specialties or programs in a particular
department. Parenthetically, people who were at Ohio State
when George Kelly was there report that lines of communication within that particular psychology department were
not well established.

Growing Popularity

But the last few years in American psychology have
seen a growing recognition that personal construct theory
may have something significant to add to psychology. Increased reference to Kelly, the 1976 Nebraska Symposium
on Motivation focus on his work, the appearance of research based on Kelly's perspectives - these are factors
that suggest that Kelly may belatedly be coming into his
own in American psychological thought.

The reasons for this change may be even more evanescent
than the reasons for the earlier eclipse of his work. Part
of it may be the very reasons that made personal construct
theory appealing to Britons. The American testing industry
has been under heavy fire from civil libertarians and
government committees for some of its methods of assessing
individual characteristics using population norms. The
public controversy about intelligence tests and personality tests seems to be only a part of a more general concern that objective tests used to make important decisions

about individuals' futures may not accurately reflect
individual situations. The repertory grid with its systematic and individualized assessment technique produces
a personality profile that is not subject to the criti-
cisms levelled at more traditional objective tests.

Theory in American psychology is changing as well. The
1975 Nebraska Symposium points out that psychology today
is in a generally fragmented state - the relatively dominant views or prescriptions that prevailed in the past
have given way to diffusion and diversity. While this may
imply confusion, it may also indicate less of a concern
than has existed heretofore with developing a central or
unified theory to underlay most of psychology. Royce (1976)
typifies the current situation in psychology with three
observations. The behavioristic perspective is currently
declining in dominance as the central theme in psychology.
Cognitive psychology has aroused increased interest and
is achieving new prominence. Consequently, there has been
a swing to a structuralist-functionalist view in psychology that Royce suggests points to 'the emergence of some
form of constructive-structural-functionalism'. He defines
structuralism as 'the approach to understanding psychological phenomena in terms of a set of elements and their
relationships' and functionalism as 'the approach to understanding psychological phenomena in terms of their adaptive
or functional significance'. He subsequently ties the term
'constructive' to the 'constructs' or 'theoretical "inven-
tions" ' of investigators. His viewpoint is not explicitly
Kellyian - he does not even mention Kelly in his presentation, though other participants in the symposium did.
But he suggests a framework of thought in psychology that
is far more in harmony with personal construct theory
than was previously the case.

To simply classify Kelly as a 'cognitive psychologist'
may make many people who have worked with his concepts a
bit uncomfortable. But the term has come to have a wider
meaning than earlier textbook use might have suggested
and implies an active-process orientation rather than a
passive-control point orientation to understanding human
behavior. And the description of psychology as moving toward a 'constructive structural functionalism' provides
a basis for understanding current interest in Kelly.

The impact of molar structural theorists like Chomsky
and Piaget in American psychology may be responsible for
some of the new interest in Kelly. Parallels between Kelly
and Piaget, in particular, have been indentified. For
example, the development of a personal construct system
has been described (Adams-Webber 1970) as 'containing
explicit parallels with the developmental models of Piaget
and Werner'. Piaget suggests that 'psychological structure
evolves through the progressive differentiation and rein-
tegration of operational schemata at increasingly higher

levels of logical abstraction' and Kelly's theory suggests
that 'the normal course of development of a personal construct system involves the progressive differentiation of
the system into relatively independent, internally organized subsystems within the overall system as an operational whole' (Adams-Webber 1970, p.36).

A functional perspective is also compatible with personal construct theory. The construing process can be
understood as a functional process. The Basic Postulate
and the Organization Corollary suggest this in referring
to the role of construct structures in the person's anticipation of events. And the Choice Corollary takes the
functional orientation a bit further when it refers to
elaboration of the system.

A detailed historical analysis of Kelly might well
find many more elements in earlier and current perspectives that are present in personal construct theory. Kelly
himself suggests (1970) that efforts to categorize personal construct theory are not particularly useful. 'I
fear that no one of these categorizations will be of much
help to the reader in understanding personal construct
theory, but perhaps having a whole lap full of them all
at once will suggest what might be done with them.' Classification for classification's sake, then, seems contrary
to the spirit of George Kelly. But the subtle shift in the
not-so-subtle prescriptions that direct much of the ex-
penditure of resources in American psychological practice
seems highly relevant to understanding and appreciating
growing prominence for the theories of George Kelly.

There is one last question to ask. Is personal construct
theory a candidate to serve as the basis for a new paradigm in psychological theory? Kelly's own writing and much
of the work that has been done with personal construct
theory suggest that no such ambitions are inherent in the
theory. For Kelly, the process of construing is ongoing -
the universality of certainty implied by the concept of
a paradigm represents a different view of the person.
And perhaps that is the answer to the question. Kelly and
personal construct theory offer a view, a perspective, a
technique - a human and humane basis for psychology in
its struggle to understand human behavior.

Acknowledgement

Marvin MacDonald, one of my students, worked with me
on some of the background issues in this paper.

DOING PSYCHOLOGICAL RESEARCH

PHILLIDA SALMON

*Institute of Education, University of London,
25 Woburn Square, London, W.C.1., U.K.*

In the job I do nowadays, as a lecturer in psychology,
I suppose my main focus is on research. Like everyone else
in the academic world I am expected to carry out some form
of research, since that is part of the traditional brief
of lecturers. I also supervise students working on M.Phil.s
or Ph.D.s in psychology. And, of course, in all the teaching I do, I am continually talking about research that has
been done in psychology. Since academic psychology is a
large and growing field, one might expect that the whole
topic of psychological research would be a widely debated
one. But questions about the validity and meaningfulness
of the vast array of work in the area, or about how best
to frame one's own research efforts or help students frame
theirs - such questions just do not seem to get raised.
It is because I feel unhappy myself about how things are
in this field, that I want to raise some issues - issues
on which, I think, personal construct theory has a major
contribution to make.

There is, I think, something basically wrong in our
traditions of psychological research. Probably few people
would disagree with the idea that research is presented
for basically communicative purposes - that is, to per-
suade others of something. But one has only to picture all
those volumes and volumes of psychological reports sitting
on library shelves to realise the massive irrelevance of
most of it for most people. It is not just that published
findings of psychological experiments and observations do
not get as far as influencing the ideas of the man in the
street. It is not even that these findings make little
impact on the understandings of other psychologists. The
fact is, I would say, that the results of research projects typically make no difference to the way the researcher *himself* sees human experience and behaviour - let alone
altering any of the ways in which he conducts his life.
It seems to me that the reasons for this rather shameful
situation probably lie in the longstanding and unquestioned
assumptions embodied in our conventions about psychological
research.

If one examines the typical ways in which research in

psychology get evaluated, some clear common denominators
emerge. This is true whether one looks at the kinds of
research study which are accepted or rejected for publication, or at the selection of would-be holders of student
research grants. One central assumption seems paramount
in judgements about whether a research project is or is
not acceptable. That is, that research is a matter of
finding answers. Perhaps this assumption is seen most
clearly in the processes that are brought to bear on an
M.Phil. or Ph.D. applicant to a psychology department. In
the usual interviewing panel, the greatest importance is
attached to whether or not the applicant can frame his
question in terms of a standard research design, and specify the form of statistical analysis he would use on his
results. The question itself is simply not seen as an
issue for discussion. If the candidate gets accepted, ex--
actly the same emphasis on findings, and neglect of questions, will be likely to operate in the way his research
project is supervised. The conscientious supervisor is
seen as one who helps a student implement his procedures -
whether these are experimental, interview or observational -
and then guides and monitors his use of statistical analyses. And the final write-up of the research as a thesis
is expected to reflect the same focus. The logic of the
design framework and of the statistical procedures is perceived as the crucial element of the work; and it is
characteristically on the basis of this that the degree
is or is not awarded.

I would not want to argue that the operationalising of
questions, the ability to put things to the test - which
these emphases partly reflect - are not important. What I
do feel is that they are ultimately *less* crucial than the
ability to ask fruitful questions. It is a truism that
answers can only be as good as the questions to which they
are adduced; but somehow this truism never seems to have
got through to our conventional thinking about psychological research. To my mind it is because the questions asked
in research in psychology are generally such bad questions
that the results of that research seem so irrelevant.

It would not, I think, be difficult to document the unsatisfactory questions underlying a very great deal of
research in psychology. One rather nasty way to do it
would be to categorise psychological research in terms of
the three headings suggested for scientific research in
general in a witty paper by Rowan Wilson (1968). These
were Bandwagon, No Stone Unturned and Fancy That; and it
would be easy to find numerous examples of each in a quick
sampling of some current issues of psychological journals.
But there are, I believe, important reasons why asking
psychological questions which avoid confusion and transcend
the obvious or the trivial is a very difficult thing to do.
Questions in psychology that are worth asking must somehow

link in to the network of assumptions about oneself and others that actually operate in the way we go about our lives. If they fail to do this, then they are bound to remain irrelevant. But actually to get at this assumptive network means achieving some grasp of what, though crucial, is typically non-explicit and intuitive - what Polanyi calls tacit knowledge. And of course, though some of our most basic assumptions are shared by others, there is no identity across individuals in the private assumptive framework within which they live.

Perhaps considerations like these seem out of place in relation to most research projects. Most projects, after all, whether they are conducted by students, lecturers or research teams, do not set out to establish once and for all the whole nature of the human condition; they are on an altogether humbler plane. But the fact is that *all* questions in psychology are bound to tie in at some point with basic personal-psychological assumptions. Any question, by raising one issue, also sets up what is *not* at issue - what is taken for granted. And the validity and centrality of these taken-for-granted assumptions are as important, for the fertility of a research project, as what is explicitly set at issue.

I would like to say something about what I think taking questions seriously in psychological research would mean. As I have related my portrayal of the *status quo* to the situation of a would-be research student, I will continue for the moment to focus my remarks on that situation. First of all, I think the assumptions governing the selection of students to do research in psychology would be very different. The nature of an applicant's research question would be seen as absolutely central. A question which is self-evident, circular, confused, or merely trivial is not a good question - no matter how ingenious the candidate may be in translating it into a complex and sophisticated experimental design. But then questions as originally formulated are often *not* good questions, and often turn out anyway not to be *the* question. I do not think, therefore, that judging a research applicant's question to be unsatisfactory should be automatically tantamount to rejecting him. To my mind, the whole of the early part of a research project should be concerned with exploring, elaborating and, almost certainly, reformulating the research question.

What seems to me to be more crucial in the decision whether or not to accept a research applicant is the student's degree of commitment to the area. It is the lack of such commitment, I think, that leads to people taking short cuts, being dishonest, or turning research into a ritualistic exercise. A little while ago I heard a paper given which described some research concerned with morality in adolescence. In his research procedures the investigator

had misinformed his adolescent subjects about the purpose
of the tasks he was asking them to do, and had without
their knowledge used a one-way observation mirror in order
secretly to record how they behaved. I think myself that
that way of conducting research can only be carried out
by someone whose research question means absolutely nothing to him personally. To fail to consider the morality
of his own procedures and relationship with his subjects,
not to see that his research topic was being explicated
just as much in his own as in his subjects' behaviour,
and that the same frame of reference applied to both -
this is only possible, I think, if you have totally separated yourself and your real personal understandings from
what you are doing in the name of psychological research.
The result, of course, is the sort of insulting and totally
unenlightening study of which there are all too many examples in the psychological literature.

I would want, therefore, to challenge the longstanding
tradition in psychology of detachment and neutrality in
research, and, on the contrary, to reject for research
studentships those applicants who have no personal involvement in their proposed research. If a student does not
actually care one way or another about what he may find
out in his research, quite apart from the doubt this may
cast on his being likely to complete the work, it certainly
suggests that he will not be able to bring to it any of
the personally significant meanings which in the end will
give it any message it may have. As I see it, it is with
exploring what these meanings actually are that the first,
long, part of any research project should be concerned.
The supervisor's role in this is the reason why merely a
shared academic interest in the topic of research is not
enough of a basis for supervision. To help someone become
aware of their tacit understandings, to explore what is
involved in any psychological issue and what would follow
from different kinds of findings - to do this it is necessary, I think, to be able to enter into the kinds of perspectives a student takes. Even given this kind of sym-
pathy, however, I think it is very difficult to explicate
why and how a psychological question matters to the person who is researching it. One device which can sometimes
help in this is an exercise described by Bakan (1967).
Before he embarks on any empirical work at all the student
writes up the research as though he had completed it. He
does this twice: first as though he had got findings in
line with his expectations, and then, as though he had got
opposite findings. Doing this can often present implications - or, sometimes, lack of implications - much more
vividly than an abstract discussion can achieve. Taking
research questions seriously also means acknowledging that
the process of operationalising them is difficult too.
It is only if you refuse really to become aware of all

that may be involved, for you, in any particular psychological issue, that it is possible to opt quickly for a
research design which will crystallise the enquiry once
and for all. To acknowledge this would again make the
selection, and the supervision, of research students into
something very different. As things are now, the complex
questions about how issues are to be posed, and what kind
of evidence will be relevant, are foreclosed in the hast-
iest of ways at selection interviews and the early stages
of a research project. Research applicants are typically
expected, at the very first meeting, to present the design
they intend to use, and provided it seems approximately
viable, it is likely to be accepted. Perhaps such per-
functory treatment would be unsatisfactory in any field;
whatever area is involved, there is probably always more
than one way of posing a question. But in psychology I
think it is really disastrous to resort quickly to a ready-
made design simply on the grounds that it 'will do'.
Psychology is about human subjects; and human beings have
values, meanings, purposes of their own. The psychological
perspectives of subjects, which may or may not be similar
to those of the researcher, or to each others', can certainly not be ignored. Neither can the fact that the encounters between investigators and their subjects are
social situations between people, no less complex than
other social situations between people. There is also the
inescapable fact that human beings do not always agree
about what a thing means, and about what is evidence of
something; and this matters just as much in making judgements about the significance of the behaviour or experience
of research subjects as it does in communicating to others
what any research findings actually mean. All this makes
it complex and difficult to set up valid investigatory
strategies in psychological research. As I see it, a recognition that this *is* difficult is a good sign in a would-be
research student. And in the early stages of a research
project I think both student and supervisor have to be
able to endure an uncomforable period of living with several possible investigatory strategies, before finally
settling for one.
   If I can try to summarise what I see as the main implication of all this for good, rather than bad psychological
research, I would argue for personal commitment as the
crucial factor. It seems to me to be the personal significance, acknowledged by a researcher, of the question he
is working on which ultimately governs the quality of what
he does. This, I think, is what determines his being prepared both to trace the question through into its implications, and to conduct his enquiry in rigorous ways.
Part of this entails the carrying through of an argument
into the kinds of procedures, design and statistical
analyses that are integral to it - something that does **not**

come about simply as a result of courses in assessment,
methodology or statistics. It also involves the willingness
not to foreclose issues or beg questions, to allow the
possibility of disconfirmation, and to draw inferences
with care. All these things can come about, I think, only
if what you are doing by way of research is something you
yourself take seriously.

How do all these questions look from the standpoint of
personal construct theory? It seems to me that Kelly's
ideas have very close links with the issues I have been
talking about, and that his theoretical position leads in
similar directions to the ones I have been urging. I would
like to relate construct theory to the whole topic of research in psychology, by dwelling briefly on each of three
distinctive emphases in the theory - emphases on the nature
of psychology, on how one might set out to extend one's
psychology, and on how such efforts should be evaluated.
In all three areas, Kelly's thinking is suggestive of particular ways of seeing and doing psychological research.

Ever since work in psychology began to be defined as
research, researchers seem always to have been trapped
within the long-standing dichotomy in psychology, between
experience on the one hand, and behaviour on the other.
Within this division, research has, I think, been pretty
clearly assigned to the behaviour pole. This has meant
that research has been viewed as being *about* the explicit
and observable behaviour of subjects, with the *method of
enquiry* being the explicit and observable behaviour of the
investigator. By the same token, what has been defined as
experience has been excluded. So what subjects think and
feel about the investigatory situation - as opposed to
what they observably do - has been viewed as irrelevant
to the 'real data'; concomitantly, the investigator, as
an experiencing person, with concerns and investments in
the research, has been totally absent in any account given.
The concept of research has been consistently restricted,
so that work which has involved the exploration of subjective meanings, whether in the investigator himself, or
in another or others - such work has typically not been
defined as research. Both kinds of effort have suffered
from this polarisation, I think. 'Research' proper has
been so concerned to be hard-nosed and objective that it
has characteristically ignored the personal factors which
could have given it meaning, and has ended in the kinds
of empty exercise I have been criticising. And on the
other side, much sensitive and potentially illuminating
work, of the case-study type, has remained merely at the
level of interesting description, because the ideas have
been diffuse, and no clear issue has been put to a test.
In Kelly's terms, the first sort of work incorporates pre-
emption and control without that prior necessity - circumspection; while the second represents only circumspection

without ever moving on to pre-emption and control. Another
way of saying this is to employ Bakan's 'duality' of terms.
'Research' involves agency without communion; the other
kind of work involves communion without agency. Ultimately,
both are impoverished.

Kelly, of course, would have to truck with the division
of man into the two categories of behaviour and experience;
and therein lies a huge advantage for the way psychological
research can be conceptualised. In the formulation that
man lives in anticipation, both the sense that people make
of things, and the way they live out that sense, are in-
extricably linked together. 'Experience' is the anticipation of behavioural possibilities, just as 'behaviour'
is the experience of creating events in terms of these
anticipations. This refusal to operate the usual dichotomy
in psychology has, I think, many profound implications.
Fundamentally, it leads to a view of research as being
concerned both with the fullest possible exploration and
articulation of a personal meaning network, and with the
submission of a major aspect of the network to a critical
test. What is distinctive to a construct theory view is
that these two aspects are integral. Without knowing what
is at issue, it makes no sense to put any question to the
test; conversely, there is little point in the most detailed and careful of enquiries into one's own psychological understanding if there is to be no test of the validity
of any of it.

As I see it, it is precisely this concern with the
exploration and elaboration of systems of personal understanding which is Kelly's most distinctive theme. This
means that his theory represents a rich source of ideas
about how to set about this kind of task. Although exploration and elaboration are essentially two aspects of the
same process, and neither makes sense without the other,
it may be easier to see the implications construct theory
has, if we look at each of these aspects in turn.

The emphasis which Kelly places on personal systems of
meaning, the thoughtful account he gives of what such
systems may entail, and the strategies he suggests for
their elucidation - all seem profoundly helpful for the
exploratory phases of psychological research. One consequence of his particular view of construct systems as
personal is the emergence of both the researcher and any
subjects he may be working with, as salient personal
figures. From a Kellyan standpoint, the convention of a
non-person, black box of an investigator, and a group of
subjects described only by some crudely defined common
denominator, is totally inappropriate. By contrast, the
particular issue and investments, with all their idiosyncratic ramifications, which constitute the research topic
for the researcher, need to be fully explored and articulated. Likewise the subjects have to be treated *as sub-*

jects, with their particular subjectivities becoming as
fully known as possible.

When it comes to ways of exploring one's own or another's network of personal meanings, what Kelly has to say is
obviously helpful. In the stress which he lays on what is
implicit and unarticulated, he emphasises the importance,
in any encounter with events, of the surrounding web of intuitive connections. It seems to have been for the elucidation of such connections that Kelly devised most of his
investigatory strategies. At a general level, there is his
concern always to articulate the implicit pole of any particular dimension of meaning, and in so doing to illuminate
the significance of whatever judgement is being made.
More specifically, the whole range of systematic enquiries
that Kelly called the repertory grid technique can reveal
the structure underlying major aspects of intuitive personal understandings. There are other broad themes in
personal construct theory which seem to suggest ways of
getting in touch with unarticulated meanings. The conceptualisation of phases in construing is one of these.
Kelly's account of the creativity cycle, and of loosening
and tightening as successive stages in thinking, promises
a potential freedom from the kinds of block that a deter-
minedly single-track pursuit of ideas so often produces.
In rather the same way, his distinction between proposit-
onal thinking on the one hand, and pre-emptive and constel-
latory thinking on the other, seems useful in enabling one
to avoid 'hardening of the categories', and to encounter
less familiar possibilities in one's own construing. That
kind of exploration is helped, too, by Kelly's invitational
mood. (In fact, this mood is of all things what psychological research has most notably lacked, just as it has also
been characteristically couched in pre-emptive terms, and
evolved through exclusively tight phases of construing.)

Construct theory also, I think, has implications for
the elaboration phase of psychological research. The logic
of the integration between exploration and elaboration
runs totally counter to the use of standard methodologies.
For Kelly, methods of experimentation are personal, and
arise out of the meaning which the question has for the
questioner. It is this meaning which defines what will be
a valid way of posing the question, and what will constitute evidence of how things stand. Hence, any idea of
a standard way of posing psychological questions, equally
applicable for all time and for all purposes, is obviously
untenable. And if the method of investigation cannot be
standardised, neither can it be imposed by one person on
another. This is one of the points, I think, at which
taking seriously the subjectivity of subjects has implications. If the subject is truly a subject, then the research
is about *his* questions, and he needs to be decisively
involved in defining what situations, what outcomes, what

criteria are critical, for him, to those questions. This is not to deny the collaboration between subject and investigator, in both exploratory and elaborative phases of research, which is so strong a theme in Kelly's own account of a psycho-therapy client, alias a research student. In every encounter, there is likely to be a great deal in the way of perspective-sharing and negotiation of meaning. But ultimately, each subject has to be granted agency in the operationalising of terms, and in the setting up of a method of investigation which he is convinced is critical to the issue - just as he has to be fully and responsibly involved in the evaluation of outcomes and the decisions about what should come next.

The third and last of the distinctive emphases in Kelly's ideas which I see as relevant to psychological research, has to do with how such research should be evaluated. This must be very much a matter of what the research is about, and here, I think, construct theory leads in a particular direction. Kelly's psychology is all about the process of making sense of things - about how people came to know what they know, and how they live out that knowledge. One aspect of this is that the process of trying to make sense of things involves much negotiation with other people. Another aspect is that the sense which people achieve is not some generalised, abstract or disembodied knowledge; it is understanding framed within personal contexts, constraints, opportunities and time-scales. Finally, the central feature of it all is the absence of any single, final version of reality.

In so far as research is - or should be - the pushing outwards of the limits of psychology, research inspired by a construct theory psychology has somehow to respect and incorporate all these features. So I would see such research as being, essentially, about the process whereby people come to make sense of things - the process, that is, rather than, in itself, the content of the particular sense they make. The importance of social interaction and exchange has to feature, I think, as research which is in some sense collaborative, and which involves working with, not working on, subjects. The experienced personal contexts that provide the framework of construed meanings have also to be present quite explicitly in any research formulations and enquiries. Finally, if constructive alternativism is to be incorporated in research, then the 'findings' obtained will be seen as less important, in the end, than the whole progress of the research itself - which, after all, represents one version of the process it is investigating. The crucial question, about any research project, would then be how far, as a process, it illuminated our understanding of the whole human endeavour to make sense of our lives, and how fruitful it proved in suggesting new exploratory ventures.

   As a footnote, I would like to raise a personal question
which I feel construct theory *does not* help to answer.
The question is, for what kinds of personal issue is research the right form of enquiry? Kelly, who illuminates
so much, does not seem to help here, because, though he
wrote so inspiringly about psychological research, he
chose instead, for himself, the alternative mode - psychotherapy. In principle, I suppose any issue at all could
be tackled through a research project of some description;
but in practice, the research approach just does not feel
right for many personal-psychological questions. It may
be that it is less a matter of the kind of issue involved
than the stage that one is at with it. Sometimes, perhaps,
one has taken a question as far as one can in one's life,
and can extend one's understanding only by subjecting it
to the more formal and systematic experimentation of a
research project. Or sometimes it may be just the opposite:
an issue has been very little tested in one's own life,
and one needs the safeguards of a relatively distanced
and limited form of enquiry. There is a further consideration; submitting a question to research means launching
into a venture that is essentially public.
   I wonder why Kelly did not choose to engage in research.
Perhaps he suspected even the best research of crystall-
izing, or reifying, what should be experienced as an end-
less, evershifting, impossible-to-capture flow of events.
If so, his own comments serve to refute this suspicion.
As they also define the whole research undertaking as a
question-asking, rather than an answer-finding, endeavour,
it seems appropriate to end this discussion with Kelly's
own voice:

> When the experiment is over the scientist picks up
> the pieces and reflects on the whole undertaking,
> wondering if his sample was unrepresentative, his
> hypotheses improperly drawn, his controls ineffect-
> ive, or if there might be something at fault with
> the theoretical foundation on which the enterprise
> was based. You want to know about the scientist?
> This is the inconclusive story of his life. It is
> also the continuing story of man. (Kelly 1970a,
> p.259).

A PERSONAL CONSTRUCT APPROACH TO LEARNING IN EDUCATION,
TRAINING AND THERAPY

A PERSONAL CONSTRUCT APPROACH TO LEARNING IN EDUCATION, TRAINING AND THERAPY

Introduction

LAURIE F. THOMAS

*Centre for the Study of Human Learning,
Brunel University, Kingston Lane, Uxbridge,
Middlesex, U.K.*

The Centre for the Study of Human Learning is a self-financing research unit within the School of Social Sciences at Brunel University. It carries out research into processes of learning as these occur in the 'natural' situations of education, industry, therapy and the more everyday experiences of living. In addition it uses its expertise in this area to offer a variety of courses, consulting and other services to industry, commerce and various government agencies. Within the wider context of self-organised learning the Centre has become especially involved with personal construct theory and the development of repertory grid techniques as aids to learning. They can be used to help learners reflect upon their own construing. Exchange grids enable people to enter each others phenomenological worlds and negotiate these into a shared reality. A variety of procedures enable grids to be compared, one with another, either for a group or for one person in time. Formulation of a 'science of conversation' has enhanced the use of grids in all these modes. Alan Radley (see Abstract No. 24) has been particularly active in developing techniques for helping psychology students become more aware of their learning skills and attitudes towards each other and their subject matter. Fraser Reid (see Abstract No. 26) has completed a major study of the nature of conversation and its implications for therapy. He has developed a novel set of techniques for feeding back the content of conversational grids and for investigating signs of personal growth and development over a series of grid elicitations. Maureen Pope (see pp. 75-86) has used the feedback grid methods as a self-tutoring technique for trainee teachers. Roger Beard (see pp. 69-74) has picked up on the previous work of Sheila Harri-Augstein (see pp. 87-101) and is using grids to assess the influence of a reading development course on both the teachers and subsequently on the children they are teach-

ing. Sheila has developed learning-to-learn courses for
education and industry. The Structures of Meaning package
which she has pioneered offers a battery of more flexible
but systematic techniques for eliciting, feeding back and
exchanging the construction of meaning. Terry Keen (see
Abstract No. 16), working with Fraser Reid in Plymouth,
has developed a package TARGET using the grid as a vehicle
for assessment and self-assessment by polytechnic teachers.
Ranulph Glanville (see Abstract No. 10) has been particularly active in exploring the non-verbal construing of
architectural space by students of architecture. Mildred
Shaw has been responsible for writing the new series of
computer packages for eliciting and analysing grids both
singly and one in relation to another. Finally, Cliff
McKnight (see Abstract No. 22) has explored methods for
attributing weightings to constructs so that grids can be
used for predicting preferences. The work of the Centre
continues with new projects on management appraisal, industrial inspection and selection interviews. This paper
by myself and those that follow by Mildred Shaw, Roger
Beard, Maureen Pope and Sheila Harri-Augstein combine to
offer an overall perspective of the work of the Centre.

A PERSONAL CONSTRUCT APPROACH TO LEARNING IN EDUCATION, TRAINING AND THERAPY

Learning and Meaning

LAURIE F. THOMAS

Centre for the Study of Human Learning,
Brunel University, Kingston Lane, Uxbridge,
Middlesex, U.K.

Education, training and therapy are all concerned with learning but theories of learning as they appear in the psychological literature would realistically more often be named theories of teaching. They are concerned with how the teachers' (or experimenters') strategies and actions influence the learner. A personal construct theory approach to learning would treat it from the learner's point of view; as the construction of new meanings or the reconstruction of existing meanings in directions which are valued by the learner. In Kelly's terms, the individual models his inner and outer worlds and tends to value those meanings which are both relevant to his purposes and viable in maintaining his transactions. Thus, in learning by reading the learner is attributing meaning to the symbols on the page and is checking how well the meaning fits with his understanding of the structure of the language in which it is expressed.

Learning-to-learn by reading involves the ability to pursue a wider variety of purposes with a more varied set of reading strategies and to be able to assess the outcomes of reading in a more flexible but viable manner. This requires the development of whole new conversational methodology. What is true of reading is true of other learning skills such as discussion, listening, writing and involvement in practical exercises.

In learning to become an effective manager the trainee has to construe a wide variety of events, people and materials in ways that allow him to achieve his purposes, more economically and effectively. In the past the emphasis in management training has been to pass on the well established meaning systems of past generations, in content oriented courses. Now, there is an increasing interest in management development seminars and on-the-job learning, where the emphasis is to encourage the manager to explore, question and review his own and others' con-

struing of situations in which he is forced to accept the
consequences of his actions. What is true for the management trainee is true for the industrial inspector, the
supervisor and the maintenance engineer.

Therapy, not only in Kellyian terms, has always been
concerned with personal awareness and understanding. But
it was not until Carl Rogers and George Kelly made the
relationship, that a continuity emerged between learning
on the couch, at a lathe and in a seminar. Pirsig (1976)
is perhaps an unconventional expression of these same
continuities. Is there, in fact, a commonality of process
to be found in all learnings? Skinner has moved from animal training to programmed instruction to behaviour therapy to token economies. In our terms, his is a theory of
teaching but the continuities are there. If we accept a
personal construct theory approach to learning, what are
the implications?

Perspectives on Learning

Learning is not something which can be assessed objectively; it is something which is inferred. It can be inferred from behaviour and experience. Inferences are made
from particular points of view. Three major perspectives
are those of:

> (i) the teacher, trainer or therapist;
> (ii) learner or client;
> (iii) another observer or organisation of observers
> (e.g. parents, employers, doctors, family).

Very different inferences about what learning has taken
place will be made when observers have different perspectives, construe situations differently and therefore exhibit different intentionalities. In addition to the point
of view of the observer there is also his or her time perspective. Learning is usually inferred against criteria
which are set prior to the learning event, that is *pro-
spectively*. But it may only be recognised *retrospectively*
in terms which did not occur to the observer until after
the event had passed. Between the prospective and retro-
spective time perspectives there is also the recognition
and inference of learning which takes place *during* the
learning process.

It is vitally important to recognise this *here and now*
perspective because, for the teacher and the learner, it
is the point of view from which they trigger the control
mechanisms of behaviour and experience. When learning is
seen from the teacher's point of view the control is ex-
erted through his method of presentation and his skill in
conducting the event. Most theories of learning have been
generated from this point of view and are, as was previously stated, more correctly seen as theories of teaching, that is, as theories about how the teacher's behaviour influences the learner's experience. When viewed

from the learner's point of view, control is generated
through an internal monitoring system which has many personal dimensions within it. Thus short, medium and long
term criteria are continuously being generated and used
to control and guide the individual's learning. It is the
nature and quality of these criteria and the way in which
they relate one to another that determines the relevance
and viability of the learning experience. These referents
for evaluating the on-going outcomes of learning are themselves just another aspect of a personal construct system.
The repertory grid is an obvious choice as a method for
exploring such systems. The position which the Centre has
taken as its starting point is to develop tools and a
methodology for encouraging the development of self-organised learning skills which are seen as relating to Carl
Rogers' view of personal knowing and Michael Polanyi's
view of tacit understanding (1958). Thus learning is seen
as the construction and reconstruction of personally relevant and viable meanings which play themselves out and
are expressed in both experience and behaviour.

Relativity, Learning and the Exchange of Meanings

From physics through to sociology there has been a
general awakening to the relativity of all knowing and
the implications of this for how man may handle the realities which he constructs. Heisenberg showed the imposs-
ibility of measuring the complete system of an entity
accurately. Einstein constructed a universe in which even
the basic dimensions of time, space and energy depend upon
the time, space and energy of the observer. Polanyi has
explored the whole nature of the scientific enterprise in
terms of the integrity of the knowing of each individual
scientist. Lorenz has progressively explored the realities
of the members of species at different levels in the phyl-
ogenetic scale until he now sees man as one probably un-
stable attempt by living matter to reflect the nature of
reality. Levi-Strauss in anthropology sees the very patterns of man's thoughts and feelings as competent reactions
to the challenge of living in the cultural, natural and
technological settings in which he is placed. Herbert Mead
and Shultz see reality as a social construction which re-
ceives much of its individual validation from transactions
with other people who share it. George Kelly has expressed
this general paradigm for psychology within personal construct theory.

But psychologists have been loathe to leave their ref-
uge in an outmoded view of the physical science paradigm
and the even more untenable respectability of the statistics of agriculture. If psychology is to continue its growth
as a major science it must joyfully accept the implications
of relativity; not only the relativity of time and space
and the sensory and motor capacity of the observer, but

also the relativity of construing, the relativity of the
very mechanisms out of which meaning is constructed and
revised. Each man and woman is not only a personal scientist but also a personal artist when it comes to the construction, appreciation and revision of meaning.

Learning is therefore a very personal process. The meanings, the differentiations and refinements which are personally relevant and viable from one position in one individual's psycho-socio-physical reality may not be appropriate from and in another. Psychologists and others concerned with learning have not grasped the nettle of subjectivity boldly enough. Meaning is both personal and
negotiable. Objectivity can be achieved within socially
and physically stable realities. Meaning can be constructed, negotiated and exchanged. But this very process is
the vehicle by which man's reality is adapted and developed to meet his needs. Our contemporary theories of learning give us very inadequate control of these processes and
have offered little in the form of a psychologically relativistic technology of learning which might transform
our educational, training and therapeutic practices.

Experience, Behaviour and Purposive Action

Psychology has been artificially divided by the behav-
iourist/humanist controversy and it has been the policy
of the Centre to attempt to use descriptions of behaviour
and explorations of personal experience together as evidence for exploring the processes by which learning can
be achieved in a variety of different situations. Kelly's
original theory certainly took behaviour into account but
the methodology of the repertory grid seems to have led
the adherents of personal construct theory into an almost
purely experiential view of psychology. Our purpose has
been to explore man's modelling of his world as the basis
for his actions and we have found it useful to use cybernetic analogies, for example, a thermostat or the Grey
Walter tortoise. (A simple thermostat can be in one of
two conditions. If the room is 'too hot' the sensor can
only *perceive* 'getting cold' and the actuator, the heater,
is switched off. Thus the experiential state of looking
for cold is directly connected to the action state of
having the heater switched off. Once the temperature drops,
the sensor switches over and the heater is switched on.
The thermostat can now only perceive 'too hot' and this
is directly coupled to the action state of having the
heater on.) Such analogies help us to understand that perception and action, experience and behaviour are always
so closely interwoven that one cannot exist without the
other. This is essential to an understanding of the implications of personal construct theory. The Grey Walter
tortoise illustrates the additional point that the connections between sensor (perception) and actuator (behav-

iour) condition the target-seeking (purposive) functioning
of the mechanism (organism). A simple light sensitive cell
connected (feedback) to the steering of the three-wheeled
vehicle enables it to behave in ways which ensure that
ninety-nine percent of observers talk about it in purposive
(motivational) terms. It chases the light! But for Kelly
the construct system mediated between the experience and
the behaviour of the construer. To change the construct
system is to change the intentionalities and motivation
of the learner. To gain the interest of a student is to
offer him terms in which to construe his subject matter.
The best position from which to start this is the learner's
own construing when this is in his own terms. The repertory grid enables this. Thought, feeling and action can be
expressed, uncomfortably perhaps, but feasibly within the
repertory grid format. The grid is the psychological equivalent of the first rough ground plane mirror.

Given this approach to combining the evidence of behaviour and experience, the repertory grid can be used as
one tool for raising awareness of the process of learning.
It can in fact be used as a psychic mirror to reflect the
state of a person's construct system back to him. This
awareness raising function is a crucial step in achieving
self-organisation and personal control of one's own learning.

The Focused Grid : A Psychic Mirror

The 'raw' grid is difficult to interpret. It is like
a kaleidoscope of construct fragments. Analysis of similarities between elements and between construct offers us
a way of re-assembling the fragments into a mirroring surface. How can the relationships between elements, constructs and the responses of the subject be most clearly
expressed? The method of *focusing* a grid serves this purpose. Each element is compared with every other element
and the ordering of the elements in the grid is changed
so that those which are most alike are clustered most
closely together. Similarly, each construct is compared
with every other construct and the ordering of the constructs in the grid is revised to place like with like.
The resultant FOCUSsed grid simplifies the data (described
in Shaw pp. 59-68).

Talk-back through the focussed grid raises the learner's
awareness of his own construing, both in terms of the
major clusters of elements and constructs and in terms of
how the ordering of elements on constructs operationally
defines the construct and how the rating of an element on
all the constructs defines that element. This mutually
reinforcing definition of meaning is centrally important
to understanding the implications of personal construct
theory for learning.

Non-Verbal Grids

The repertory grid uses elements which are segments of an individual's experience and although the use of verbal labels often misleads us into believing that two people using the same words have access to the same experience, this is by no means always the case. The exploration of sensory and perceptual experience is enhanced when physical objects are used as elements and the grid elicitation is carried out in non-verbal terms. For example, two art students can each choose six art object (possibly their own work). They sit facing across a table. The first orders his objects to represent one construct. The other decides one by one where each of her objects should be placed to 'fit' the first student's ordering. Neither talks, one places her objects 'in the other's construct', the other nods or shakes his head. This continues until all twelve objects are ordered. Now the second student orders her objects and the first discovers her construct. The negotiation continues alternately. The experience of taking part in such a negotiation is that the visual and textual properties of the objects take over. If the partipants avoid sub-vocalisation and the temptation to 'talk to themselves' in verbal terms the whole experience becomes a creative encounter in non-verbal terms. The ordering of the objects can be recorded without verbal labels and the resulting grid focused and talked-back in the usual way.

The two-person exchange described above can be used to provoke the participants into negotiating in non-verbal terms but it is not essential for the elicitation of non-verbal grids. One person can sit with a set of objects and negotiate a non-verbal grid on his or her own. We have used this method with industrial inspectors to explore the perceptual organisation upon which their acceptance or rejection of products is based. A number of our consulting projects have been based on these techniques. Work measurement engineers evaluating performance, distilling experts blending whisky, clothes manufacturers assessing the quality of women's underwear and confectioners producing crackle toffee have all learned a considerable amount about the hidden sensory basis of their perceptual skills by using non-verbal grid methods.

Exchange Grids

The two-person procedure is not essential to the non-verbal grid technology but it illustrates the essential characteristics of a battery of techniques which can be used to enhance the quality of conversational exchange. We have called these procedures exchange grids. If a person elicits a grid of any kind the content can be taken to represent an operational statement about his or her construing. For example, a teacher may construe his stu-

dents in grid form, a foreman engineer his apprentices,
or a therapist her patients. The resultant grid contains
a pattern of relationships between elements and constructs
which uniquely defines the person construing. If the grid
descriptions are now copied out so that only the verbal
descriptions are given, that is, the ratings are all deleted, the empty grid may be offered to another person
for completion.

The second negotiator can approach the task of filling
in the grid in a number of different frames of mind. He
may wish to test his understanding of the first person's
point of view. If so, he will attempt to fill in the grid
as he thinks the other has already completed it. Careful
analysis of the difference grid (i.e. the remainder when
one grid is subtracted from another) reveals the areas
of understanding and misunderstanding revealing certain
elements and/or constructs as the sources of the problem.
Agreement and/or disagreement can be explored when the
second negotiator completes the first's empty grid with
ratings which represent his own construing of the meaning
of the element and construct descriptions. The negotiation
of the differences between the two grids can now be used
to reveal areas of agreement or disagreement. Various
computer analysis techniques PAIRS, CORE and DIFFERENCE
can be used to enhance the process of negotiation (described in Shaw and Thomas pp. 59-68).

Sociogrids

The relationship between two grids is not simple. Even
when both elements and constructs are shared as in the
exchange grid the pattern of similarity and difference
cannot easily be expressed as a single numerical measure
of similarity. The CORE analysis establishes which elements
and constructs are most shared between two grids and extracts a core grid which can be used as a referent for
relating one grid to the other. The more difficult problem is that of relating two grids which share a group of
common elements but have individually elicited constructs.

PAIRS ignores the verbal labels attached to the constructs and simply treats them in terms of how they order
the elements. All constructs in one grid are compared with
all constructs in the other grid and a measure of commonality of construing is obtained. Again a shared or 'mode'
grid can be identified. This consists of all the shared
elements and those constructs from either grid which are
most shared. PAIRS leads on to SOCIOGRIDS in which the
pattern of relationships between the grids from a group
is identified. This yields one 'mode' grid for the whole
group or a set of 'mode' grids representing cliques or
nodes of shared construing within the group. It also yields
'socionets' in which the measures of similarity between
all combinations of pairs of grids are used to produce a

sociometric description of the pattern of shared construc-
ing. Thus PAIRS, CORE and SOCIOGRIDS open up the possibility of exploring those socially defined realities which
form the basis of public knowledge.

Computer Aided Conversations with Oneself

The real-time data processing capacity of the computer
can be used to enhance the quality of the elicitation and
talkback conversations. If the participant sits at a computer terminal and it 'converses' with him or her in plain
language, the on-line interactive mode can be used to
derive a grid elicitation program, (PEGASUS). If, further,
the program continuously analyses the responses, the results can be used to provide a commentary on the nature
of the construing which is being revealed. As the participant becomes more and more aware of the implications
contained in his or her own construing, he or she can be
offered more and more choice about the direction which
the conversation should take. Careful distribution of the
choices between the computer and the participant can be
used to control and enhance the quality of the ensuing
interaction. Thus the computer becomes a powerful aid in
our exploration of the mysteries of conversation.

Teaching and therapy can be investigated not experi-
mentally but 'conversationally', since the computer program can be 'content free' articulating only the essential
skeletal decision-making structure of the conversation.
The content of the conversation is contributed by the
participant in the form of elements, constructs and the
ratings of the one on the other. Thus the computer offers
the content-free form in which the participant may have
an articulated conversation with himself or herself. But,
the paradigm can be taken further. Suppose two participants
sit at two computer terminals. The program (INTERPEG) can
begin to elicit grids from each. Not only can each grid
elicitation be interactive in itself but the computer can
compare and contrast the two grids one with the other
using the exchange grid theory to articulate the negotiation. We begin to be able to really investigate the properties of 'conversation'. Can teaching and learning, even
therapy (say non-directive counselling), be made to yield
their secrets?

Again, the paradigm can be expanded. Why must the conversation be restricted to two people in the here and now?
Why should not the 'experts' grid be stored in the computer? Participants may then converse with him in his absence (PEGASUS BANK as described in Shaw pp. 59-68). Why
should 'the expert' be one static grid? The computer store
can be systematised and continually updated by the conversations in which it participates. Why should the store
be constrained by the two dimensional tabular qualities
of the elements and constructs of the grid form? If ele-

ments define constructs and constructs define elements,
network theory, directed graphs, hierarchical and heter-
archical structures can all be recruited into the conversational exploration. (I am tempted to write PSYCHPEG but
perhaps that is enough to indicate some of the exciting
possibilities for extending personal construct theory and
giving form to the idea of an expanding grid technology.)

Constructing One's Internal World

The procedures of non-verbal grid games, coupled with
conversational technology implied in the previous section,
begin to slide a thin wedge into the doors of perception
and consciousness. Suppose you were asked to elicit a grid
using only those constructs which can be directly related
to your sensory experience. Designate those constructs
C(S)1, C(S)2 and so forth. Now suppose you were asked to
elicit a grid containing the same elements (or some related population of elements which share a subset with
the previous grid) and told to elicit constructs which
directly relate to your perceptual categories. You will
obtain a second set of constructs C(P)1, C(P)2 and so
forth. Now the two grids can be *focused* together and the
relationships between the C(S)s and the C(P)s explored
to reveal some of the structural forms of your construing.
The perceptual-motor basis of skill is open to exploration.

These techniques form the technology for some of our
industrial training projects. The techniques can be extended further. Experience in eliciting C(P) type-grids
shows that the types of construct elicited are not all
of the same form. Some are purely descriptive representing the socially agreed designations of what are taken to
be common perceptual experience. Coupled with the more
sensory and therefore potentially negotiable constructs
of the C(S) grid we can perhaps explore the quality of
socially stabilised realities. Other types of C(P) constructs are not purely socially descriptive, they carry
implications for what the participant infers from previous
experience. Inferential constructs proliferate and can be
focused, sorted and sifted to reveal the inferential structure of the construct system in the participant's own
terms. Kelly's claim that each of us models our own reality and uses this to anticipate the outcomes of our actions becomes open not to experiment, but to conversational
investigation. This can be illuminated by the computer-
based methods outlined previously. Skill, competence and
creativity are open to investigation. The tacit knowing
of Polanyi becomes available to conscious scrutiny.

The Investigation of Behaviour

Earlier in this paper it was claimed that personal
construct theory is not a purely experiential psychology
but can be made to heal the wound, close the gap, between

the humanist and behaviourist traditions. Behaviourists
are moving into the realms of self control; by handing
over the reinforcement schedule into the hands of the subject the gap between mindless manipulation and personal
autonomy is bridged. The expanding technology which is
here outlined starts bridge-building operations from the
other end. Records of behaviour, for example the video-
tapes of micro-teaching or sports coaching, can be used
to talk the learner back through sequences of his own
behaviour which are usually only open to observation by
the teacher or another observer. Technology for making
explicit behavioural processes normally hidden from the
observer and the observed can also be recruited for learner
talk-back. Records of reading behaviour and blood pressure
are but two obvious examples.

Thus, systematic conversational talk-back conversations
can be used to enhance the participants capacity to re-
construct and re-live his experience. This expands his
capacity for reflection and self-review. The talk-back
through behavioural sequences can be coupled with the personal construct technology to produce a more harmonious
relationship between the views of learning which arise
from the experiential and behaviourist viewpoints. Com-
puter-driven tape-recorders, video-tapes, slide projectors
and so on, allow us to dynamically link the grid based
conversational elicitations of personal construct systems
with these behavioural talkback techniques.

What possibilities are opened up if we add physiological
measures to our behavioural repertoire and link these into
the computer conversations. Perhaps the bastions of psy-
chosomatic diagnostics and the Eastern techniques for
achieving control over mind and body can be explored and
made available to investigation. Perhaps the skills of
the couch, the lathe and the seminar are continuous and
are open to investigation. Learning and the perspectives
from which it can be observed may offer the pathway to an
understanding of more than the trivialities of the memory
drum, the statistical relationships between I.Q. and examination results or the misleading complexities of much
educational technology.

The Science of Conversation

Humanist personal construct theorists often construe
the whole area of technology and computers with grave
suspicion. Inspection of the construct systems of many
technologists shows that in practice this suspicion is
often justified. But such problems arise from the social
realities in which the different groups live. A more
serious question is whether the socially negotiated physical reality which enables the computer technology to be
constructed has properties which justify the doubts of
the humanists. In other words, does the process of con-

versation involve more than the permissive information
passing and decision making which enables PEGASUS and
others, to articulate the interaction between two systems
of personal constructs? It obviously does! Carl Rogers
for example would claim that congruence, empathy and un-
conditional positive regard are essential to therapeutic
conversation. Each person needs to acknowledge and rely
on the person that 'lies within' (or is it contains) the
other construct system.

Part of the Centre's work is concerned to investigate
the personal properties of conversation and in this context the computer is seen merely as a temporary store of
some small part of a science of conversation. Without
elaboration I will finish by outlining the directions in
which this work is progressing. Any effective Learning
Conversation is thought to involve at least three different levels; the central one is of the 'tutorial conversation' in which the content of learning is negotiated
and learning contracts are defined. When learning seems
to be losing its relevance a 'life conversation' is required in which learning needs and purposes are negotiated
to map the results of learning back into the personal
knowing required for living. If a participant is unable
to achieve the learning contracts he defines for himself,
a 'learning-to-learn conversation' is required. Here the
skills and competences of learning are explored, reviewed
and developed.

The whole Learning Conversation can also be seen as
composed of three related dialogues. The first relates
to the 'process of learning' and is concerned to raise
awareness of process, bringing it into consciousness. The
second dialogue is concerned with providing *'support'*. This
creates the atmosphere in which emotions can be expressed
and blocks to learning can be dissolved. Finally, the
cybernetic examples were used to raise the issue of control. The monitoring or referent systems by which the
individual controls his own learning are often an imped-
iment to his personal growth and development. The *'referent'* dialogue explores the question of how the person
constructs and maintains this control system. A change in
the system of referents can transform the whole learning
process.

INTERACTIVE COMPUTER PROGRAMS FOR ELICITING PERSONAL MODELS OF THE WORLD

MILDRED L. G. SHAW

*Centre for the Study of Human Learning,
Brunel University, Kingston Lane,
Uxbridge, Middlesex.*

The Centre for the Study of Human Learning is interested in encouraging self-organisation in learning by helping people to investigate, expand and rebuild models for construing which will enable them to be more successful learners and users of experience. This paper describes how conversational methods are used which are content free, and which lend themselves superbly well to the real-time data processing of a computer. The application of these model building facilities has been in areas such as learning skills; psychotherapy and 'becoming'; management selection and development; industrial inspection and quality control; art and architecture; the maintenance of electronic equipment; career guidance and the training of counsellors; and in the education of both children and teachers.

Conversations may take place between two people, in a group of people, or within one person such as Perls' (1969) 'top dog' and 'underdog', or Pask's (1973) 'P Individuals'. Conversational heuristics have been embodied in content free computer programs which have the capacity to encourage and control conversation as rigorously and systematically as traditional experimental methods are monitored and controlled. In this context the Centre can be seen as a psychological tool-making unit.

The Programs

The repertory grid is used as a conversational tool to help people to become more aware of the patterns of thought and feeling implicit in their responses. The FOCUS program takes a completed repertory grid and re-orders it for talk-back purposes. The elements and constructs are sorted in such a way as to highlight the pattern of responses in terms of the similarities and differences. FOCUS is described later in more detail.

PEGASUS is an interactive program which elicits a grid using a conversational heuristic. Feedback commentary is given immediately the responses are entered. Again, it will be described in detail later.

SOCIOGRIDS is a method for examining the commonality of construing in a small group. The area of interest is represented by the shared elements, and from each individually elicited grid a pattern is constructed showing the subgroups of people who are construing in the same manner, and the content of construing which leads to these patterns.

ARGUS elicits six grids simultaneously from one person from different points of view, which are then processed on SOCIOGRIDS to explore the relationships of these viewpoints.

CORE examines the change between two grids with the same element and construct names. Details are given in 'Notes on Computer Programs' (Shaw 1977).

FOCUS - Grid Analysis for Feedback

The traditional methods of grid analysis have been factor analysis and principal component analysis. Later, multidimensional scaling was used, and more recently methods of cluster analysis. The method developed and used by the Centre is called FOCUS and is a type of non-inclusive two-way cluster analysis (Thomas and Shaw 1976).

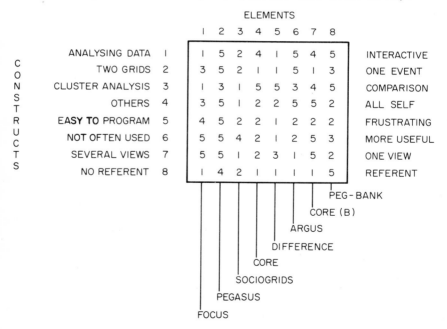

Fig. 1. Raw grid showing the construing of the programs.

The method was devised mainly for use in feeding back

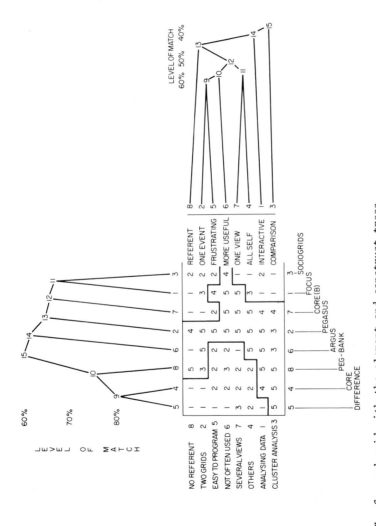

Fig. 2. The focused grid with the element and construct trees.

the analysis of the grid to the subject without displaying
any mathematical 'magic', complex computer output, or general problems of naming factors or components. The focused
grid retains the raw data, (shown in Figure 1) but presents it in a re-ordered form with tree diagrams indicating how the re-ordering was derived (shown in Figure 2).

   This is an example of a focused grid elicited using
the PEGASUS program. (For purposes of explanation the elements are in fact the programs discussed in this paper as
construed by the author using a 5-point scale.) The element tree above the grid is examined first. Initially
each element is considered as a cluster of one, and the
first combination to be formed is cluster 9 which contains
element 5, DIFFERENCE and element 4, CORE. Clearly these
are similar on all constructs but construct 1: they have
no referent, use two grids, were easy to program, are not
often used, incorporate several views, concern others
rather than just self, and are comparisons rather than
cluster analysis. PEGASUS-BANK then joins CORE to make
cluster 10. Again the differences are only on one or two
constructs. Looking down the patterns of ratings, element
2 (PEGASUS) is most different from DIFFERENCE, and the
progressive change in patterning across the grid shows
that SOCIOGRIDS on the right hand side is quite similar
to DIFFERENCE on the left. So that, if the constraint of
the linear re-ordering was not necessary, and another
dimension could be allowed in the representation, the
ends of the grid would swing round the back and come quite
close to each other.

   Looking now at the constructs, the first peculiarity
is that none are highly matched. In fact clusters 9, 10,
11 and 12 are all happening at almost the same level. The
types of construct also vary. It seems that 3, 1, 4 and 7
are descriptive, 6, 5 and 8 are subjective and 2 is not
very meaningful. Some indicate the point of view of 'me
as user', and others of 'me as programmer'. Thus Figure 2
shows how two-way clustering re-orders the grid responses
for easier and more meaningful feedback. This is the ess-
ence of the FOCUS technique. The majority of our other
programs use the FOCUS algorithm as a base.

PEGASUS - The Grid as a Cognitive Mirror

   Used in ways similar to this, the grid is acting as a
cognitive mirror. It is an empty, content-free structure
which reflects back to the user himself, his models of the
world, and his constructions on the world. In the PEGASUS
grid elicitation procedure, real-time data processing by
the computer allows the feedback to be immediate and interactive. In practice, the computer terminal takes the place
of the psychologist/therapist in the elicitation procedure.

   Kelly's view of 'Man as Scientist', or as it is now
being described 'Personal Scientist', shows man as modell-

ing reality in order to anticipate and act on the basis
of this anticipation. The quality of a person's models
will determine the level of skill, coping, competence and
creativity he will be able to achieve, and the PEGASUS
grid is a useful tool for heightening awareness of the
world. On the one hand it can be used in a 'grid-centred'
way, that is as a grid elicitation package with interactive feedback during the elicitation and analysis of
the results on completion of the grid. On the other hand
it can be used in a 'learning-centred' way. Learning must
necessarily involve changes in construing, and PEGASUS
encourages the user to review and revise his model as he
becomes able to differentiate in ways he previously was
not doing, and hence become more able to learn from experience. By giving the learner continual feedback when
constructs and/or elements are being used in a very similar way, the computer is doing what few human beings can
do with any degree of accuracy.
Figure 3 is a user's flow diagram of PEGASUS (Thomas and
Shaw 1977). It does not demonstrate the flow of the program but only the interaction between the human user and
the computer. It is divided into six sections. The first
one is the 'Basic Grid' in which explanations are given
and the first four constructs are elicited. The choice of
elements largely determines the depth of interaction that
can be achieved. The elements must relate to the purpose
the user had in mind, and represent as fully as possible
the universe of discourse which is to be explored. As each
construct is elicited, the poles are named and ratings
assigned to each of the elements on this dimension. The
elements are then grouped according to the ratings given
to highlight the patterning and allow the user to revise
his ratings or pole names if he wishes.
    The second section 'Construct Match' provides feedback
when two constructs are being used similarly. The options
given are to add an element to split these highly matched
constructs; to delete a construct if the user feels that
one subsumes the other; to combine the two constructs into
one; or to continue leaving both constructs in if he feels
that they are contributing differently to his grid. In
the earlier example of the grid in Figure 2, the on-line
feedback led me to split the constructs 'recent - long
standing' and 'not often used - more useful' by adding
the element PEGASUS-BANK. Later, however, the two constructs 'recent - long standing' and 'easy to program -
frustrating' were highly matched, and I chose to delete
'recent - long standing' at that stage.
    The third section is 'Element Match' which gives feed-
back on elements which are being construed similarly. The
options given here are to add a construct which puts one
of the elements on the left pole and the other on the
right pole; to delete one of the elements, which may or

may not be appropriate depending on the type of element being used; or to carry on leaving both elements as they are.

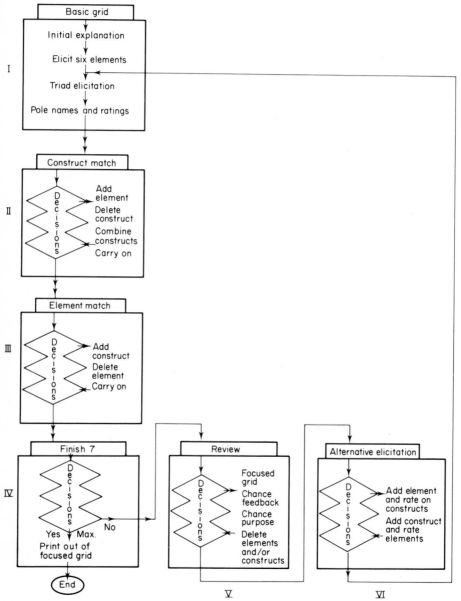

Fig. 3. Flow diagram for the PEGASUS interaction.

Since elements are less often deleted than constructs when a high match occurs, the resulting grid usually displays more highly differentiated constructs than elements as in Figure 2. If a construct or element has been added, the ratings of the other elements on that construct, or that element on all the constructs, must be entered.

Section four is 'Finish?'. This gives the user the opportunity to complete his grid at this stage during the elicitation. If he chooses to do so he is offered a choice of printout of either the results of the analysis or all the analysis. If at this stage the grid is maximum size the user must finish, but if he has the maximum number of elements he may add constructs to bring it to the maximum size.

The fifth section, 'Review', allows the user to see his grid in focused form. He may also adjust the intensity of feedback, and review or refine his purpose for eliciting the grid. As the elicitation proceeds the addition of elements and constructs may shift the boundary of the universe of discourse, and the purpose may need to be modified. The user may also wish to delete elements or constructs which he feels to be outside the boundary of his grid.

In section six 'Alternative Elicitation', the user is given more freedom to add an element, or a construct without using a triad. In the previous example, as the elicitation proceeded it became clear that CORE was being construed in apparently inconsistent ways. This was due to the fact that there are two main uses for this program: for comparing two grids done by the same person on two separate occasions, and for investigating the shared understanding between two different people. The problem was solved by splitting the element CORE into two elements - CORE being the version for two people and CORE (B) the version for one person over time. In the analysis, if these are in fact being used in the same way they will be highly clustered, which is not so in this case.

The user is also invited to choose his own triad for eliciting a construct, but if he chooses not to do this a pseudo-random number routine is used rather than fixed triads.

This is the basic structure of PEGASUS. An alternative form is MIN-PEGASUS which allows constructs to be added or deleted but does not give feedback commentary on matches between them. This version is used when one wants to discover how the user is construing in the situation rather than pushing him to differentiate highly matched elements and constructs. PRE-PEGASUS allows the user to start his grid on one occasion and continue or complete it at a later date.

PEGASUS-BANK is an addition to the PEGASUS program. It allows a bank of constructs to be stored in the computer

representing an 'expert' view of an area of public knowledge. As the processing takes place, continual comparison
with the bank gives feedback on how the user's constructs
map on to the expert's construing of the same elements.
Since the comparison is made in terms of how the construct
orders the elements rather than in terms of the verbal
labels, it is often found that although a person may have
only a vague idea of the expert's terms, he may in fact be
using very similar constructs. One example is that of a
grid using animals as elements. The biologist had elicited
a grid which was stored in the bank, the user had elicited
a construct which he called: 'horrible creepy crawlies -
nice, soft cuddly ones'. The computer's feedback response
was that 'horrible creepy crawlies' was highly matched
with the biologist's term 'arachnida', and 'nice, soft
cuddly ones' was being called 'warm-blooded mammals'.
Very often the user is both surprised and enlightened to
find the similarity between the patterning in his grid
and that of the expert. This technique therefore provides
a sound basis for assessment and a useful starting point
for training.

SOCIOGRIDS is a program which analyses the results of
common experience and/or training in a small group (Thomas,
McKnight and Shaw 1976). The negotiated elements represent
the subject under discussion and each person elicits his
own grid using personal constructs. The constructs from
each person represent similar or different thoughts and
feelings on the subject. Any pair of grids can be matched
one with the other to obtain a measure of overlap or
commonality of construing. The FOCUS algorithm provides
a simple method for doing this. All possible pairs in the
group are analysed in this way and a series of sociometric-
like diagrams are drawn, designated 'socionets', to illustrate patterns of similarity and dissimilarity of construing within the group. In addition, all the constructs
from each individual are classified in terms of the extent
to which they are shared. A 'mode grid' is constructed
from those constructs most frequently used by members of
the group and is used as a common referent with which
each individual is compared.

The Delphi technique used in conjunction with SOCIO-
GRIDS makes use of the mode grid to allow each individual
in the group to clarify his thoughts and feelings in the
light of the constructs most used by the group, and to
revise his constructs to highlight his position in the
group if he wishes to do so.

The ARGUS program describes a conversation between
several roles or points of view within one person. The
user is asked to name six people who are central to him
in the area under consideration, and he is then asked for
three constructs about these people. Taking the point of
view of one of his elements he is asked to re-rate all

the elements on the existing constructs and add a new construct which he thinks would be important for that person.
This is done from the position of each element in turn.
As the elicitations continue, he builds up six grids each
with the same element and construct labels, but with different ratings in the grids. If the elements represent a
set of significant others, each of the six grids captures
an important personal perspective for the elicitee. These
six grids are then processed on SOCIOGRIDS to investigate
how these personal perspectives relate one to another.

The CORE program compares two grids in which the same
constructs and elements are used, to identify the stable
or common component. It does this interactively, allowing
the user to delete alternately the element which is construed most differently and the construct which is used
least similarly, until he decides to stop. The remaining
stable elements and constructs constitute the 'core grid'.
One application is that of 'exchange' grids used to explore the extent of understanding and/or agreement between
two people; another is to chart change in one person over
time, to assess the effectiveness of therapy or training
for example.

In conclusion, these programs offer a facility that
turns the repertory grid back into a useful and developing technology. Other projects include the possibility of
extending the technology of learning-centred structures
to non-grid techniques. These might include different
ways of discovering personal constructs at different levels of organisation; and alternative ways of representation
such as Venn and Carroll diagrams from mathematics, and
hierarchies, heterarchies, networks, trees and linked
lists from computer science.

TEACHERS' AND PUPILS' CONSTRUING OF READING

ROGER BEARD

Centre for the Study of Human Learning,
Brunel University, Kingston Lane,
Uxbridge, Middlesex.

Introduction

In recent years there has been an increasing emphasis
in the educational world on the need for the 'development'
of children's reading skills. This has been most notable
in junior and middle schools (9-13 year olds). The increase
in book-based project work in the curriculum of many
schools catering for this age-range calls for a varied
and flexible range of reading skills. This project work
is carried out under a variety of labels: topic work,
thematic studies, centres of interest and others. Generally, children are required to use a variety of sources
to compile an individual 'special study' folder in a certain subject area.

In organising work of this kind, I feel that there will
always be uncertainties in the teacher's mind. How much
choice should pupils have in deciding the subject area to
be studied? Some boys may choose 'football' term after
term. One girl I knew compiled a project folder on 'horses'
three years running with different class teachers. Another
uncertainty is connected with the nature of the 'study
reading' skills which children need to deal most effectively with a range of written sources. Robert Dearden (1972)
has remarked how classes of children involved in project
work can resemble anything from an 'embryonic university'
to something like a 'wet playtime which lasts all day'.
This difference reflects underlying attitudes to books.

For book-based project work to be effective, children
may need to be involved in accessing and surveying information, defining specific purposes for reading, comprehend-
ing written texts at more than just a literal level, responding imaginatively to literature, constructing and
evaluating a variety of types of reading outcome and so
on.

Underlying these skills is a view of reading as an
active, generative process, as proposed by Thomas and
Harri-Augstein (1976). When such skills are absent the
project founders. Indeed, it can be argued that it is
only when embedded within a battery of these skills that

reading becomes really beneficial to individuals of all
ages in virtually any circumstances, whether in school or
college or more generally in learning whilst living. The
need for the development of these and other skills has
been emphasised in various publications including the
Bullock Report 'A Language for Life' (1975). Significantly
the Open University's reading courses have been called
'Reading *Development*'. The B.B.C. are soon to begin an
in-service course for teachers called 'Reading After Ten'.
   There are certain difficulties in trying to assess the
effect on teachers of courses about these skills and in
trying to evaluate the effectiveness of teachers' subsequent attempts to encourage their growth in children.
Firstly, we may over-estimate the maturity achieved by
teachers themselves in their use of 'reading as a learning
skill' and the empathy that this gives them with their
pupils' problems. A well-known paper by Perry (1959), for
example, highlights the relative inefficiency of Harvard
undergraduates in their ability to study by reading.
Secondly, by incorporating our own selective views into
our measuring instruments, we may also fail to do proper
justice to what children 'make' of the many reading tasks
which can be experienced in school and of the reading
materials to which they have access.

Application of Kelly's Ideas

   I hope that this brief introduction allows you to envisage the potential value of Kelly's repertory grid technique, and the recent extensions of this developed at the
Centre, to the evaluation of reading competence. The research in which I am engaged uses the grid technique to
assess how junior and middle school teachers' construing
of reading materials and reading activities is influenced
by an intensive, eight-month, part-time, in-service course
on the teaching of reading.
   In the coming months, grids will also be used to examine how the 'views of reading' of a sample of the pupils
in these teachers' classes, change as the ideas from the
course begin to be implemented by the teachers.

Aims of the Research

   The aims of the research are:
   (1) to elicit teachers' personal construct systems relating to reading materials, purposes and outcomes before
they begin their in-service course on reading;
   (2) to repeat these elicitations during and after the
course;
   (3) to assess the nature of any changes in constructs;
   (4) to relate these changes to the nature of the course,
through discussion with the teachers;
   (5) to elicit children's personal construct systems
relating to reading materials, purposes and outcomes when

they first enter the classes of these teachers in the
Autumn term of the year in which the teachers complete
the course;
    (6) to repeat these elicitations later in the school
year;
    (7) to assess the nature of any changes in constructs;
    (8) to relate these changes to the nature of the read-
ing for learning activities devised by the teachers and
thus indirectly to the content of the teachers' course.
Discussions with the teachers will take place and also
with the pupils if this is found to be practicable.

Methods

It was decided to concentrate on the constructs of
teachers and pupils relating to three aspects of the reading process. Three grids are being elicited:
    (i) reading materials
    (ii) reading purposes
    (iii) reading outcomes (acceptance of written, spoken,
conceptual, behavioural).
These three components derive from a model of the reading
process developed at the Centre.

The Grids on Reading Materials are based on six 'common
elements', the same six pieces of material being used in
all grid elicitations:
    an encyclopaedia
    a dictionary
    a well-known story for children
    a comic
    a book on a general subject
    a book on a specific subject (within the same sub-
    ject area as the general one)
Respondents are asked to add other types of material
to this list, if they wish to, before elicitations begin.
A tick and cross rating is used.
The common elements allow the SOCIOGRID computer analysis (see Shaw 1977) to be used to reveal and measure
commonality of construing. Construct systems and changes
in them can be compared between teachers, between a teacher and his or her pupils and between pupils.

*The Grid on Reading Purposes and the Grid on Reading Out-
comes* are both based on individually negotiated elements
and five point rating scales are used. These grids are
analysed using the FOCUS and CORE programs (see Shaw
1977). Changes in individuals' construct systems in the
year of the teachers' course or, in the case of the pupils,
in the year following it, will be closely monitored.

Report on Progress

At the present time, only the first set of grids has
been elicited with the teachers before they began the

course, and with a number of teachers not taking the course who are being used as controls.

The proposed elicitations with the children are currently being developmentally tested. The *materials* grid, using the same six examples of reading matter, has been elicited from children without many snags being discovered. They were interested and involved in the sorting and labelling activities, treating the grid like a puzzle or a challenging 'game'. When asked about the different *purposes* which they can read for in school, some anecdotal prompting has sometimes been necessary: 'Think of the different things you read or *could* have read at school yesterday or today' and so on..... The *'outcomes'* grid at first proved more difficult: but introducing the term 'effects of reading' and some non-directive prompting has enabled children to complete these grids without too much difficulty.

Early Analysis

Early analysis of the first four teachers throws up some interesting findings.

In the 'materials' grids, elements *added* to the initial six, as *other types* of reading material used in school include:

>   a reading laboratory card
>   a maths book
>   word games
>   wrappers
>   a newspaper
>   a postcard
>   a poetry book
>   a crossword book, and
>   an activity based English textbook.

The maximum number of constructs elicited in the materials grids was 9, the mean 7.5 (I have had my own constructs elicited on this grid and in spite of having been involved with reading courses for a number of years, only managed twelve from a total of twelve elements).

In the 'purposes' grids, the maximum number of constructs elicited was ten, the mean 6.25. The maximum number of elements negotiated was 9, the mean 7.8.

In the 'outcomes' grids, the maximum number of constructs elicited was 10, the mean 6. The maximum number of elements negotiated was 9, the mean 8.

The SOCIOGRID analysis includes the assembling of a 'mode' grid made up of those constructs from different grids which best represent the shared construing of the group.

As Laurie Thomas explained in his paper, *Focusing* involves re-ordering the rows and columns of constructs and elements in a 'raw' grid, in such a way as to produce a re-sorted grid in which every pair of adjacent rows and columns has more in common than in any other arrangement.

In focusing the 'mode' grid with those of each individual's reading materials' grid, the closest match was 85.7%. It is interesting to note that this match involved the grid of a teacher who appears to be the most unsure of her performance on the course and who is most keen to work with other students in informal study groups! All the teachers so far analysed have at least a 70% match with the mode grid. It is also interesting to note that my grid (as a course tutor who had been through all the 'reading for learning' course components) only had a 52% match with the mode grid.

The 'socionet' analysis provides a further commentary on the relationship between my construing of reading materials and those of the teachers. This analysis involves the focusing of all pairs of grids and the computation of similarity measures which can then be expressed as a sociometric-like diagram (i.e. socionet). A rank ordering of similarity measures enables an evolving sequence of socionets to be extracted. My grid was involved in the two highest similarity measures (links one and two), and with teacher number 2, I also seem to be the person who most relates to the other four (see link 8).

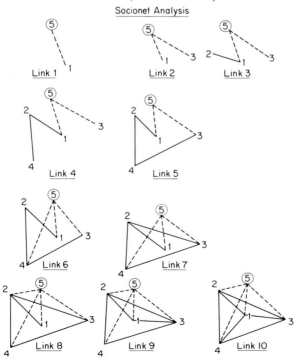

Socionet Analysis

Fig. 1. Socionet diagrams showing relationships between the participants.

Finally

The great bulk of work in this research has still to
be done but it is hoped that the results will help contribute to the understanding of the *transfer of ideas* in
teaching and learning, both at the level of professional
in-service training and in school classrooms. The repertory
grid allows the construing of reading to be explored in
the teachers' and the children's own terms. The SOCIOGRIDS
analysis will reveal the commonalities and differences in
construing both between people and over time. Thus, this
approach to the evaluation of a course avoids the more
obvious pitfalls which derive from measuring instruments
that embody only the researcher's views of the terms in
which 'change' or 'improvement' should be measured.

MONITORING AND REFLECTING IN TEACHER TRAINING

MAUREEN POPE

*Centre for the Study of Human Learning,
Brunel University, Kingston Lane,
Uxbridge, Middlesex.*

The training of teachers has long been a subject of much debate in educational journals, political papers and the national press. In this year of 'The Great Debate' on Education one can hardly fail to be aware of the great diversity of opinions and attitudes prevailing about what Education is or should be; how pupils should be taught, how teachers should be trained and how educational research should be conducted. The last two are of particular concern in this paper, although in effect many of the issues are inter-related.

Willey and Maddison (1971) in an enquiry into teacher training, commented that the Department of Education and Science and the Local Education Authorities had emphasised the quantitive demands of the service 'at the expense of the qualitative nature of much of the training'. At a time when several Colleges of Education are faced with closure, many argue that there is still a pre-occupation with quantity rather than quality. Demands for 'more research' into teacher training are frequent. However there is growing dissatisfaction among those in education with the outcome of traditional research on teachers and teaching. Teachers often resent the presence of the researcher who conducts his research solely from his vantage point without reference to the teacher's criteria. An example of this was the publication in the national press that large classes had little effect on pupils' performance. Teachers questioned the lack of regard for the stress caused to the teacher in dealing with large numbers of pupils within a classroom.

Biggs (1976), in discussing the relationship between Psychology and Education, is critical of the findings of educational research based largely upon an outmoded physical sciences paradigm. He shares with teachers the disillusionment with traditional psychology. Thus he says of education and psychology: 'Let us face it: The frustratingly long honeymoon is over'. I also would like to suggest that the marriage between a psychology based on the idea of absolute truths and education is finished. However I would argue that psychology based on personal con-

struct theory offers a new relationship with education.
One in which the views of those actually involved in the
educational process are paramount and not subordinate to
the elegance of experimental design.

Education research has largely consisted of mass sampling techniques where certain variables, notably IQ or
social class, of a sample have been measured and related
to performance - often under 'controlled' environments
such as selective or comprehensive schools or streamed
versus non-streamed classes. Barker-Lunn's (1970) report
on such studies has shown that in one half of a sample of
72 matched primary schools, pupils in non-streamed schools
made better progress than pupils in streamed schools,
whilst in the other matched half the reverse was the case.
Barker-Lunn concluded that the differences must be due to
some unknown factor and that 'it is possible that teachers'
attitudes have something to do with it'.

It is my belief that the constructs of teachers and
pupils are more important than 'the System'. The 'System'
or 'method', be it comprehensive, grammar streamed, de-
streamed, setted or whatever, is probably not the opera-
tive variable. It is surely the constructions of the people
within the system that is the real source of influence on
any outcome. Runkel (1958) suggested that the 'frames of
reference' of the teacher was an important determinant of
classroom behaviour. Ben Morris (1972) echoes this in his
review of objectives and perspectives in education over
the last few decades. He notes a shift from a subject-
oriented approach to the 'Perspective of the Personal'.

The 'Perspective of the Personal' is central to the
work of George Kelly. This is implicit in the title of
his theory - Personal Construct Theory - and explicit in
his writings, for example: 'We start with a person. Organisms, lower animals and societies can wait' (Kelly 1970).
According to Kelly each person erects for himself a representational model of the world which enables him to
chart a course of behaviour in relation to it. This representational model is subject to change over time, since
constructions of reality are constantly tested out and
modified to allow better predictions in the future. To
understand an individual it is not as important to know
what his early childhood experiences were or what environmental circumstances he is now in, as it is to know *what
he feels and thinks about those circumstances*, that is,
to come to some understanding of his representational
model.

Kelly's theory and methodology form a coherent approach
which is consistent with many of the current ideas on education. Despite this, relatively little use has been
made within the educational sphere, of the techniques he
evolved. Reid and Holley (1972) have applied Repertory
Grid techniques to the study of choice of university and

the technique formed a basis for Roy Nash's (1973) work
on teachers' perception of pupils' performance. It would
seem that the tendency is still towards nomothetic studies
and particular difficulties in obtaining access to schools
and colleges for educational research has resulted in researchers adopting the form of grid technique, where elements and constructs are provided rather than elicited
from the individual concerned. Whilst I agree that, provided adequate groundwork is done in obtaining representative (hopefully) elements and constructs, the analysis
of such grids can often provide more useful information
than the conventional questionnaire, I feel that the most
powerful use of repertory grid technique lies in the elicitation of elements and constructs.

There have been many studies aimed at assessing the
attitudes of student teachers, using conventional questionnaire and attitude scales, for example, McLeish (1970).
The 'frame of reference' of the student teacher is an
important factor in his teaching behaviour. It would seem
therefore that this is an aspect that needs to be monitored
and that the student teacher could benefit from *reflecting*
on the way he/she construes teaching.

Laurie Thomas discusses the need to consider changes
in the learner's perspective when evaluating a learning
process and has suggested the use of repertory grid technique as a 'psychic-mirroring' device to aid the learner's
self-awareness of his process (see p. 51).

The following case study is an extract from a research
project aimed at using repertory grid technique to monitor
the viewpoints of student teachers before entering a major
teacher practice session, during the teaching practice and
on return to the college course.

Some brief details of the main project may be necessary
at this stage. Volunteer subjects within two teacher training establishments were obtained and then randomly assigned
to one of three groups:

Group 1 - Subjects interviewed before and after teaching practice.

Group 2 - Subjects interviewed before and after teaching practice, plus completion of 3 grids, one before, one
during and one on return to college after teaching practice.

Group 3 - Subjects completed the same schedule as Group
2 with the addition of feedback sessions during which the
analysis of their previous grid was discussed.
Each person in Group 2 and Group 3 provided their own elements and constructs. The elements were those things which
the person thought of when he/she had 'teaching' in mind.
Tape recordings of interviews and feedback discussions
were made. The grids were analysed using the FOCUS programme (see Shaw p. 60).

Figure 1 shows the hierarchical element 'tree' or

cluster diagram for a subject belonging to Group 3 above.

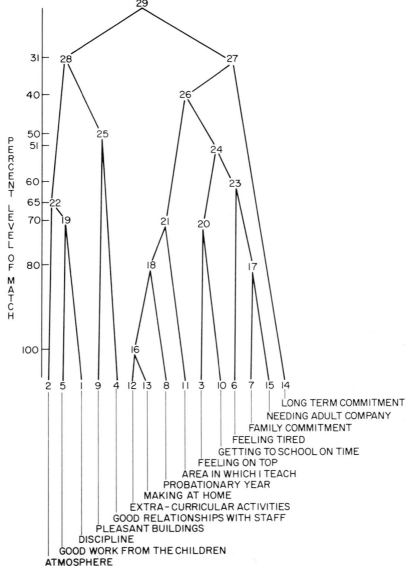

Fig. 1. Element tree for grid completed prior to teaching practice.

On obtaining the list of elements at the outset I was
immediately struck by the fact that, despite many conversations with student teachers before this study, I would

not have provided *needing adult company* as an element.
This however proved to be a very important element as far
as this student teacher was concerned. It was one of the
reasons behind her decision to enter teacher training.
Family commitments were also important, as these could
affect her performance as a teacher. This particular subject was divorced, with a young child.

The 'tree' diagram (Figure 1) was shown to the subject
during the feedback session and she was asked to comment.
Individual groupings, for example *marking at home*, *extra-
curricular activities*, *probationary year* and *area in which
I teach*, were discussed. The emphasis being on the *subject
providing the labelling or rationale* for the cluster rather
than the researcher naming the factor, which is often the
case in other studies. As I was interested in monitoring
possible changes due to experience and reconstruction
during teaching practice the subject was given her original list of elements and constructs, was allowed to add
any elements or constructs and then was asked to re-rate
the elements on the constructs. Thus one had a base comparison between original elements and constructs on each
occasion plus a monitoring of any additions.

Figure 2 is from the second grid from the same subject,
completed in the middle of her teaching practice. She
decided to add *relationships with the children* to her element list, as she now realised this was an important factor in teaching. One can see that there was a tight cluster - *feeling tired, family commitments, needing adult
company, marking at home* and *feeling on top*. In describing this the subject explained that she was very pressur-
ised during teaching practice and found it difficult to
cope with both family and school work. She now realised
how important the *atmosphere* in the classroom was for
the general *discipline* of the children. She commented on
the fact that *good work from children* and *pleasant building* seemed to be linked - she was not surprised by this
and felt it represented her feelings and experience during teaching practice, as the following extract from her
tape recording indicates:

> It was a Victorian school with very high ceilings,
> and very little display space, and it was very diffi-
> cult to organise the classroom so that it looked
> attractive. The vast ceilings, and you had to stick
> things on the wall with sellotape and it looked
> messy. There weren't any nice display boards. You
> felt you wanted to - it would be more incentive to
> get the classroom looking nice and get the children
> producing stuff if you could in fact have displayed
> it nicely, but it was very difficult.

Her comments on the new link between *good relationships
with staff* and *long term commitment* were also revealing:
> When I was at the school that I was on teaching

practice at I found that staff..... Well I just was
not compatible with them at all and I just couldn't
imagine teaching for a long time in that situation
with that kind of company.

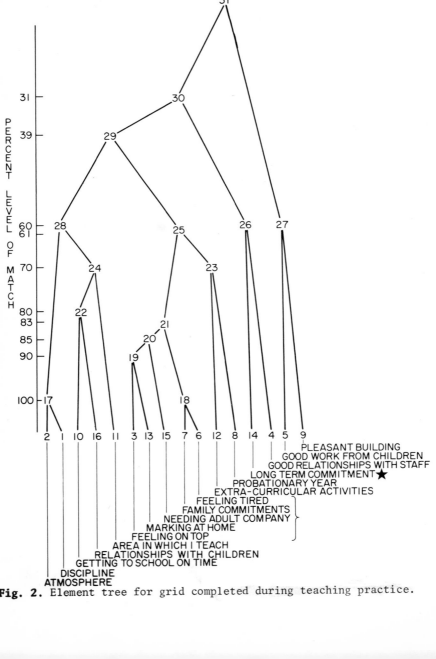

Fig. 2. Element tree for grid completed during teaching practice.

I would really find it very off-putting unless there
was staff there that I felt I fitted in well with.
I don't think you can isolate yourself in the classroom all day, I think you need to have some kind of
feedback from the staff which I just didn't have at
that school..... I really do think I need to be,
feel inspired. You know I just found the staff exceptionally dull, exceptionally unimaginative and I
just felt completely an outcast. You know they weren't
antagonistic towards me, I just had absolutely nothing in common with them at all which is quite horri-
fying. I couldn't possibly consider doing a job if I
felt like that about people.

In addition to using the clusters and changes in cluster
as a basis for generating further discussion, the changes
in ratings for each element on the two occasions were explored. If one keeps the constructs constant and enters
the ratings for the element on two occasions in the same
raw grid, one can compare the ratings for each element.

	1st occasion					2nd occasion		
	E1	E2	E3	E4.........E15	E16	E17	E18.........E30
C1 ⁻	3	4	1	5...........4	5	2	3.............4
C2 ⁻	2	3	4	3...........5	4	2	4.............5
C3 ⁻	4	5	2	5...........3	2	2	3.............3
⁻	.	.	.	....	.	.	....
⁻	.	.	.	....	.	.	....
C15 ⁻	3	3	4	3...........3	4	3	4.............5

Fig. 3. Diagram showing the combination of two grids.

For example, Figure 3 represents a portion of a 30 x 30 element matching score matrix derived from one 15 element and
15 construct grid given on two occasions. Thus one can see
that element 15 ratings have changed very little compared
with the changes on element 1 ratings. By putting the ratings in in this way one can obtain a matching score matrix
for elements. Figure 4 is a portion of a 30 x 30 element
matrix which highlights the different matching scores obtained for each element with itself for the subject in
this case study.

Whilst there was not a great deal of change in the elements, three were somewhat different, namely *atmosphere,
long term commitment* and *area in which I teach*. Again, the
verbatim report of the subject was of interest:
And the *area in which I teach* I did change my mind
about that actually, because I was thinking more of
travelling, and yet when I was teaching in this sub-
urban area I started thinking of the areas in terms

of social class, which I certainly wasn't thinking of to begin with. I would be far happier to teach in an area where I felt comfortable, where I felt I was achieving something, than to teach in a school which was very dull close by.

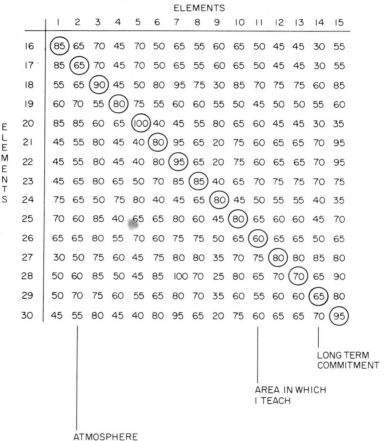

Fig. 4. Portion of 30 x 30 matrix of element matching scores indicating change in particular elements.

This case study illustrates that using grid analysis as a base one can gain a great deal of insight into how the person feels about teaching in *his/her own terms*. I would suggest that these extracts tap issues of personal importance to the student teacher which will have significant bearing on both her performance as a teacher and her own career choice. The discussion of such learning experiences could be a valuable addition to tutorials or counselling sessions.

Having had some subjects complete grids without feedback I was able to assess how useful I felt both methods were. I believe that the majority of subjects in Groups 2 and 3 enjoyed reflecting on their thoughts about teaching - many reported that it was probably the first time that they had sat back and reflected on their personal approach. This is supported by Terry Keen's work using Repertory Grids as a basis for feedback to teachers about their views on effective teaching (see Abstract No. 16). He reports that teachers often said that they had not really given much thought to their personal viewpoint and that the exercise gave them valuable insight into their own perspective. However, I felt that Group 3 subjects gained more from the exercise having had sessions where the analysis of their grids were discussed. Apart from the additional benefit to the subject, I feel that the researcher gains enormously by adopting the strategy of discussing the analysis with the subject. In this way the interpretation can be as the subject sees it rather than that of the researcher 'with his hat on'.

Whilst the major aim of the project was to gain some insight into the representational models of the individual student teachers, the data obtained raised some other interesting points. Given that there was a common set of elements and constructs on the three occasions that subjects completed 'grids', it was possible to obtain, for each subject, a crude numeric for the amount of change between any two occasions by the summation of the differences between ratings on the two occasions for each cell of the grid and expressing this as a percentage of the theoretical possible difference between the pair of grids. In this way it was possible to explore when the largest amount of change occurs.

Figure 5 indicates that the greatest change occurred between the occasions 'prior' to 'during' teaching practice since the difference between grids 2 and 3 for many subjects was less than the difference between grids 1 and 2. Many investigations into teacher training have emphasised the importance of teaching practice for the student teacher. It would appear to be a time of considerable reconstruction for the individual. Indeed the subject of the case study given in this paper emphasised that, although she had been made aware of sociological factors involved in teaching from lectures on sociology, it was experiences during teaching practice that had turned these 'sociological facts' into personally relevant issues. This represents a shift from public to personal knowledge (Polanyi 1958).

Morrison and McIntyre (1974) note that, in almost every investigation of student teachers' attitudes, any changes induced by college courses are relatively short lived.

MAUREEN POPE

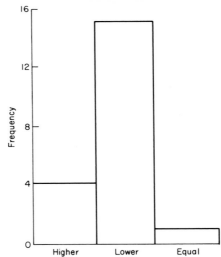

Fig. 5. Difference between grids 2 and 3 compared with the difference between grids 1 and 2.

Runkel and Damrin's (1961) study of student teachers noted a loose-to-tight-to-loose construing cycle throughout training. Figure 6, from the present study, shows a slight trend for the students at the end of their college year to be closer to their original position than to their point of greatest change reached during teaching practice. I feel that this issue is worthy of a more thorough investigation than was possible within the framework of the present study.

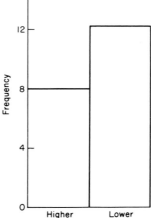

Fig. 6. Difference between grids 1 and 3 compared with the difference between grids 1 and 2.

Earlier in this paper I mentioned that it was important
to consider the learner's perspective when evaluating a
learning event. This is not to say that the tutor's appraisal is irrelevant. It is relevant to the tutor and is often
relevant to the student. Figure 7 represents the Teaching
Practice Assessments for the three groups of students at
the two colleges who took part in this study.

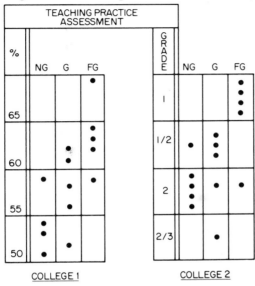

Fig. 7. Teaching practice assessment obtained by subjects within each
group.

It can be seen from this that the trend is for those within the 'grids with feedback group' to obtain higher Teaching Practice Assessments than those who completed grids
and that those who completed grids only had higher assessments than those who were interviewed without completing
grids. Given that there was no contact between myself and
the college staff as to who volunteered to take part in
the study and that the staff were unaware of the full details of the project, these results are encouraging.
    I have already stated that I believed that Group 3 sub-
jects gained in personal awareness from the 'conversational approach' (Harri-Augstein and Thomas 1975) adopted with
this group and that the researcher is able to incorporate
these discussions into his analysis. These latter findings,
albeit with a small sample, may well indicate that the
raising of student teachers' personal awareness has impli-

cations for the external criteria applied by the tutors.

Within the context of this study I feel that the results suggest that the methodology allows one to attack
the qualitative aspects of teacher training. It provides
a framework within which the 'person' can emerge and their
attitudes can be examined in their own terms. Changing
viewpoints throughout the course of training are significant aspects of the student teacher's learning and should
be of interest to those responsible for guiding their
learning. Feedback on academic performance is usually
given as a matter of course - I would suggest that reflection on their change of ideas about teaching is also of
importance to the student teacher.

Personal construct theory and repertory grid methods
are consistent with the new emphasis on relevance in educational research and the 'Perspective of the Personal'
(Morris 1972). The wider implications of the theory and
methodology within the educational context have yet to be
fully explored.

REFLECTING ON STRUCTURES OF MEANING:
A PROCESS OF LEARNING-TO-LEARN

E. SHEILA HARRI-AUGSTEIN

*Centre for the Study of Human Learning,
Brunel University, Kingston Lane,
Uxbridge, Middlesex.*

General Introduction

Personal Knowing and Public Knowledge

The culture of any given society (its Arts, Science, Technology, Religion and Social System) is characterised by a vast array of artifacts; products which represent the ways in which individuals and groups have sought to express and record meaning. A Tibetan 'thangka'* (illustrating The Peaceful Buddas, the Buddas of Knowledge and the Wrathful Buddas) which summarises Tantric-Buddist-iconography offers one pertinent and beautiful example. Equally relevantly, one could have chosen a Welsh love spoon, a Bob Dylan folk poem, the Great Pyramid of Cheops or a 3-dimensional model of D.N.A. These artifacts represent a store-house of society's strongest and most enduring systems of public meaning; the mindpool of a culture, (to draw an analogy from the neo-Darwinist concept of the 'gene pool').

A personal construct psychology must inevitably concern itself with how each individual interacts with this mindpool to construct personally satisfying, significant and viable meanings' Such 'meanings' will enable the individual to continue transacting effectively with the events, people and objects which make up the realities of his or her world. These personal understandings offer better insights into individuals' own processes and enhanced communication with the processes of others.

In slow changing societies the equilibrium between processes of socialisation and self-actualisation is such that the structures of public meaning and the purposes embodied in these, remain fairly stagnant. The 'mindpool' stabilises into a system of meaning which is preserved as ritual and dogma. Within such societies the individual, for example an architect, is expected to learn the rules and content of the mindpool and to practise these in the ways specified by the culture. In our contemporary society, partly because of the pressures created by the fast-changing social and technological conditions and partly because

of the person-centred philosophical creed of the times,
the balance is much more towards the renaissance of the
individual. There exists an increasing emphasis on inno-
vation, on a questioning of existing realities and on a
celebration of awareness as Illich ardently expounds.

Within the crisis-ridden conditions which prevail in
current societies, the structures of meaning of today can
become the chains of tomorrow's mind. Emphasis needs therefore to be given to the processes whereby personal understanding is achieved rather than to content of knowledge
per se. Awareness and control of the process by which
meaning is attributed enables the individual to develop
a mode of construing which facilitates competency in ongoing transactions with chosen realities. It is this which
becomes the selective factor in the struggle for personal
growth and social survival, not knowledge and expertise
in the content of the mindpool itself.

Learning how to learn therefore has a central function
to play in contemporary education, and a self-organised
learner can create personally viable structures of meaning
from within a repertoire of idiosyncratic needs and purposes. Both the content and the purpose of the mindpool
become changed as individuals seek to personally express
and find themselves within their social context. Becoming
a self-organised learner depends on overcoming the basic
tendency towards the maintenance of stasis and the practise of habitual mechanisms of thought and behaviour, so
that alternate ways of acting on, and experiencing the
world can be sought. The robot-in-man then becomes servant
rather than master, and the learner is freed to explore
and develop competence. An individual can then stroll
around the system of public meaning in a given society and
remain free to interact with it in personally meaningful
ways. Despite this fairly obvious argument, current educational practice gives much too much emphasis to dogma
at the expense of personal knowing. Ranulph Glanville's
work with architectural students is a particular exception
which proves the rule (see Abstract No. 10).

A Multi-faceted Approach to Meaning

Individuals experience and express thoughts and feelings in many forms. Meaning is expressed in the kinaes-
thetic sense of the voluntary muscle system, in the visual,
auditory, tactile and olfactory sensory systems as well
as in a symbolic pattern of relationships which are continually being constructed as a person interacts with the
world through the mediation of language. In riding a motorcycle, chairing a meeting, or reading a book, the emphasis
given to each form within the total system of meaning will
differ, but each plays its part, within the person's construing.

Our use of language plays a key role since the symbolisation of things, events, people and ideas relates richly and complexly to our sensory and behavioural experiences. Often we are only partially aware of this vast and complex system of meaning within which we operate. It becomes difficult to communicate this meaning to oneself or to others. To attempt to teach another to ride a motorcycle shows one, that although this understanding is represented in our personal knowledge, very little of it is in symbolic form. Rather the meaning is in the muscle sense and organisation, in visual experience linked to balance and motion, in the feel of the hand on the throttle and the foot on the brake, and the visual perspective of the road. Similarly, the architect's appreciation of space is largely non-verbal.

This partially tacit understanding influences the ways in which we anticipate, act out, and revise our views of our personal world. Attempts at the outward expression of this multi-faceted and tacit system of meaning can facilitate the construction of more personally significant and viable representations of knowledge. This depends on the development of an awareness of the 'self in process' and of 'others in process'. The outward expression of meaning can be used as a MIRROR of process and reflecting on this reflection can enable individuals to review and develop their competency as learners. This mirror should reflect meaning in terms which are compatible with the original experience.

Unfortunately, education gives too much emphasis to symbolic forms of meaning, these cease to be means becoming ends in themselves, a pattern of abstract relations divorced from other forms. This monolithic concern with symbolic understanding, particularly in the middle school and in higher education, may well result in other aspects of meaning degenerating into vestigial modes of representation so that an individual's potential for creating a wide-ranging system of personal meaning becomes impoverished. The word 'academic' often conveys this. Also, too little emphasis is given to developing insights into personal processes, so that a high percentage of 'the educational product', society's youth, end up as fairly effective robots, totally vulnerable and unable to cope in a rapidly changing and stringent environment.

Examples of Ways of Representing Meaning

During socio-psychological evolution, man has devised means of expression which have become very powerful instruments for embodying different classes of meaning. A few selected examples of how meaning can be represented serve to illustrate the wide variety of ways of construing that can be generated by man and woman.

A Christian view of the act of creation as interpreted by Heronymus Bosch depicts Adam and Eve in the original garden. On the other hand the shri-yantra which is the most powerful meditative yantra in Tantric-Buddish philosophy, interprets creation as a reversal of genesis depicting time as a projection of human experience and knowledge.

The idea of 'womanhood' has been represented in infinite ways within various cultures. Kirchner within the movement of German expressionism and Corot within French impressionism, depicts woman in her daily life, smoking a cigarette in a cafe and reading at home. In Tantric art Radah awaits Krishna, adorned for her daily life, and the woman as Goddess is depicted in the Tantric Kali.

The relationship between man and woman has been expressed in sculpture, painting, and in symbolic prose. Maillol illustrates the pair as a loving couple, Henry Moore as a family unit and Tantric Art as joint seekers of self-actualisation within a sexual relationship. The Tantric view of psychological process depicts man and woman (Shiva and Shaki) in complete union joining in the totality of experience and separating into an acceptance of a subjective - objective view of the world.

Another completely different class of meaning is represented in the findings of science. The double-helix model of D.N.A., the structure of the Retina are two typical examples from Western science. A Talisman for tapping the vitality of the brain represents an Eastern example.

Within different cultures a variety of ways exist for exhibiting the structure of knowledge. Gordon Pask (1975) has developed the Entailment Structure and Laurie Thomas the Focused Grid. Within biochemistry, flow diagrams describe the complicated pathways of physiological processes. Lama Govinda depicts the structure of consciousness as pyramidal planes of existence, and Chinese calligraphy represents 'happiness' in one hundred different symbols.

Two very different ways of representing the human body are epitomised within the physio-anatomical systems in the tradition of analytical Western medicine and as a system of energy forces or chakras in the tradition of Eastern psychology.

Again, in verbal language there exists a vast range of different forms of representation from Joycean prose, Bardic stances, Haiku poems to Sufi tales. Noh or Pinter drama, ballet, mime, mathematical proofs, chemical formulae, maps, plans, temples, Zen drawings, and Islamic carpets are all equally valid forms that man and woman have sought to express meaning.

Each example is highly selective, enhancing some aspects of meaning at the expense of others and represents an end point in a specialised search for expression. *The problem is that such particular artifacts or final forms have become objects of knowledge rather than examples of how personal meaning is sought.*

Even when examples show the processes of expression quite clearly, as in some Art sequences, mathematical proofs or music, the teaching emphasis is toward selling existing languages, rather than in creating wide-ranging personal means of expression. Often in educational curricula, attempts at the exploration of meaning have been packaged *into separate historical studies*. Education fails to emphasise the importance of early attempts at grappling with knowledge, whereas it should consist of such battles. The 'discovery method' should be implemented within a pedagogical framework describing the conversational interaction of 'the learner in process' exploring the chosen resource. This is quite a different view of discovery learning to that embodied in the Nuffield syllabus and to that held by those exponents who believe that the process itself needs to remain semi-mystical.

Reflecting on the Reflection

Individuals can be encouraged to experience the processes whereby meaning is created and hence learn to learn by systematically reflecting upon the terms in which they think, feel and act. This depends upon a conversational interaction which accepts both the learner and the tutor, therapist or researcher as potential equals. Each represents a semi-autonomous mode of communication and control. Whilst the contributions of each may be of a different kind, they are of equal value. The learner can tap his or her own experience aided by the researcher's technology and conversational skill. This technology must enable the researcher to mirror the learner's processing so that this can be made at least partially explicit. The mirroring device must be capable of tapping the multi-faceted resource of personal meaning experienced by the learner.

Many of the artifacts in society can be recruited as mirroring devices. Either by constructing such artifacts or by attributing meaning to the artifacts created by others, individuals can be helped to become aware of, and review, process. The contemplation of a Gerald Manley Hopkins' poem, writing an article, building a boat, reflecting upon a Surrealistic Still Life by Griz or Dali, can be equally powerful ways in to process. Again, observing the strivings of others, for example the paintings by Van Gogh from 1886 to 1890 or the drawings of Leonardo de Vinci as recorded in his Notebooks displaying experimentation with the visual representation of beauty through perspective, light and shade, can lead to insights of personal process.

The problem with using these artifacts as 'mirrors of process' is that they represent highly developed and content focused devices and one level of purpose is embedded in their form and content. Unless the individual learner is capable of transcending this to arrive at a meta-des-

cription of the processes involved in constructing or
attributing meaning to these artifacts, he or she will
remain imprisoned in content and therefore almost totally
unaware of process. Specialist psychic mirrors on the
other hand can be designed so that the learner is elevated
to a description of process. But, what kind of descriptive
system and display device best captures the psychological
processes of construing?

Psychology has fallen into the trap of continually producing statistically-based descriptions such as Personality
categories, IQ and Creativity measures, and Semantic Differential scales, with which the individuals concerned feel
uneasy as descriptions of 'the self'. Rogers' gigantic
step inwards into process laid the foundation for exploring the conditions of change but he pays little attention
to the modelling facility itself, the unique inner processes which initiate, sustain and restyle the 'cognitive
maps' of a person. Husserl opened up a new vista of phenomenological investigation, but psychology had to wait
for Kelly's metaphorical conception of 'man the scientist'
for the development of the personal biography and the
repertory grid as tools for the personal description of
meaning. *It was through Kelly's craft that a breakthrough
was achieved into a Humanistic Technology that allows
meaning to emerge in individual terms and yet retain some
systematic form.*

Let us consider very briefly the necessary attributes
of a psychic mirror. The device must be capable of:

(i) exhibiting meaning as part of a hierarchically
organised system;

(ii) tapping personal meaning in all its fullest
aspects, as experienced by the individual;

(iii) enabling the individual to become aware of the
intentionality which influences thought, feeling and action;

(iv) allowing the exploration of meaning in its most
bizarre or idiosyncratic form;

(v) realising the anticipatory nature of the construing process.

A Review of Three Psychic Mirrors

Within Humanistic psychology a number of mini technol-
ogies have emerged for facilitating awareness and change.
The encounter group movement, psycho-drama, and role playing are some examples. Within personal construct theory,
the personal biography and the repertory grid represent
two powerful devices.

The Personal Biography

This allows a personal self-image to emerge and uses
the complexity and innovativeness of the free form of
natural language, but this linear form of expression is

so well practised that it may fail to raise new levels of awareness and the learner remains within a robot-like routine of thought, feeling and action. As a free form of self-observation the biography presents a useful tool once the person has experienced more systematic procedures for awareness-raising and control.

The Repertory Grid

This allows personal constructs to emerge as a representational model of an individual's world. These constructs are hierarchically organised into a system within which meaning is attributed, stored and applied. But, the use of the grid as a mirror of process depends on the skill and sensitivity of the elicitor. *As an interpretive image of personal meaning the grid only partially captures the model building and 'acting out' process of construing.* The technological and methodological innovations developed by members of the Centre for the Study of Human Learning, serve to develop the grid as a more encompassing tool for psychic mirroring, so that the software aspects of its use are steered into hardware. This provides greater rigour and precision and ensures validity within the conversational paradigm. The period of apprenticeship in its effective use as a mirroring device becomes therefore minimised.

The advantages of the grid can be briefly summarised:

(i) the elicitation process is explicit and systematic;

(ii) meaning is embodied and displayed within a relatively simple format;

(iii) a structure emerges, particularly when the grid is focused (elements and constructs clustered so that they are displayed in a new relationship), which shows that a person's model may be much simpler than one might initially believe;

(iv) the structure of meaning so displayed enables the individual often for the first time to become aware of the tacitly known experiences which influence construing;

(v) the structure is so systematic that the individual can easily begin to explore, review and develop control of the construing process.

However, by its very nature the grid is limited in terms of its sensitivity in tapping meaning, its failure to exhibit the relationships between items of meaning and by its low predictive powers. The disadvantages can be summarised as follows:

(i) It does not display the natural hierarchy of meaning within a given range of discourse; (even in a focused grid, the hierarchical tree diagrams only serve to indicate the closeness of relationship between elicited items (example given in Shaw p. 61).

(ii) the grid matrix restricts the pattern of meaning to a 2-dimensional format;

(iii) the process by which the description of meaning is arrived at tends to be reductionist, with the analysis of parts gradually built up into a wholistic pattern;

(iv) the compare and contrast bipolar differentiation of elements into similarities and dissimilarities in the ways a person perceives and conceives the inner and outer world may push meaning into convergence very early on in the conversational elicitation, so that much of the potential richness is lost;

(v) the grid fails to display the kinds of relationships between items of meaning; rather it expresses the characteristics of these items. A construct expresses one dimension of meaning only. This limitation can be partially overcome by means of a 'relationship grid' in which constructs represent dimensions of relationships, but this would be a special case. Even so, it is only when a construct refers to two specific elements that the relationship, such as 'cause and effect' or 'a contains b' represents any real meaning. When applied across all the elements this becomes an abstraction;

(vi) intentionality is not expressed in the grid, although it is implicit in the range of elements selected and in the repertoire of personal constructs. Every aspect of meaning has a purposive component to it which influences the directionality of construing within an n-dimensional non-Euclidean space. Exhibiting purpose is an important aspect of mirroring, which is lacking in the grid;

(vii) as an expression of meaning at one given time it fails to take the sequential process of construing into account. The anticipatory and predictive aspects of 'man the personal scientist' constantly inventing models of his own reality and using these as a basis for anticipated action, and revising these models in the light of ongoing experience, are not made explicit in the grid.

Although the grid can be a very powerful device for confronting an individual with tacit ways for modelling the world, it has serious limitations as a mirror of a 'person in process'. Many 'grid tricks' have been developed at the Centre to overcome these; the weighting of constructs to exhibit intentionality by means of the Raiffa technique, and a method for comparing grids in a temporal sequence, as well as computer-aided conversational feedback, represent some of these innovations. Clearly, there is scope for the further development of the grid to become a 'harder' and more universal tool for mirroring process.

However, the time is also ripe to stand back and consider the development of other descriptive devices. What needs to be developed is a whole library of descriptive systems, each with its own characteristics, to be recruited

by the two conversationalists, (the participant subject
and the participant elicitor), as they negotiate the
directionality and intentionality of what is to be brought
into awareness and control.

The Flow Diagram

One such device is the Flow Diagram Technique. This
displays the multi-dimensional relationships between units
of meaning, within a chronological or time sequence. This
is therefore one advantage over the grid. The horizontal
axis displays the descriptive categories and the vertical
axis displays the sequence. The arrows specify the relationships between items. Levels of description of meaning can also be displayed in successive flow diagrams. The
elicitation of the display is more 'wholist' than the grid,
since each unit of meaning has to be considered in relation to its sub-units and also in the context of the supra-
ordinate units before it can be categorised within the
descriptors of the flow diagram. Its major disadvantage
is that the categories for classifying the items of meaning (the descriptors) are arrived at early on in the elicitation process, whereas in the grid the categories (the
constructs) are open to exploration throughout.

Again, it is possible to adapt the grid format to give
two systems for arriving at a non-Euclidean description
of relationships. If one takes a very large grid with
many non-applicables, a complex of mini-grids within one
maxi-grid is displayed. One series of constructs apply
across all elements, others split the main grid into sub-
clusters. Once one begins to consider the positive and
negative attributes of each display device, it becomes
possible to design and develop additional devices, the
specific characteristics of which serve some particular
function within the learning conversation. Alan Radley
uses conversational triads to raise awareness of how each
of three learners respond to written or spoken utterances.
At another level of awareness and control, the wide variety of bio-feedback devices can be effectively recruited
into the learning conversation. Heart rate, blood pressure,
and smooth muscle response can be brought under greater
control, as this has been demonstrated by Neil Miller and
others. The Tibetan wheel, yantras and mandalas are equally
proven devices within Buddist cultures.

Within the context of this relativistic approach towards the development of mirroring devices, it is useful
to briefly review their attributes:

(i) The items of meaning should be 'naturally occurring' and exhibited within a hierarchical system of meaning, capable of tapping the multi-faceted forms of representing and experiencing personal meaning.

(ii) The relationships between items should be explicitly displayed and these should also be 'naturally occurr-

ing' and not constrained by logical thought.

(iii) The device must be capable of expressing thought and feeling as a pattern in time. Causal models, from repetitive cycles, probabilistic, as well as those from the physical science paradigm and general systems theory need to be explored and displayed.

(iv) The intentionality influencing thought and action must be made explicit.

Simulation by computer systems tied to a graphic display may be the best yet for displaying the construing process in its totality. This has the advantage of displaying process faster than real time. But other cultures have arrived at effective systems in other ways. The realisation of a Tantric model of all thought and time represents one such way.

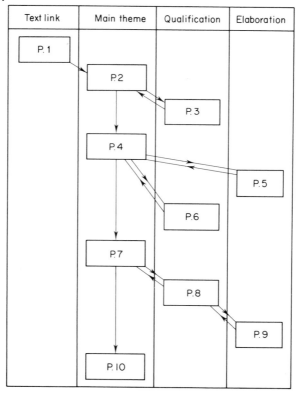

Fig. 1. An example of a Flow diagram

Towards a Library of Devices for Displaying Structures of Meaning

We have developed a kit of mirroring devices aimed at

meeting the four preceding criteria (Thomas and Harri-Augstein 1977). This kit serves two different learning-to-learn purposes.

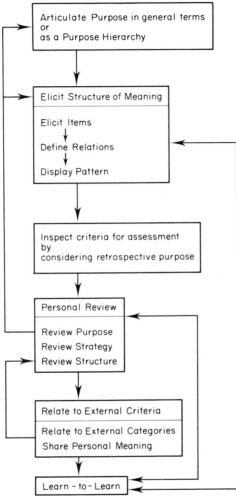

Fig. 2. An algorithm for displaying and assessing structures of meaning.

(i) It is devised to make explicit the mechanism of externalising personal meaning for self-reflection and the mechanism for the exchange of meaning in communication with others.

(ii) Because of the unusual nature of the techniques and procedures it raises awareness of personal process at

a meta-level of description.
The underlying principle is flexibility and relativity
for elicitation and display of meaning within a conversational paradigm. *PART A* of the Kit facilitates the self-
reflection of personal processes. It introduces a battery
of procedures for:

    (*a*) the elicitation of items of meaning,
    (*b*) sorting these items into a structure of meaning,
    (*c*) displaying the structure, with items of meaning in
a specified relationship,
    (*d*) reviewing the whole process.

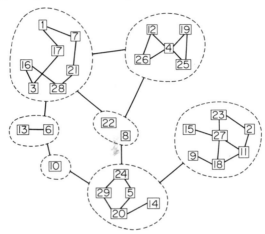

Fig. 3. Diagrammatic representation of a "net" structure of meaning.

These procedures are summarised in the algorithm in Figure
2, and a diagrammatic representation of one structure of
meaning is shown in Figure 3.
    Seeking specific relationships between items and par-
ticular modes of display leads inevitably to selectivity.
The criteria underlying the selection of structures will
relate to the person's intentionality. It is of crucial
importance to bear in mind the relationship between purpose and the structure of the display. A highly purposive
display device can be very selective and refined. Architectural plans, and Electronic flow diagrams are examples
of such devices. Whereas in less purposive more open-ended
devices as in structures of meaning displayed in Art,
intentionality is more freely expressed. Each device may
have a role to play within the conversational encounter.
PART B of the Kit is concerned with exchange of meaning.
Figure 4 illustrates a procedure for two-person exchange,
and Figure 5 illustrates in diagramatic form a structure
of meaning resulting from such an exchange. One learns
to learn not only in the context of one's own personal

process but also with reference to the processes of others.

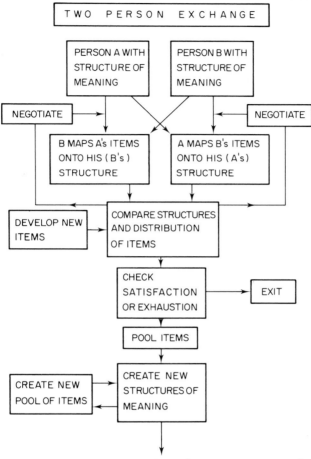

Fig. 4. Diagrammatic representation of a two-person exchange of meaning.

Techniques and tools for negotiating shared meaning may involve entering completely into another's world, compromising or truly creative encounters. Individuals are encouraged to choose appropriate referents (people and multi media resources) for developing their personal understanding. By remaining firmly within their own meaning attributing processes individuals can begin to relate these within the wider perspective of public experience, the mind pool of the culture.

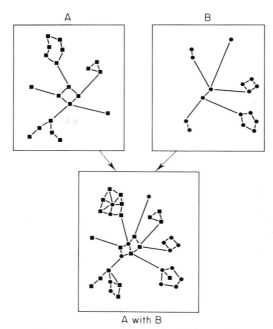

Fig. 5. Diagrammatic representation of a "shared" structure of meaning resulting from a two-person exchange.

Purpose and Structure

Whilst the maverick or the fully developed learner can take-off within the artifacts offered by a culture, so that these become a tool for arriving at a meta-description of process, most of us fail to achieve this. Education is partly to blame. The Kit aims to systematise the meta-description of processes within a social context. The conversational paradigm it offers becomes a mode of articulation of experience which can be applied to all other forms of expression of meaning. The individual is freer to question all existing artifacts and the content these embody. Such artifacts can then become tools for the expression of meaning, and for the exploration of personal processes. Everyone can be encouraged to achieve this level of freedom. It depends on the recruitment of the appropriate tools and the internalisation of the conversational procedures.

Learning-to-Learn

Education and Therapy often fail to elevate people to a level of awareness of process, whereby they can free themselves from the shackles of dogma, self perpetuating cycles of activity and absolutist construing. Learning is best defined as the quest for personal construction and exchange of viable models of meaning to act on and within the world. Learning-to-Learn depends on developing a capacity to reflect on such personal processes of construction. The search for appropriate structures for embodying meaning, will itself facilitate the modification and extension of these structures within the ongoing experience. Such structures become viable as they enable the individual to transact effectively with the people, objects and events in the personal world. Structures of meaning need to be brought under review during certain phases in a person's life; otherwise habitual mechanisms of construing may once more take over. Not only does the conversational paradigm need to be internalised, but it must also be extended outwards in a person's life space from learning-to-learn to overall learning contracts and to conversations in life.

Footnote

Throughout the verbal presentation of the paper coloured slides were used to provide alternate non-verbal stimuli for construing.

THERE IS MORE TO STUTTERING THAN MEETS THE EAR: STUTTERERS' CONSTRUING OF SPEAKING SITUATIONS

URIEL MESHOULAM

*Department of Psychology, Merrimack College,
North Andover, Massachusetts 01845, U.S.A.*

The field of stuttering has been explored from the perspective of a variety of contradictory theories, yielding equivocal findings. It is the contention of this report that the contradictions are rooted in the formist and mechanist world views (*cf*. Pepper 1948) which underlie the mainstream approaches to the study of stuttering. Further, it is argued that the contradictions are reconcilable within the framework of a contextualist theoretical approach, of which Kelly's (1955) theory of personal constructs is an exemplar. A study of stuttering within the context of personal construct theory (Meshoulam 1977) may demonstrate the utility of the contextualist-constructivist approach to the study of phenomena such as stuttering.

Approaches to the Study of Stuttering

Formist Approaches

Much of the formist research of stuttering is devoted to a search of 'empirical uniformities', that is, 'statements of observed correlations in concrete existence, (which) contain no reasons why the regularities should occur' (Pepper 1948, p.182). Following these notions, a large number of anatomical, physiological, and psychological traits were studied as possible variants upon which stutterers could be distinguished from non-stutterers.

An anatomical 'empirical uniformity' was suggested by Aristotle, who speculated that stuttering is due to an impaired tongue (Aristotle, translated by Loveday and Forster 1913). Similarly, Deiffenbach (1841) has argued that in stuttering the tongue cleaves to the roof of the mouth, a condition which is treatable by cutting out a triangular wedge from the base of the tongue.

Twentieth century researchers have given up hope of finding anatomical correlates to stuttering. The search for empirical uniformities, however, was not forsaken. Many researchers turned to *dysphemic* research (Ainsworth

1945), looking for physiological or biological correlates
to stuttering. West (1958), for example, studied the extent
to which stutterers differ from non-stutterers in their
blood-sugar level. Travis (1931), on the other hand, suggested that stuttering is associated with late acquisition
of preference for one hand over the other, resulting in
confused messages from the brain's two hemispheres. Still
other investigators attempted to correlate stuttering with
childhood brain damage (Schilling 1966), infectious dis-
eases of the respiratory system (Berry 1938), and scores
of other factors.

There is a considerable discrepancy between the per-
sistance of physiological researchers in the field of
stuttering and the little encouragement dysphemic approaches have received from research results. The link between
blood-sugar level and stuttering was not demonstrated,
neither was handedness shown to be connected to disfluency.
Nevertheless, these theories maintained their popularity
for a few decades. Perkins (1970), reviewing more than two
hundred physiological studies of stuttering, concluded
that 'no evidence points convincingly to differences between the stutterer as a person and the normal speaker as
a person, yet this is the trail that most physiological
research has chugged along for many years' (Perkins 1970,
p.221).

A large number of researchers relied upon psychological
tests in their search for traits which correlate with stuttering. The search for empirical uniformities led to the
investigation of stutterers' intelligence (Carlson 1946),
motoric skills (Burleson 1949), need Achievement, or nAch,
(Richardson 1944), trait anxiety (Boland 1953), hostility
(Santostefano 1960), sense of humor (Staats 1955), and
scores of other traits. However, none of these traits consistently differentiate between stutterers and non-stutterers. On the basis of hundreds of trait studies, Sheehan
(1970) concluded that 'although the parade (of trait studies) will no doubt continue, its goal, the search for simple personality differences is likely to be illusory'
(p.125).

Considering the meagre contribution of the formist approach to the 'study of stuttering, one may wonder why the
'parade' has been going on for so many years, and why it
will no doubt continue? Sheehan (1970) comments on this
puzzle with the following blunt words:

> If there are no differences between stutterers and
> non-stutterers that hold up on repeated samples, why
> do so many people continue to search, and why do
> they continue to report differences where none exist?
> The answer here appears to lie not in the person-
> ality problems of stuttering but in those of the
> investigators (Sheehan 1970, p.125).

More specifically, the answer may lie in the world view

of the formist investigator which implies persistence in
face of negative results. As Pepper (1948) puts it:

> If most of what we call scientific knowledge is, we
> suspect, merely description of empirical uniformit-
> ies, and therefore liable to error, that does not
> alter the situation, according to the formist.....
> According to the formist, the principle of success-
> ive approximation noted by Lenzen as characteristic
> of scientific method is a series of descriptions of
> regularities of nature successively approximating
> to the actual necessary laws of nature which subsist
> (Pepper 1948, p.184).

It has been shown that the formist position has not yet
succeeded with its task to show consistent differences between stutterers and non-stutterers. Some investigators
turned to a mechanist paradigm in hopes of finding a more
useful approach to stuttering.

Mechanist Approaches

Mechanism, by virture of its insistency on natural laws,
promises stricter guidelines for research than does form-
ism, and offers the possibility of integrating separate
empirical uniformities into a single system. Dreyfus (1971)
defined the mechanist metaphor as 'a device obeying laws'
(p.81). The mechanist assumed that the organism can be
viewed as responding to 'discrete, context free, unambig-
uous, and uninterpreted elements. Where the context and
meaning of objects experienced seems relevant, the mechanist assumed they can either be ignored without loss or
translated into elements which make no further appeal to
context or meaning' (Dreyfus 1971, p.82). In psychology,
the mechanist world view found expression in both psychoanalysis and behaviorism.

The complex psychoanalytic interpretation of stuttering
is based upon innumerable and conflicting assumptions.
Schneider (1922), for example, believes that stuttering
results from displacement of *anal* libido to the speech
organs, and that there is a symbolic connection between
stuttering and the retention of bowel movement. Coriat
(1943), on the other hand, sees in stuttering an *oral* fixation, repressed sexual experience, fear of betrayal of
the Oedipal mother, a denial of hatred to father, and a
fear of pronouncing sexual taboo words. Other psychoanalysts attempt to explain stuttering in terms of oral conflict (Stein 1942), defense reaction (Murphy and Fitzsimons 1960), or experienced sexual pleasure when stuttering (Blanton 1930).

Psychoanalysts often refer to 'lauber's (1958) paper
as a comprehensive presentation of psychoanalysis and
stuttering. However, no one explanation is singled out by
the paper, developed, and defended. It seems that the
author implicitly assumed that by 'shooting' many inter-

pretations almost indiscriminately he increases his chances
to hit the target. Not less than eight independent interpretations are accompanied by two old studies. Unfortunately, conflicting psychoanalytic ideas and poor experimental support, as exemplified by Glauber's paper, are the
rule rather than the exception.

The behavioral psychologist studies stuttering as if
it were a learned behavior acquired and maintained in the
same fashion as are all behaviors. Proceeding on the assumption that stuttering differs from disfluent speech only
in degree, Shames and Sherrick (1963) argued that disfluencies - mild as well as severe - are controlled by
their consequences. Stuttering is assumed to be maintained
by some kind of reinforcement, and thus expected to be
avoided when punished. Following this notion, Flanagan,
Goldiamond and Azrin (1958) reported success in reducing
disfluencies when these disfluencies were followed by an
aversive loud tone. Other experimental studies demonstrated
a lower rate of stuttering in situations where disfluencies were followed by an electric shock (Martin and Siegel
1966), or by an aversive verbal response such as *not good*
(Martin and Siegel 1966) or *wrong* (Quist and Martin 1967).

Many experimental results, however, seem to be contradictory when interpreted within the framework of learning theories. While Rickard and Mundy (1965) reported a
decrease in disfluencies following verbal approval of
fluent behavior, Cooper, Cady, and Robbins (1970) reported
the same result - reduction in the rate of disfluencies -
following the verbal approval of *disfluent* behavior.
Further, the results of punishment studies do not necessarily demonstrate the inhibiting effect of aversive contingencies upon disfluent behavior. It has been shown that
neither contingency nor stimulus aversiveness is necessary
to bring about reduction in rate of disfluencies. Biggs
and Sheehan (1969) found that loud noise presented *at ran-
dom* was as effective as disfluency-contingent loud noise
in reducing the frequency of stuttering. Cooper, Cady, and
Robbins (1970) found that the words *tree* and *right*, con-
tingent upon the subject's disfluent behavior, were as
effective in reducing stuttering as the word *wrong*. The
assumed aversiveness of disapproving words used in punishment experiments cannot explain this effect.

The behavioral approach to stuttering is based upon the
assumption that the study of disfluencies *is* the study of
stuttering. Treating stuttering as divorced from the meaning it may have for the person who stutters may well be
the reason why the behavioral approach did not lead to an
unequivocal and consistent explanation of research findings. Bloodstein and Shogan (1972) succeeded in demonstrating that disfluency and stuttering, although *behaviorally*
indistinguishable to the experimenter, *are* clearly dis-
tinguishable to the person who stutters. In this study,

twenty stutterers were instructed to force stuttering under various conditions. The authors found that the subjects produced utterances which fit the behavioral definition of stuttering but at the same time the subjects did not regard them as such. 'Without exception, the subjects clearly indicated that they experience real stuttering as a phenomenon quite different from faking (Bloodstein and Shogan 1972, p.184).

The discrepancy between the experimenter's definition and the experiencer's definition of stuttering cannot be resolved within a mechanist framework. One cannot escape incorporating into a definition of stuttering the interaction of the experiencer and the phenomenon being experienced, that is, the relation of the stutterer to his stuttering. This solution, however, violates the mechanist requirement of objective definition in terms of 'independent (context free), neutral elements' (Dreyfus 1971, p.94). To this end, it is suggested that the contextualist paradigm will provide a more useful approach in the understanding of stuttering.

A Contextualist Approach

Unlike the formist and the mechanist, who assume that 'any whole can be analysed completely and finally into constituent elements' (Hahn 1972, p.21), the contextualist denies this possibility.

> The patterned event or affair with which the contextualist starts is not a discrete atomic unit but rather a complex inter-relationship of tendencies all interwoven into an integral whole of its own individual character or quality (Hahn 1972, p.7).

A contextualist view of a spoken sentence is that of a unified structure which has a coherent entity or a total meaning. According to Jenkins (1974):

> The total meaning of the sentence in that context is the quality of the event. We might note that the event persists in time over some period but that all of it at once forms a single, unified psychological moment (Jenkins 1974, p.785).

Goldman-Eisler (1968) acknowledges the complexity involved in the production of speech and its unity, and argues that 'the different processes involved and levels of control engaged fuse into a well-blended single phenomenon, so often described as stream of speech' (Goldman-Eisler, p.9).

In his book *The Tacit Dimension*, Polanyi (1967) argues that attending *away* from the overall unified structure *to* the components which make it up disrupts the meaningful structure. Polanyi's thesis is that we normally attend *from* the particulars *to* the coherent entity, rather than attend to the particulars themselves. 'Scrutinize closely the particulars of a comprehensive entity and their mean-

ing is effaced, our conception of the entity is destroyed'
(Polanyi 1967, p.18).

Stuttering, analysed along these lines, is seen as a
breakdown of the total meaning of the speech structure,
a structure disrupted by attending to the particulars of
speech. Polanyi (1967) specifically argues that the *voice
sounds* one produces (particulars) are shaped into *words*
(coherent entities) by one's vocabulary. If one worries
about the technical production of words and struggles for
fluency by switching attention to the phonetic level, his
speech may be temporarily paralysed and a fluency impaired.

What are the qualities of the *interaction* between the
speaker and his speech which may channel his attention to
the particulars rather than the coherent entity? Mancuso
(1977) argues that attention is regulated by incongruity
between the stimulus input and the person's anticipation:

> Where there occurs a discrepancy between input and
> existing structure - 'expectations' - the input to
> the disrupted channel is shifted to the central pro-
> cessor. This stimulus occupies 'attention' until the
> incongruity is resolved.....These periods of 'prob-
> lem solving' are accompanied by physiological arous-
> al, and when the incongruity has been resolved, there
> is 'habituation', marked by a diminution of the phys-
> iological activation (Mancuso 1977, p.65).

This thesis is in complete agreement with Kahneman's
(1973), which states that 'a stimulus which is novel, complex, or incongruous certainly demands greater processing
effort than a stimulus distinguished by none of these
properties' (p.54), and 'normally elicits a response of
physiological arousal' (pp.42-43).

Under the assumption that the stutterer, unlike the
normal speaker, construes disfluency as incongruent with
his self-definition, disfluent speech is expected to demand
greater processing effort of the stutterer. Central processing of speech, however, disrupts its structure as a
coherent entity. Thus, a vicious circle is established.
The attention which is directed at incongruent stimuli
produces more incongruities, accompanied by an increase
in the level of arousal; this, then, channels attention
to the incongruent stimuli; and so the cycle continues.

Two assumptions underlie the contextualist-cognitive
explanation of stuttering as presented here. The first
assumption (the *incongruity assumption*) is that stuttering
is construed by the stutterer as incongruent with his self-
definition. The second assumption (the *attention assumption*)
is that channeling of attention to one's own speech performance disrupts its quality as a whole and results in
disfluencies. The following provides empirical data relevant to these assumptions.

The Incongruity Assumption   Stuttering, as construed by
the stutterer, involves implications which are incongruent

with his self image, the social presentation of his self,
or the role he attempts to play in certain situations.
Fransella (1968) instructed male stutterers and non-stutterers to rate the concept *me* and the concept *stutterers*
along nine semantic differential scales (Osgood, Suci and
Tannenbaum 1957). Fransella's conclusion based upon a factor analysis of the ratings of the concepts, is stated as
follows:

> There is no relationship between the way stutterers
> see the group formed by other stutterers and the
> way they see themselves.....Thus the stutterer seems
> to view other stutterers in the same way as everyone
> else does, but this is not the way in which he views
> himself. It is as if he were to say: 'Yes, of course
> I stutter, but I am not like the general run of
> stutterers, as an individual I am unique' (Fransella
> 1968, p.1533).

For example, Fransella's male subjects regarded the concept of *stutterers* as negatively related to *masculinity*,
whereas they rated themselves (the concept *me*) as highly
masculine. In a more recent investigation, Fransella (1972)
studied the ways in which stutterers construe *stuttering*
and *themselves*, and found 'surprisingly little agreement
between the construct dimension used for construing the
self and those used for construing *stutterers*' (Fransella
1972, p.124). The author regards her results as evidence
that the ideas a stutterer has about himself as a stuttering being are often incompatible with the ideas he has
about his self. She has gone on to show how, in two subjects, this incompatibility is resolved as successful
treatment progresses (Fransella 1977).

One of the implications of the discrepancy assumption
is that the severity of stuttering would fluctuate with
changes in the construed incongruity between self and
stuttering. It is indeed a well established phenomenon
that in situations where the speaker takes a non-self role
(*cf*. Sarbin and Allen 1968), such as acting on stage or
talking in an accent foreign to him, stuttering is dimin-
ished considerably. On the other hand, stuttering increases
when self role is taken. Sheehan noted that 'most stutterers have difficulties with their names, their addresses,
their occupations....., and other self-referent terms'
(Sheehan 1970, p.12).

The Attention Assumption Goldman-Eisler (1958, 1968)
studied the hypothesis that central processing of the particulars of speech disrupts the stream of speech. She examined the relationship between hesitation in normal
speakers and the degree to which the speech demands processing effort. Twelve sentences uttered by four subjects
were sampled. An assumption was made that words which carry
'greater information' offer 'greater freedom of choice'
(Goldman-Eisler 1958, p.97), implying that their selection

is centrally processed. Proceeding on this assmuption, the
amount of information inherent in each word was estimated
by its predictability. The procedure followed Shannon's
(1951) guessing technique. Each word had to be guessed by
a number of individuals, on the basis of a part of the
sentence. The relationship between the guessers' predictions and the subjects' pausing behavior is summarised by
Goldman-Eisler as follows:

> Fluent speech consisted of sequences of words which
> were easily predicted from the context by guessers
> .....In most cases, however, where guessers found
> themselves at a loss for predicting the next word
> as spoken originally....., the original speaker also
> seemed to have been at a loss for the next word, for
> it was at those points that he tended to hesitate
> (Goldman-Eisler 1958, pp.104-105).

Schlesinger, Forte, Fried and Melkman (1965), following a
similar procedure, demonstrated that stutters, like normal hesitations, decrease with transitional probabilities
as estimated by word-by-word guessing.

If the attention assumption is valid, it would follow
that directing of attention away from speech performance
to irrelevant non-speech stimuli would result in a decrease
of disfluencies. Newly introduced stimuli should occupy
the central processor by virtue of their novelty so long
as their novelty does not wear off (Kahneman 1973, p.42).
It has also been shown that almost any form of novelty
added to the speaking situation serves to reduce stuttering. Novel or unusual patterns of speech - such as talking
with an object in the mouth, whispering, and cursing -
often have a diminishing effect on stuttering.

In order to study the effect of novelty on stuttering,
researchers increased situational novelty in various ways.
Noise has been introduced in a number of studies (Adams
and Moore 1972; Conture and Brayton 1975; Webster and
Dorman 1970), and was shown to eliminate stuttering. A
similar effect was achieved by the amplification of the
subject's voice (Ham and Steer 1967), or by instructing
the stutterer to speak rhythmically (reviewed in Beech and
Fransella 1968).

By the same token, so-called punishment experiments
which frequently result in reduction of stuttering (e.g.
Flanagan, Goldiamond and Azrin 1958) can be re-interpreted
as situations in which the speaker's attention is diverted
by the introduction of 'nonrelated discrepancy' or coercion
(Mancuso 1977, p.78). Diverting stimuli, whether aversive
or not, interrupt the central monitoring of the particulars of speech and result in elimination of stuttering.

In addition to experimental studies, the attention
assumption derives support from studies which investigated
stutterers' own conceptions of the moment of stuttering.
Stutterers often report that they attend to their own

speech and process disfluencies prior to the stuttering
moment. Bloodstein (1975, p.18) referred to it as a 'per-
nicious speech consciousness'. He and many others have
demonstrated that stutterers can predict that they are
going to stutter on a word before they say it.

The contextualist does not restrict himself to the
study of the characteristics of stutterers, neither does
he limit his investigation to that of 'objectively defined' stuttering behavior. He does not, therefore, concentrate on the stutterer's traits, physiology, or 'dynamics', and neither does he try to manipulate speech fluency
for the purpose of identifying situational factors which
control stuttering. Rather, the contextualist focuses on
the study of the relationship of the person who stutters
to his speech. Kelly's theory of personal constructs con-
centrates on the relationship of the person as a construer
and an experiencer to his world's events.

Stuttering and the Theory of Personal Constructs

In accordance with the contextualist world view, stuttering must be studied within the context of the situation
in which it is taking place. It may be assumed that stutterers' speech performance is closely related to the ways
in which they construe speaking situations. Stutterers try
to make sense of their stuttering and to anticipate changes
in its severity. In the process of construing stuttering,
stutterers look for themes which are replicated over situations, and which are possible to anticipate. In terms of
the theory of personal constructs, stutterers may be said
to employ a finite number of bi-polar speaking situation
constructs which enable them to distinguish between situations where stuttering is likely to be evoked, and situations where stuttering is unlikely.

Constructs are not employed independently of each other;
rather, some constructs may imply others (Hinkle 1965).
One may assume that the stutterer builds ordinal relationships among his speaking situation constructs for his convenience in anticipating his stuttering. If this assumption
is valid, a relationship would be expected between a construct which permits a prediction of failure to speak fluently, such as *I am likely to be disfluent* vs. *I expect no
problem when speaking*, and situational constructs such as
ones which may describe the listener or the location of
the situation. This relationship should be such, that when
situational constructs are applied, the construct which
predicts difficulty in speech is implied. In other words,
a convergence of constructs is expected with a *speech difficulty* construct located at a higher level of superordin-
ation.

Although no causal relationship between arousal and
stuttering was demonstrated, or even assumed for that
matter, physiological arousal was shown to accompany stutt-

ering (Berlinsky 1955; Brutten 1963). Furthermore, people
who stutter often refer to anxiety as playing a circular
role - that of cause *and* effect - in the process of stuttering (Bloodstein 1975; Frankl 1969; Fransella 1972). The
belief that stuttering is caused by anxiety and at the
same time provoke it should be reflected in the stutterer's
speaking situation construct system, by way of *reciprocal*
implicative relationship between an emotional arousal construct, such as *I am anxious* vs. *I am relaxed* and a 'speech
difficulty' construct.

Although it is very likely that 'all people have *some*
constructs to do with the way they speak, such as loud-
ness, tone, or speed, of speech' (Fransella 1968), one
would expect stutterers to be concerned with additional
aspects of speech which are of no concern to fluent speakers. Following these notions, the speaking-situation construct systems employed by stutterers are expected to be
complex and well integrated, to allow efficient discrimination and anticipation. In the words of Fransella (1968):
'The stutterer has a highly elaborated system of constructs
to do with speaking'. Fransella (1972) supported this contention by a study of stutterers' construction of speaking
situations. Each of the fourteen stutterers who participated in her study was asked to rank order twelve speaking
situations in terms of nine constructs, including the construct *situation in which I am most likely to stammer*.
On the basis of the interrelationships between the rank-
ings, Fransella concluded that 'there was marked similarity (among stutterers) in some aspects of construct
patterning' (1972, p.154).

To Recapitulate: a Constructivistic Theory of Stuttering

On the basis of the discussion thus far, a contextualist theory of stuttering can be summarised in terms of the
theory of personal constructs, as follows: the stutterer
is assumed to have a complex construct system which he
employs for his convenience in anticipating the severity
of his stuttering in different speaking situations. This
system includes a functional construct upon which a direct
prediction of stuttering can be made. When this system is
employed in actual speaking situations, it evolves into
an expectation of fluency or disfluency, as the case may
be. When stuttering is implied and anticipated by the construing process, the discrepancy between the anticipated
behavior and the self role definition increases. The increased discrepancy is assumed to channel the stutterer's
attention to the particulars of his speech performance.
This, in turn, destroys the coherent structure of speech,
bringing about decrement in fluency. The evoked disfluency,
then, validates the constructs which have made the anticipation possible. In cases where stuttering is not expected, or in situations where stuttering is not highly dis-

crepant with one's self definition, the stutterer's attention is not forced to the particulars of speech performance, the coherent structure of speech remains intact, and
thus no disfluencies occur. Once again, the constructs
which led to prediction of fluency are validated.

Meshoulam (1977) examined the construct systems employed
by stutterers in their construing of speaking situations.
Sixteen stutterers and 32 non-stutterers (of whom 16 had
speech problems other than stuttering) construed speaking
situations and nonspeaking situations. The procedure followed Kelly's role construct repertory test (reptest), and
Hinkle's (1965) laddering technique. The implicative
relationships among the sampled constructs were examined
for each construct system, following a modified implication grid (impgrid) procedure (Fransella 1972; Hinkle
1965).

The picture of stutterers' speaking situation construct
systems emerging from the results is that of construct
systems which are geared toward anticipation of speech
difficulties and which are attentive to the level of the
construer's emotional arousal. Among the characteristics
of stutterers' speaking situation construct systems are:
(*a*) a large number of constructs; (*b*) a high degree of
implicative interdependency among the constructs; (*c*) a
high degree of organization of the construct system, by
way of convergence of constructs' implications around a
single superordinate construct; (*d*) a *speech difficulty*
construct, superordinately located, which allows direct
prediction of stuttering; (*e*) a superordinately located
construct which deals with the stutterer's arousal, and
which often implies, as well as implied by, a *speech difficulty* construct; and (*f*) a superordinately located construct which deals with the flexibility of the speech task
and the degree to which the stutterer is free to choose
what he says and how he says it.

This research demonstrates that the personal construct
approach allows for the study of aspects of phenomena
which other approaches, in particular behavioral analysis,
do not. For example, the fact that stutterers construe
stuttering and emotional arousal as implying each other
could not be investigated by way of observing overt behavior. The concordance of physiological arousal and stuttering can be (and has been) noted; but the beliefs of
stutterers regarding the implicative relationship between
the two can only be determined by interogating the stutterer. The theory of personal constructs proved to provide
efficient, fruitful, and quantifiable ways of inquiring
into such questions.

The results of Meshoulam's (1977) study demonstrate the
shortcomings of conventional definitions of stuttering:
they point at differences between stutterers and non-
stutterers in other than overt speaking behavior, namely,

in the way in which they construe speaking situations. It
is conceivable that a stutterer who manifests a relatively
low and unimpressive rate of disfluencies may yet define
himself as a severe stutterer, basing his self definition
upon his attitude toward his speech performance as he experiences it. Mild stutterers often feel that their difficulties are worse than what meets the eye - or ear. For
example, one of the stuttering subjects in Meshoulam's
(1977) study informally expressed this notion by saying:
'I am a bad stutterer, but very few people know it. The
thing is that I am good in substituting words and in doing
other tricks which help me to avoid blocks. You may call
me a "closet case" stutterer'. On the other hand, so-
called normal speakers are often disfluent in their speech,
but they do not regard their disfluencies as stutters in
that they neither attempt to predict them nor do they try
to control them. In both cases, understanding the speakers'
construct systems which deal with speech performances is
far more illuminating than their rate of disfluencies,
the description of the types of blocks they manifest, or
the identification of the contingencies of their stutters.

Along the line of contextualist approach the stutterer,
in order to speak without disrupting the quality of speech
as a whole, would have to change the way he construes
speech events. In principle, any approach with contextualist overtones would focus on the relationship between the
experiencer and his experience, rather than focus on one
or the other. Thus, it is neither the stutterer-divorced-
from-his-stuttering that has to be treated (as psychoanalysis and general psychotherapy may imply), nor is it
the stuttering behavior independent of the speaker who
experiences it which has to be unlearned (as behavioral
approaches may have us believe). After all, stutterers
have not been found to be more 'neurotic' than non-stutterers; why subject them, then, to the general process of
dynamic psychotherapy? Further, stuttering was not shown
to plague all stutterers all the time - every stutterer
can speak fluently in some situations - so why try to
teach stutterers to speak fluently, something which they
can already do well in some situations?

One alternative therapy of stuttering - paradoxical
intention - is suggested by Frankl (1969; 1975). Paradoxical intention is contextualist in that it aims at changing the person's attitude toward his experiences, in cases
where his attitudes bring about the behavior which he
fears. Taking the paradoxical intention attitude, the person is essentially encouraged to take some distance from
his problematic behavior - by way of humor - and to paradoxically intend exactly that which he had previously
tried to avoid. When applied to stuttering, the stutterer
is instructed to paradoxically 'wish' for more stutters
to occur. Thus, rather than construing stuttering as some-

thing which is incongruent with his self and therefore undesirable, the stutterer is given the opportunity to practice a different way of construing his speech performance, and a chance to demonstrate to himself that there is more than one way of looking at his problem.

Kelly's (1955) fixed role therapy also involves taking an unconventional role upon oneself. Here the client is told to pretend, for a limited number of weeks, that he *is* a different personality, described by a credible role sketch. Thus, for a limited time, he would have to 'try to interpret his experience in terms entirely of this "person" ' (Bannister and Fransella 1971, p.134). In fact, in the treatment of stuttering, paradoxical intention may be looked at as a private case of fixed role therapy, a case in which the fixed role sketch is that of a person whose attitude toward disfluencies is different from that of his usual self.

Fransella (1972) describes her treatment of stutterers along the lines of the theory of personal constructs. Although she did not specifically utilise the fixed role therapy principle, her treatment resulted in reconstruction of stuttering and fluency by her clients, and an increase in their rate of fluency. No doubt, further research is needed before the reconstructivist therapies can be evaluated. The reptest and related methods of sampling construct systems should prove to be sensitive measures of progress in therapy, and should help in our understanding the stutterer more than overt behavior measures can.

THE ROLE CONSTRUCT REPERTORY GRID AS A PROCESS FOR FACILITATING SELF-AWARENESS AND PERSONAL GROWTH

JOANN KERRICK-MACK*

*Department of Anthropology, University of Washington;
Counselor, Division of Adolescent Medicine,
School of Medicine, University of Washington*

I discovered a few years ago, as I conducted a clinical research project concerning adolescent development, that the repertory grid process had a number of inherent features that could be used in personal growth settings. Since that time I have used the grid with groups of adolescents and adults, deriving strategies that elaborate mini-lectures and group experiences. These strategies focus on, among other things, 1) developing effective communication skills, 2) enhancing trust, intimacy, and self-disclosure among members of the group, 3) discovering more fully ideas and beliefs about the self and others, 4) gaining information about the ways in which others view their interpersonal world, 5) clarifying and understanding one's interpersonal values and goals, and 6) learning more about one's assumptions and expectations of self and others ..... the latter being explicated through analysis of construct system structure.

The process of eliciting constructs and sharing information from the grid has seemed to be especially effective with adolescents who have had few, if any, experiences giving form to their ideas and beliefs about 'self' and sharing those ideas with an attentive, non-judgemental listener. The task-oriented nature of the grid helps to focus attention and to relieve the anxiety encountered in a more open-ended, unstructured approach that seeks answers to the question, 'Who am I ..... in what kind of world ..... in relation to whom?'.

My personal goal for this seminar is to share information, concerning the use of the grid as a process for facilitating self discovery, with interested and/or experienced clinicians and facilitators. I will have detailed information that describes the strategies I use available for demonstration, discussion, or distribution.

Footnote

*It had been hoped to include JoAnn Kerrick-Mack's full paper, but she was most regretably prevented from completing it by a sudden illness.

THE OPPOSING SELF

ALAN RADLEY

*Department of Social Sciences,
University of Loughborough, Loughborough,
Leicestershire LE11 3TU.*

The title of this paper refers to the feeling of inner resistance which we sometimes sense when we set out to do something which we have resolved to do, and find that our good intentions are dissipated in the very preparations for our action. Somehow we just don't get down to beginning the particular job we meant to start that day, or we don't say the things to the other person which we'd planned to say. These are examples of occasions when the resistance to action cannot be located in the external situation, for our failure to act seems, mysteriously, to be our own. I expect that many people have had this experience at some time or another.

Now it has crossed my mind that this inner experience may be a pseudo-problem, inasmuch as the failure to do this particular thing was really the achievement of doing something else, and that the answer lay in the external situation relating to this other activity. For example, the letter which must be written, the television programme which is almost certainly not to be repeated, are the reasons (excuses?) for doing something other than what we had intended. And yet this argument is unconvincing, for it omits altogether the fact that we are capable of ordering our priorities and constructing various means of self-discipline. However, the really striking reason why the problem succeeds in being taken seriously is that, in its purer form, the person just doesn't succeed in doing something else. Failure to get down to doing what we know we want to do can leave us sitting at our desks, shuffling papers and biting our nails in a daze of abstraction. Attempts to force ourselves to try to do whatever it is, to exert some self-discipline, may then evoke in tangible form this feeling of inner resistance. At this point the paradoxical nature of this situation is often apparent to us - that we want to do something which, when attempted, is somehow hindered so that the attempt fails. We seem to be standing in our own way, which is, of course, a ridiculous but surprisingly natural thing to have occurred.

Now this paradoxical situation has long been noted as

a feature of certain neurotic conditions. Karen Horney
(1945) described this problem and Victor Frankl (1960) has
suggested a technique for dealing with it within his logo-
therapy approach. More recently, Watzlawick and his co-
workers (1967, 1974) have described a method whereby people
may be helped to overcome such situations by, in a sense,
giving up the attempt to try to achieve their ends. However, my purpose in this paper is not to review or to
suggest ways whereby an individual can break out of this
seemingly intractable problem. What I would like to do
instead is to pursue the theoretical questions which arise
from recognising the problem, and to refer the discussion
to some issues with which a personal construct psychology
might deal.

A Closer Look at the Problem

My reason for focusing on this problem of inner resistance is, as I hope to show, its usefulness in highlight-
ing a number of quite important issues concerning behaviour, and more particularly concerning personal construct
theory. At its centre the problem seems to turn upon the
question of consciousness and choice in action, and the
relationship between what we would normally term construing and what we would normally term behaviour. More specifically, an examination of some examples from my own and
other people's experience led me to the following points.

Inner resistance seems to follow from an attempt to
act in such a way as to achieve a predetermined end. By
this I mean that the person's efforts continue to operate
with respect to a set of criteria which exist prior to
what he is trying to do. The activity itself - the actual
doing of it - is experienced as merely a means towards
this end. The felt ridiculousness of the conflict partly
arises from this 'fact' that the person knows exactly
what he wants to do, but somehow he can't get down to
doing it. Subsequently, when he feels frustrated by repeated failure, he may experience this paradox in a slightly different way; so he might say: 'the whole damn thing
is a complete irritation and the sooner I get it out of
the way the better'. The shift in emotion here - the
difficult effort giving way to frustration - also marks
a point of change in the manner of working. At first the
end result seems to be in mind, and initial efforts just
don't seem to come. Following this, the features of our
action in the situation become the focus of attention and
we may try to operate on these directly. In a simpler example, when confronted with a door which won't open we
sometimes begin to pull at the handle itself as if it were
responsible for the trouble. Often, the handle is just
below the little sign marked 'push'.

These, then, are three features of 'inner resistance'
which are first noticeable, and of course were well known

to the gestalt psychologists working in the general areas
of problem solving and frustration. (Duncker 1945; Wertheimer 1961). They are again:

(*a*) that the form of action is as a means towards a
predetermined end.

(*b*) that there is a shifting of consciousness from
the problem field onto oneself or one's ability as part
of that situation.

(*c*) there is often an attempt to work on the 'blockage'
- on one's action - in some direct manner.

At this point, one possible perspective offered by
personal construct theory would invite us to look at how
the person construes the problem. The *choice corollary*
states that 'a person chooses for himself that alternative
in a dichotomised construct through which he anticipates
the greatest possibility for the elaboration of his system'. Using this as a guide, one might examine the various implications of the choice of this activity over
others, and seek to explain the person's failure in terms
of the relationships of that alternative with respect to
other elements in the system. In that sense, the inner
resistance in which we are interested would be explained
(and in a sense located) in the structural features of
the person's construct system. In addition to this, one
might use methods based upon Kelly's idea of acting 'as
if', employing dramatic metaphor in order to elaborate
the alternative courses of action in order to fill out
the picture of this opposition.

Recently Mair (1977) has used the metaphor of the 'self
as a community' as a technique for exploring the alternative 'selves' which a person uses to define himself.
Using this approach, the question of inner resistance
might become explicable within the terms of the perspectives offered by the various 'selves', and the relationships between them. The person's failure to act, the
inner resistance, would be a function of his being essentially a divided person, one aspect of self opposing the
action of another aspect. This, I think, is a fairly close
approximation to the feeling one gets in the actual situation, but I believe it to offer an incomplete account
for our purposes in this discussion. For there are two
further aspects of the problem of inner resistance which
are useful in offering a different perspective on the
problem, and invite us to take a rather different standpoint from the two which I have briefly (and rather in-
adequately) described above.

The first is what happens when the resistance disappears
and the person gets on with the activity at hand. Apart
from the accompanying disappearance of self-consciousness
and direct effort there is what we can call an involvement
in the task itself. The situation is not so much one of
the individual operating upon the problem, but is rather

one of a person having entered into the problem so that
his activity is, at base, spontaneous. This does not mean
that it is in any way unstructured, but that the freedom
of activity arises within the changing features of the
situation as they appear to him. Clearly this different
way in which the person relates to the problem at hand is
an important clue in trying to clarify the original question of opposition.

The second, as yet unmentioned aspect, is one which I
think fundamental to an understanding of the problem and
is only revealed to the individual subsequent to the removal of the resistance and in the execution of the activity. It is this. That in the period of failure, frustration
and effort, the way in which the person represented the
activity to himself is afterwards seen to have been only
an approximation to the lived experience of performing
the task. Now while in retrospect this may sound a truism
it is not at all apparent while we are striving to carry
out the activity. A person trying to write a letter knows,
in a certain sense, just what he wants to convey and yet
he might still make several attempts and be dissatisfied
with what he is actually writing. Only when our action
passes beyond the point of resistance do we see our original intention in a different light, the reason for which
may remain unclear to us at the time or simply be brushed
aside as we lose reflective awareness concerning the frustrating situation. This is brought out by Henri Bergson
(1910) in his book *Time and Free Will*, in an example which
is a variation on our particular problem because the person just avoids the action which would give rise to frustration, reflection and effort. He writes:

> But then, at the very minute when the act is going
> to be performed, *something* may revolt against it.
> It is the deep-seated self rushing up to the sur-
> face. ...in the depths of the self, below this most
> reasonable pondering over most reasonable pieces of
> advice, something else was going on - a gradual
> heating and a sudden boiling over of feelings and
> ideas, not unperceived, but rather unnoticed. If
> we turn back to them and carefully scrutinize our
> memory, we shall see that we had ourselves shaped
> these ideas, ourselves lived these feelings, but
> that, through some strange reluctance to exercise
> our will, we had thrust them back into the darkest
> depths of our soul whenever they came to the sur-
> face. And this is why we seek in vain to explain
> our sudden change of mind by the visible circum-
> stances which preceded it (Bergson 1910, pp.169-170).

For Bergson this is an example of the opposition of
that aspect of ourselves which he equates with 'the whole
of our inmost feelings' against reason in the form of an
'external, superficial idea'. While the general gist of

Bergson's statement is in line with what we have been considering, his analysis offers little help. We need to try to state more precisely what our problem is and which questions we might usefully ask.

Based upon the earlier discussion, we might inquire further as to the way in which the person relates to the problem or task, the difference between an activity which is likely to lead to inner resistance and one that is not. As part of this question we might pay attention to the form of relating by which the whole activity, or parts of it, are designated means or ends for the person involved. Secondly, what is happening in a case where a person is striving to achieve something and failing? What is the hindrance, and does it have a different effect before and after the person becomes aware of it? Finally, what are the changes in the person's activity and in his experience of it, as he passes from the point of inner resistance to involvement in the task? More specifically, we might take particular note of the person's conceptualisation of what he is trying to do, and how this changes in relation to the ongoing action.

Before tackling these questions, it seems useful that we should keep in mind their relevance for personal construct theory. What, in a sense, we are asking is what is the relationship in personal construct psychology between thought and action, as manifested in situations where there is difficulty in fulfilling what we have chosen to do? Do the grounds of choice - the person's relationship to the task - determine how he will approach it? Does the person's failure to fulfil his commitment to the chosen alternative mean that he did not make 'an elaborative choice' in the first place? And even if a person makes a poor start, why is there an internal opposition to what might better be left to a process of reconstruction through coming to grips with events in the actual situation?

Reformulation of the Problem

So far we have discussed this question from the standpoint of the individual's experience of what it is like to fail repeatedly in the execution of what he wants to do. This has led us to elaborate the question in such a way as to locate the problem for inquiry - really, locate the opposition - in the feeling of resistance which the person has on attempting to act in the way that he has decided upon. We might go on from here to ask questions about these alternative selves - experienced as alien blockages - and their relationship to the chosen course of action, with a view to seeing how they might be overcome if the person is to act freely. Or else we might re-examine all the alternatives to inquire as to whether the person had elaborated them sufficiently; that is, that his original choice was made with respect to a reasonably full understanding of the implications of his choice. This second option could lead to the person reconstruing the whole affair and perhaps deciding that his original choice wasn't such a good idea after all.

Now, I find both of these options unsatisfactory, because they seem to bypass the question of why such a state of affairs should have arisen, and they also seem to be based upon the assumption that if you just get your view of the thing sorted out then action follows freely. From this perspective the relationship of the construing of the course of action to the activity itself just doesn't arise. For the real nub of the problem as I see it is in just this changing relationship of the person's view of the problem to how he really acts in the situation. To limit our inquiries to the person's view of it - his interpretation of the action - and to limit our practical efforts to eliminating the dilemma seems to me to miss an invitation to look at the whole question in a different way.

Kelly himself points to this way when he talked of construing man as 'a form of motion'. If we do this, then we see that understanding what a person does can be a matter of seeing in which directions he moves - hence, the analysis of personal constructs. To pursue the metaphor, this particular problem of resistance to action can be seen as one of 'inner friction' related to movement. Now the solution to the problem of movement and falling bodies was made possible by Galileo (Wertheimer, 1961) posing the question from a standpoint contradictory to all familiar experience. Where experience framed a beginning point concerning the relationships between pushing objects, their subsequent movement and their eventual coming to rest, the Galilean/Newtonian perspective conceived an ideal state in which bodies moving with a constant velocity will never come to rest if no external forces are applied. So, to say that man is a form of motion and *mean* it, could have implications for how we approach the problem of the opposing self.

I use this as a parallel to what I think we find with the problem of inner resistance. From the perspective of our own experience the problem is either one of strange forces that militate against our rational choice, or else of other selves or aspects of self which vie with us over what we should do. We are divided within ourselves, and the problem field is delimited by the machinations of these counter-aspects of self. The question of action itself (of movement, if you like) remains always slightly mysterious from this point of view, inasmuch as action somehow follows a person's construction of the problem. In the remainder of this paper I would like to approach the question from the perspective of the person *acting* in the world. By this I mean that instead of beginning with assumptions about construing and alternative selves, we assemble, if but sketchily, a standpoint which has as its basis construing as a practical, social, and temporal activity. (This is in opposition to it being essentially cognitive, individual and spatially arranged.) Having achieved this perspective, it may then be possible to re-phrase some of the questions pertaining to the original problem.

The Standpoint Described

If we assume man as active, then we see him active *in the world*. We need to begin by realising that action - con-struing if you like - is directed towards something outside the person. When we are engaged in any task, when we commit ourselves in any way, we make changes in the world through our actions which in turn make changes in us. For that reason I propose that we see construing as primarily a practical activity, through which we engage events through our discrimination of particular features of the world in which we live. I do *not* mean by this that we 'see' events towards which we subsequently 'behave' - for that is to separate out activity into perception and behaviour, and lays the groundwork for the intractable problem of how these two factors are to be described within a single framework of construing. No - if we assume a whole organ-ism which is active, then construing at base must be grounded in our description of what we believe the nature of that activity to be. Through action we make differences in the world in which we live, and simultaneously differ-ences are made in us so that construing is an organised, two-way process of discrimination.

Through discrimination, particular events in the world arise in relation to the person - they become distinct to him. By this I mean that the particular features of the world which stand out and the particular discrimination which the person makes are in relation to one another.

Such a relationship exists between the person and the event, and defines the standpoint of his action. It there-fore has an objective reality, to the extent that it has arisen prior to any interpretation which he might sub-sequently make of it. The relationship between person and event - which I am still calling a practical one - also defines the person's perspective from which he acts in the situation. Therefore we should not see the perspective as being in the person, but *the person as being in the per-spective*. That is what, I contend, makes construing pri-marily a social affair - that it arises *in relationships between* persons or between persons and aspects of their world. Furthermore, I also suggested earlier that we treat construing as a temporal process rather than as if it were a spatial affair. Certainly the notion of change is not strange to personal construct theory, but it often seems

to conjure up the idea of a system which, if measured at
t_1 and subsequently at t_2 will be seen to be different
in certain respects. Instead of this I would like to point
to that quality of construing in which objects (and we
ourselves) *endure*. When Kelly talks of living in anticipation or of construing as bringing together the past and
the future into the present, that is the meaning of temporal to which I wish to draw attention. In the passage of
time we experience individuals and objects as enduring
even as they pass from one system of meaning into another.

To summarise so far, the standpoint which I have sketch-
ed out is one of construing as being alive in the world -
that is, acting in relation to events rather than looking
upon events. It is relational in a fundamental way, insofar as the discriminations which we make through our actions are mutually defined within ourselves. The perspectives which these practical relationships define are therefore not subjective - not of our own construction, if we
mean by this that they are our interpretations which we
place upon the world. Neither the events in the world, nor
the discriminations which we make are ready-structured.
The former view is the positivist position which Kelly so
vehemently rejected; the second is the tendency to sub-
jectivism with which construct theory occasionally seems
to flirt. If this latter position were to be adopted it
would precipitate us into difficulties concerning how a
person acts on the basis of his interpretations, and even
how he comes to know any particular thing at all. For the
important thing about persons is that they are discriminating beings, and that they adjust to events as they
emerge in their activity. (I emphasize here the idea of
discriminating *beings* rather than individuals who make
perceptual distinctions.) So then, in the course of action,
new features of the situation arise in relation to the person, and these call for adjustments in the discriminations
which he makes. This need not involve self-consciousness
if we argue that this view of construing involves an organising process - what Kelly calls re-construing. Again I
would only mention that reconstruing is a feature of the
process in which persons are involved in change - exchange
- in relation to events. Reconstruction is not, within
this perspective, necessarily a matter of re-interpre-
tation or even of my choosing to construe something in a
different way.

Now, we are aware of this situation in retrospect when
we refer back to activities in which we have been absorbed
to a marked degree. In carrying out such activities - be
it painting a picture, cleaning out a dirty carburettor or
listening to music - the aspects of construing to which I
drew attention do seem to be in evidence. We experience
ourselves as drawn into the activity - of being involved -
and while conscious of what we are doing we need no con-

sciousness of ourselves doing it. Furthermore, our absorp-
tion in the task may be signalled, if only at the end, by
an awareness of how time has slipped by during our involvement. We endure, with respect to that activity, in a way
which is clearly different to our awareness of the general
passage of events and of ourselves within it. It would be
of interest, in these examples, if one could interrupt the
person at several stages along the way to ask him about
what he was doing, and how the particular events of that
moment fitted into the whole situation. Of course, this
would only make the individuals conscious of themselves
doing it - which would interrupt the flow of action - and
it might also necessitate some nonsensical questions. So
we might ask the listener what he thought of the symphony
so far, what he had made of the first movement, and how
did he think the second movement would finish. Or we might
ask the artist about a fresh brushstroke, to inquire as
to its place in the whole picture. It is possible that
these people might give cogent answers, but it is more
likely that they would say something like: 'I'm not sure
how - I don't quite know why this follows what's just gone
- wait till the end and I'll tell you'. Or the mechanic
might explain that he only thinks at the moment that the
engine noise means the carburettor is blocked, but he's
not certain. The musical phrase, the brushstroke, the
engine noise are all particular features of the situation
which are clearly meaningful for the individuals concerned,
although their final meanings, if we can call them that,
are far from clear.

In all of these examples, there is a gradual evolution
of the person's understanding with respect to the new
features of the situations which emerge. Going back to our
description of construing as acting in the world, what is
there as a particular feature takes its meaning through
the anticipatory movements of the person - that is, the
organised discriminations through which he lives. Similarly, as new features emerge in the situation - say a
fresh brushstroke - there is a simultaneous change in the
discriminations which are part of the painter's basis of
action. This is because the painter and canvas are *in relation* - rather than the painter subsequently making distinctions between marks which are held to exist quite sep-
arately from him. This is not to say that the painter does
not reflect upon his work or does not stand back from it
to review his efforts so far. All I want to say here is
that this is not necessitated by each stroke of the brush,
and that construing is not primarily a mental reflection
on what we have done just previously.

A discrimination, therefore, *is an act* through which
we may be conscious of making differences in the world,
and no less important, of differences being made in us.
So, for example, a fresh brushstroke changes the artist's

relation to the emerging picture in its expression of a
discrimination - an act - come into being. A previously
unheard engine noise transforms what was a routine carburettor maintenance into a problem. The new brushstroke,
the new engine noise are, therefore, not merely differences
which are made to the existing situation, but in making
distinctions within us become part of the organised basis
through which we then approach the situation again. The
next stroke is made with respect to what is now there on
the canvas; listening to - (as opposed to just hearing) -
the new engine noise leads to a reformulation of the problem. The adjustment, if you like, which we make to the
appearance of a new feature is its inclusion within the
basis of our action. It is, at one time, a part result of
what we have done, and yet a pointer towards that which
is yet to be. However, I do not mean by this that the
final picture is in the head of the artist any more than
the problem is under the bonnet of the car. What I do mean
is that there is a change in the relation of that aspect
of the situation to the person's action, so that the painted contour takes its place as part of the basis from which
the remainder of the picture is to be painted. The reconstruction of the picture to accommodate that new brushstroke and the anticipation of the painting about to be
done are aspects of the single process to which I am draw-
ing attention. So, we now have another way of describing
how construing involves bringing the past and the future
into the present. *Reconstruing is that adjustment by which
new features of the situation become part of the person's
organised basis of action, and in which he endures through
the transposition of past distinctions into anticipatory
discriminations.*

Opposition as a Relational Act

Up to now, what I have been attempting to sketch out is
construing without interpretation and deliberation. However, much of our activity is, indeed, marked by our reflection upon what to do next, in which we consider the
various possibilities of action. This often arises in
cases where action is hindered in some way, or where we
feel it best to appraise alternative ways of proceeding.
To use a simple example again, if we begin to open a door
which then jams our attention is brought to the door as a
distinct object, where before it was merely a part of the
flow of events leading to where we were going. By being
sensitive to where and how it jams we might deduce how it
can be freed. That is to say, the physical hindrance to
our efforts at opening it becomes a pointer toward understanding why the door won't open. This is the situation
which I described previously, except that on reflecting
about a problem we are able to reformulate it from alternative perspectives which we can adopt. This reformulation

of the problem in reflection involves taking alternative
perspectives towards the situation, so that distinctions
made previously become the basis for discrimination and
we act through them rather than upon them. The earlier
example of the transformation in activity of the engine
noise illustrates this particular point. So it is that,
in reflection, we *work with* perspectives which are the
interpretations which we make of our situation (Radley
1978).

Now, on occasions, we find that a person faced with a
problem situation continues to 'pull at the door' so to
speak. The door, the handle, remain as objects to be pulled
at from the action perspective through which he approached
it. The door remains merely a means to a further end which
he continues to seek. Another way of describing this is to
say that he continues to seek validation where his construing has proved unsuccessful - Kelly's definition of hostility. There will be no attempt on his part to enter into the
problem of why the door is jammed until his relationship
to the situation is changed - until he enters into what
Duncker (1945) called the 'grounds of the conflict'. In a
sense, the 'hostile' individual continues to live through
(or act from) that action perspective in which opening the
door was (or should have been) a passing event. Living in
that time (for time is relative in a thoroughgoing psychology of construing) he projects, as it were, the 'should
have been' onto the present situation, so that construing
in an active, emergent sense is hindered. However, the
angry and frustrated person is still not necessarily a
self-conscious individual, and when extremely emotional
is even less likely to be. So while the nature of hindrance
which we find in the example of the jammed door approaches
our problem of inner opposition, it does not satisfy it.
For here the situation is one where the person clearly
sees the blockage and yet does not realise the problem.
In contrast to this, inner opposition seems characterised
by *his awareness of what is yet to be done*, accompanied
by *a frustrating ignorance of what it is that resists his
every effort*.

This would seem to be the special feature of the problem, that we know what we want to do and yet are unable to
do it. In attempting to carry out such an activity - perhaps just writing a letter - the words which get on to the
paper, even after such difficulty, are felt to be inadequate. In a sense, part of the problem is that we are
trying to wrench out, to display as finished products particulars of a whole message or argument which is yet to be
realised. As we noted previously, a novel feature of a
situation serves both as a new element in the system in
which it arises and also as a pointer towards the system
which is coming into being. Such an element - a personal
quality or an abstract idea - has a different place within

the system of understanding which emerges from the place
which it enjoyed in the previous system. At base, that
system is a practical one, so that through such trans-
positions (or reconstruing) may we subsequently experience
not only the idea but ourselves in a new relationship to
the problem as a whole.

It is this process which is hindered to the extent that
we continue to organise our words so as to justify the
particular conception which we have of the task at that
time. It is as if, by trying to operate directly upon
those tangible aspects of what we want to say, we hope
that the whole meaning will come clear. Then these particular features remain as objects to us, words which
when written down are but a superficial indication of the
deeper meaning which, remaining as yet unexpressed, they
simply cannot convey. Now this last point seems to rest
upon a paradox, for the words in being written down *are*
the forms of expression. And yet, when we try to force
the argument it is as if we want to organise them with
respect to a meaning which is in some sense already attain-
ed. In effect, what we are tyring to bring into our awareness through reflection is the argument all-of-a-piece,
inasmuch as we attempt to express it in the present as if
it were there, ready-made. More exactly, what we do have
in our awareness is our construction - *our interpretation*
- of what it is that we want to say or do. As we shall
see in a moment, that construction is not to be confused
with the task which is yet to be done.

However, objectifying our aim in this way also serves
to distance ourselves from it. Our attempts to assemble
the arguments directly are attempts at reconstructing the
problem, but not in the sense in which we described reconstruing in the practical sense. The reconstruction
involved in reflection is the re-organisation of perspectives with respect to the problem as objectified. The
parallel here is with the man pulling at the door handle,
insofar as it remains merely a means to a predetermined
end. In Wertheimer's terms, there is no re-centering of
the problem, because the person continues to act through
a particular perspective which remains unchanged. There
need be no self-consciousness in this - our efforts are
directed towards the problem from the practical perspective through which we act. However, subsequently, on reflecting about our difficulties, we often do experience
it in a particular way. The problem, we say, is that we
can't get this done or that said. There, in our awareness
we have ourselves as separate entities trying to do something to that which exists apart from us. We (as unchanging entities) are trying to organise the words to meet
the particular ends we have in mind (which are also unchanging entities).

As I have said, there is no necessity for self-con-

sciousness when we try to do something, although our subsequent reflection will tend to formulate the activity in
this way. The important clue in this, however, is in the
relation of the unchanging nature of self and aim. For
this suggests that the whole activity takes place within
a perspective in which we are placed in a particular relation to the world. To illustrate, I would again suggest
that the problem often arises when we treat the task simply
as a means to an end, that in forcing the paint into particular forms on the canvas or in organising the words
towards a predetermined meaning we are trying for a good
painting or an admirable argument. Indeed, the relationship between task and ego-involvement has long been recognised by field theorists. For us now, it points towards
what I think is an interesting phenomenon. It is this.

In making such efforts, the aim of the activity (the
painting, the essay) is held as a fixed form - an invari-
able means - within a practical perspective defining our
relationship to the world. The form of this relationship
is the maintenance of particular distinctions which we
have attributed to ourselves in relation to what we do,
as ways of anticipating events. So, for example, the picture which the person strives perfectly to paint is there
as a form within the practical perspective devolving from
his desire to paint 'good pictures'. The whole activity
lies within this perspective, which we see as characterised
by the maintenance of distinctiveness of the basis of his
action and the end-product towards which he strives. His
efforts to mould the problem - to shape it - have an instrumental use in which, as tools (Schon 1967) they are
unchanged in relation to the material on which they work.
In effect, the picture or argument lie within distinctions
which are preserved, so that they have the quality of
being aspects of a past to be imprinted on the present.
So, as our frustration grows with failure, there is an
impatience to be done with it, a heightened awareness of
the things which might be delayed because of our inept-
itude, of it interfering with our time. Indeed, the spat-
ialisation of time in such forms of action is, I suspect,
a product of it stemming from an apparently ready-made
system of meaning which is, in its reflective form, a
system of past distinctions being maintained.

Having said all this, what then is the nature of the
opposing self? We can now see, (if we return to our New-
tonian analogy for a moment) that man as a form of uninter-
rupted motion is construing as we described it earlier.
The pushing and pulling are clearly the efforts which we
make to operate upon the task directly. What, then, is the
'inertia' which we have to overcome? What has stopped reconstruction so that we need to get it moving again? I
think the answer to this is there in our previous analysis.
The inner resistance, the strange opposition *is the prac-*

tical perspective in which distinctions are maintained as
we relate to the task at hand. And it belies most fundamentally that relationship in which meaning would evolve
through the transition of emergent features. Then the person exists in a paradoxical relationship constituted by
the negation of his avowed aims by the practical perspective through which he engages the task at hand. That is
why when I say 'belies fundamentally', I mean not in our
thinking but in our being. Therefore, *within that perspective*, it is quite possible for us to bring to bear with
all honesty and effort every resource available to express
what we are trying to say. There is no such contradiction
in our striving, (though we do experience opposition)*,
although in retrospect we know that what we were trying
to do was in some way wrong. Then, often through ceasing
to try, when we are into the problem so to speak, we see
what we were aiming for with such difficulty to have been
a substitute - a mere fiction - compared to what has now
been said or done without such fulsome effort. However,
its meaning only changes in respect to the new system of
relations which has subsequently emerged. Indeed, when we
are involved in reconstruing - in transition - we often
do sense that our labels for things are just that. They
serve as signposts directing us towards those things which
emerge through our relating to events, be they in the outside world or within ourselves as part of what is yet to
be expressed.

Interestingly enough, when we do strive after events
directly their guise cannot be known, except inasmuch as
we subsequently feel that what we have done is not what
we really wanted to do. Yet even there, to the extent that
we are in the perspective which we have described, the
argument, the painting or whatever is only what it is with
respect to the system in which we are living. At that time,
with respect to that system, these events are neither
pointers nor cloaks for anything else. If we are in the
perspective of end-gaining then there is no emergence, nor
can we invoke a final meaning awaiting expression. That
practical relationship, not being present, is not there
to be considered. The actual task cannot be realised just
for that reason, because we have confused what we have
grasped as a distinction in reflection with what is yet
to be discriminated through action. We are in the situation
of trying to make positive adjustments to a problem field
which has been negated inthe practical relationship through
which we act. And how we see the problem is preserved
because the relationship defines the perspective; and our
activity within it, though unsuccessful, serves only to
make us redouble our efforts. Inasmuch as we reflect upon
our efforts within this relation, then we also see these
objectified as part of the problem. Coupled with the lack
of any external blockage to our action it is not surprising

that we conceptualise the problem in the way that we do. We have a 'self' which wants to do, and a 'self' which opposes, and that is where, *in individual experience,* the question arises.

However, in terms of the foregoing discussion the question of the opposing self in our awareness is a *product* of a process of construing which underlies it. It is not, I submit, the basis from which our inquiry into the problem should start. If persons are practical, temporal and social beings then we cannot envisage them equipped only with systems for looking and thinking. Nor, I would argue, do we advance theoretically by reifying individualism within the person, so that we approach the question from the inner experience of 'opposing selves'. Instead, I would suggest that the examination of this problem invites us to take our standpoint, not in the individual construct system, but in the relational and practical acts of persons - that is, in *construing.*

Footnote

*For a discussion of the difference between 'paradox' and 'opposition' as forms of contradiction, see Wilden (1972).

OBSESSIONAL CONSTRUING AS ACTIVITY INTERACTING WITH SURROUNDINGS, ACTIONS AND CONTENT: IN TRANSITIONS, BRIDGES AND SEMI-EMPTINESS

NILS SIVERTSEN

Rødbråtbakken 5, Oslo 8, Norway.

The regulating variables in personal construct theory are properties of one's own constructional content, as one predicts the changing world. Regulating variables in the field of shifting activation levels and information processing capacity are not incorporated in the Kellyian system. Construing from that point of view could be called 'construing as activity'. Regulation by the surroundings are also sparsely treated by personal construct theory.

The phenomenon 'vacation' can be used to illustrate these concepts. As constructional content 'vacation' can happen in different centuries; it can be positioned inside or outside the range of convenience of constructs; it can wander across sub- and superordinate levels, and to a greater or lesser extent realistically replicate the situation at the moment and the future. Vacation as constructional activity is placed within a context of the other actions and the activation level of the moment (e.g. daydreaming of vacation when one is tired in the working situation). Other activities which can constitute the vacation is also bound to the time and place where they are happening (e.g. trying to look after the children while reading a book). The surroundings with regard to 'vacation' are, on the one hand, the norms and interests of others (e.g. wants from one's family), and, on the other, the physical environment (e.g. distance to recreational areas), both of which put limitations on and open up possibilities with regard to when, where and how one could spend the time.

The SAC model (surroundings, activity and content), operates in the field of interaction between these variables, with the framework of transitions as one of its conceptual tools.

Transition and Obsession

An example of a transition would be when the capacity taxing feature of some activity is decreasing, and is being kept at a new level (e.g. listening to a speech which is getting less interesting), and activity in other

structures makes for constant activation level (e.g. superordinate self-instruction to listen attentively). Then one
could have 'replacement' as another, dependent, activity
increases (e.g. one moves restlessly in the chair, or
starts daydreaming). If for some reason the dependent
variable lags behind in its change, then 'deprivation discrepancy' (e.g. boredom) could follow. A 'replacement
transition' like this is one among a series of transitional
structures not presented here. It will be used to describe
some obsessional problems.

   There are many obsessional forms. One of them refers
to the emergence of an unsolved and structurally simple
content relation during a transition (e.g. 'Is the cheque
really signed?'). This could be seen as filling an empty
period (after having sealed the envelope) with constructional activity. This transitional form appears in different contexts and with a variety of contents. When one has
gone round a corner on a bicycle: 'Did I hurt someone in
that street?' (Flatten 1965, p.79). Some time after one
has removed a stone from the road: 'Absurd reason I did
it. Must put it back.' (Freud 1909, p.190). When day has
passed (bedtime): 'The shoes should stand at right angles'
(puts them that way), 'No, side by side' and so on. (Rado
1974, p.200). When one has finished a trip on a scooter:
'Did it get any marks?' (Kvilhaug 1965, p.46).

   Having to return to check the gas, or the door, or anything else when leaving one's home (e.g. for vacation),
can be seen in the same light. The decrease could come
about by the loss of differentiated, constructional activity closely tied to the home, as well as by the construct
of 'vacation' having few implications. Before going on
with the above example, some assumptions with regard to
contrast, 'wideness' and time have to be presented.

   The contrasting of elements is fundamental for the
building and use of constructs in personal construct
theory (Kelly 1955, p.51, pp.59-61, 370-1; 1969, p.9).
It seems reasonable to propose a *contrast-dimension* with
values ranging from pseudocomparing (vague fusing elements
as when one's self constructs 'not clever', 'not happy',
merge to 'all bad'), through abrupt slot-change with limited contact between poles, (e.g. from 'all bad' to 'all
good'), to the simultaneous grasping of indpendent elements (e.g. seeing one's 'goodness' and 'badness' in perspective). Kelly's main dimensions, construct-theory-
defined feelings, and his recommendations with regard to
therapeutic experimentations can all be seen as related
to the regulation of contrast value between elements. In
line with Kelly's warning against premature dilation
(1955, pp.836-47), or experimentation (1955, pp.1104-10),
it is not implied here that high contrast value is always
an advantage.

   An additional variable, 'wideness' of elements, is seen

as regulating the constrast value. Wideness is the seg-
mental area of the encircling space of elements placed
around one's position. Its values should range from 'small'
(in the environment, for example, this would be like a
person some distance away), to 'wide' (a large part of
the field, like the bus one is about to board, or a person leaning over one's shoulder to inspect one's work),
to 'encircling' (the surrounding field, like the room one
is in, or being surrounded by a group of people).

The first part of the fourth question in Galton's
famous questionnaire on imagery (1883) would fit here:
'Call up the image of some panoramic view (the walls of
your room might suffice), can you force yourself to see
mentally a wider range of it than could be taken in by
any single glance of the eyes?' (p.378). The macroptic/
microptic posthypnotic instructions of Aaronson (1968)
that 'everything you look at will seem twice (/half) as
large as usual in each dimension' (p.162), would only
partly relate as it also implies size.

Wideness of any given element in a set is seen as inversely related to contrast values between those same
elements. Small elements are therefore easily compared,
while those in the middle range relate by the way of slot-
change (e.g. either focusing on one's own view, *or* 'understanding' that of another, at a given time). Encircling
elements merge (e.g. vague identification). Huttenlocher
and Presson (1973, p.298) conclude from their experiment
on mental rotation that there is a problem of representing views from spatial positions other than one's own.
That problem could be a part of the more general difficulty of comparing encircling views.

Time should also be considered in relation to wideness.
Encircling wideness with regard to time would mean the
position of *now*, while 'small' wideness would mean a point
in time some distance away.

The example of obsessional problems on leaving one's
home, could now be developed further by description of a
time-dependent reason for emptiness. The elements 'being
at home' and 'being on vacation' could be within the same
focus of convenience, and could, a few days before the
scheduled departure, be compared easily. However, as the
planned time of departure comes ever nearer, the representation of holidays could 'widen' until forming an encircling element at the point of departure. The two elements
as represented at that time, could be outside easy comparison, even being down at the slot level on the contrast
dimension. To the degree that the meaning of 'vacation'
was defined mostly in relation to 'being at home' one
could now go through a sequence leading to constructional
emptiness. First, one would have difficulty construing
holidays when still being at home, and then when leaving,
one could for a while find oneself positioned in between

the two poles, that is, outside the door but inside the
gate (or garden fence), one being neither at home nor away
on vacation. That could come about through the constructional activity being related to space structures. It could
be called a 'subjective no-man's-land'.

However, even when encircling wideness hinders contrast,
'at home' and 'on vacation' are still inside the Kellyian
focus of convenience. Without thoroughly treating the two-
dimensional interaction, one could unpretentiously mention
this as an example of an interacting relationship between
a SAC and a personal construct theory variable (wideness
and focus of convenience).

Sequences of Transitions

Not only the structure of transitions, but also sequences of transitions can be related to obsessional problems.

Downward Sequence

If a transition is repeated, the local rise in activity
need not be at the same level each time, but could be
ordered in a descending hierarchy. When one is reading
the newspaper, for example, one starts by reading the
stimulating headlines, and after a short pause searches
automatically for the next highest item, the cartoons perhaps. And if for some reason one does not leave the situation, one could go on in this way ending up repeatedly
reading meaningless advertisements, maybe wondering why
one has become tired and lethargic.

One could expect compulsive repetitions of wide elements (like walking back to pass a specific location once
more) to have the same effect, by the progressive loss of
newness with repetitions. After performing some rituals
one can indeed be in a worse mood, as Walker and Beech
conclude: 'Rituals do not always improve the patient's
mood, and indeed often cause it to deteriorate; such deterioration is more likely to occur the longer the ritual
continues, (1969, p.1262). However, the quotation does not
directly relate to the example mentioned above as the
activities studied by Walker and Beech were handwashing
and haircombing, and the variables covarying were measures
of hostility, anxiety and depression.

Level-Sequence With Negation

To eat piece after piece of cake, or to do other self-
stimulating activities which maintain their value over a
period of time, can sometimes be construed as unwanted.
When the actual eating of a piece of cake is finished,
and no other activities are readily available, the rising
new activity can be in the form of negation of the next
item ('I must not take one more piece of cake!'). However,
being complex units, negations are not easily seen in perspective. So, when a negation has to be held, no other

alternatives easily come forth. It then becomes monotonous and will soon fade out. After a short uncategorized pause, the stage is set for the really automatic reaching for another piece of cake. This new element requires just as much activity and gives as much stimulation as the one before, thus the term level-sequence.

In a ritual like this, one's best course of action would be to leave the field, but one or more of the different SAC variables could interfere with such a solution: one's activation level could be too low (being too lethargic to rise and leave); one could be constructionally locked into ambivalent passivity (having an 'implicative dilemma' as described by Tschudi 1977, with regard to some waiting work); or the environment could be too poor (not enough sources of encouragement or variation available in the surroundings).

These fields could interact, as examplified by the following relation between content and activation: To have an implicative dilemma, could be static constructional activity which lowers the activation level. On the other hand: The pain in rising while having a low activation level, could be construed as a disadvantage of changing one's position, and as such be part of the dilemma.

The space of alternatives defined by a certain level of required effort, however, broadens and narrows through the sequential process; the field being easier to leave when eating, as one is not then mentally locked up by fully attending to a negation. Unfortunately one is attending to the different qualities of eating cake at that particular moment. One solution would be to use the growing emptiness just after finishing a piece of cake to make a decision to leave the field during the consumption of the next one. In addition to the future effect, such a decision would make for a simultaneous opening of the field, as planning to leave is an easier starting point for varied construing than an absorbing negation.

Bridges

A series of obsessional activities can be seen as local solutions to problems in passing transitions. They could be called 'bridges'.

Three Counting Bridge

Of the different obsessional number manipulations, the repeating of actions three times is often found in the literature: turning the spoon three times on the empty plate after having eaten the soup (Raymond and Janet 1903, p.322); seeing to it that the soap lies three different places on the back of the hand when washing (Kvilhaug 1965, p.47); not doing 'anything' without first having turned around three times (Gadelius 1896, p.212). How can one explain this? On trying to leave one activity,

and getting a fresh start on a new one, which has few implications (e.g. leaving one's home), it can be difficult
to get one's previous situation totally out of mind (without boredom or intrusion). A solution could be to finish
the first activity by a constructional structure which
would give few possibilities for associations by being
relatively empty with regard to content, and which would
have some self-sufficiency by being complex and referring
back to itself. A combination of SAC and personal construct
theory could explain three-counting as such a tool.

The first element of such a series of isolated ritual
markings (e.g. knocks) would be vulnerable to fading away
and replacement. With regard to information, the second
would be rather different, in that it would to some degree
establish the phenomenon. As the English philosopher
Francis Bradley wrote in 1883: '[I]f one feeling is no
feeling, perhaps consciousness first wakens with a complex
presentation, and gets by a circular process the result
together with its premise. The first feeling, which is the
reason why we experience the second, itself becomes explicit in the product, and is thus both starting-point and
goal' (Bradley 1883, p.444). And as the Norwegian philosopher Dag Østerberg says: 'For this reason our experience
never begins, but is given to all of us as something which
is already begun. In paradoxical form: To know is to recognize for the first time' (1966, p.64, trans. 1977).

Three elements would parallel the three date points
which are the minimum context of a baseline (Øst 1974,
p.5), as it reveals a directional trend: two subsequent
relations opens for a relation between their directions.
Somewhat parallel is the Kellyian minimum requirement for
construct building, that is, a property attributable to
two elements should immediately be contrasted by a third,
(Kelly 1955, p.61). If one 'were not immediately concerned
with such a negation one's current reference to a common
property would be indiscriminate and psychologically foot-
less' serving 'no human purpose' (Kelly 1969 p.9). With
regard to activation, the addition of a third conforming
one could also make the sequence a little monotonous,
making the transitional upsurge of a meta-level more
available.

So, by knocking three times, one would have an econom-
ical structure which would (*a*) open for some self-sufficient endurance through its complexity (which makes variation possible), (*b*) give little associations to other
than the immediate field through its content-meagreness
(knocks are non-verbal), and finally (*c*) be relatively
immune against intrusions through its self-reference.
Having these properties comprises help when it is problematic to leave a field.

Hierarchical Bridge

Checking when leaving a place can sometimes partly be
ordered in levels, as in the following much simplified
and rather edited description of rituals occurring when
rising from the table (acted out for the present writer).
1st level: (Action multiplied by elements). Looks at tobacco pouch. It looks all right. Puts in pocket. Does the
same with lighter and cigarette paper. 2nd level: (Verbal
sequence multiplied by elements). 'The tobacco is okay.
It's in the pocket. That is okay. The lighter is okay....'
and so on. 3rd level: (Verbal unit multiplied by elements)
'The tobacco is okay, the lighter is okay....' and so on.
4th level: (All inclusive verbal). 'Then all is okay with
these things.' 5th level: (Non-verbal knocking signal).
Three complex sequences plus one hard knock. Freedom to
go on to other matters then ensues.

This individual explained that he felt he had to know
where his belongings were because he had a need for control, being afraid of losing it, of being mentally 'in-
vaded', of fainting, maybe even of dying. SAC would point
out that an absolute form of control would be to have all
content matter gathered and effectively isolated in one
single non-content phenomenon (the knocking), and then
make an effective negation of this phenomenon easier by
making it (the knocking signal) satisfying with regard to
variation (complicated), thereby diminishing the possibility of intrusion.

Three Plus Two Bridge

A person could have an implication void when just having left the building the last day on a job (1st element:
construct of 'job'). Such a person could construe in the
following manner: 'I shall get another job' (2nd element),
'and still another' (3rd element). 'And all these jobs,
including the one which I am now leaving, I take to earn
money' (1st meta-element). 'And all these jobs I also
take because I like to work' (2nd meta-element). The first
element which was originally difficult to leave, could be
made less dominating, maybe almost unavailable, within
this operation. The 'three plus two', consisting of two
levels, would be stable through its complexity, tied to
concreteness, and future-oriented, as one does not leave
the first level in favour of a fully developed Kellyian
construct (three elements) at the meta-level, but makes
more than a tentative start (the two meta-elements). The
whole construction makes a kind of platform, and could
be seen as a technique for Kellyian 'loosening' and creative work.

Stepping Stone Bridge

A less useful solution could be presented by what one
might call a 'stepping stone bridge'. To say: 'You can

have a new job, then earn money, then go on vacation',
and so on, could turn out to be a futile effort to console
the person. By continually moving on to new elements,
while irreversibly leaving the passed ones, one never gets
enough constructional complexity to both rest and make
controlled 'framebreak' (go beyond one's conceptual framework of the moment).

Luggage Bridge

Many important benefits are closely tied to the position of being a wage-earner in our society, and it can
come as an enormous shock to suddenly lose this position.
In our culture such a transition can be accompanied by
rituals. Job ending rituals can include wearing plain
clothes, getting presents, good wishes, being given reassurance of a welcome on future visits, and accompaniment on
the road (Adams, Hayes and Hopson 1976). This could be
called 'luggage bridge' as elements from one situation
are carried along to the next.

Use of Transitions

Some reactions to transitions have been discussed.
Some examples of the active use of transitions in therapy
are presented below.

The creator of direct decision therapy, Harold Green-
wald, in a therapeutic demonstration described the feelings of the audience to the client. In doing this, he
raised the intensity of his voice and content to a dramatic climax, and then, after a moment's passivity, said in
a low voice: 'including you'. Here he implied a possible
likeness between the described audience and the client.
This sequence could be described as (*a*) raising the client'
activation level (the raising voice), and (*b*) making for
a replacement transition by sudden lowering the client's
surroundings (silence, passivity), and (*c*) steering the
content carefully just as the client's level of imagination automatically increased (by the words 'including
you').

A comparable technique of raising and steering the construing of the client would be to (*a*) get her to accum-
ulate many independent elements and (*b*) then simplify representation of the items by getting her to raise one level
to a simple, superordinate construct, and (*c*) thereby
release some imagination activity which can then be steered. Milton Erichson (Haley 1973) seemed to do this in a
successful thrust to gain the confidence and co-operation
of a woman with a strong negative self-construct. He
reeled off twelve relatively simple, colourful and extremely negative statements about her looks, made a simple
conclusive statement, and then immediately advanced to
the steering of content, as illustrated in the excerpt
below:

Your forehead is too hideously low. Your hair is
not even decently combed. And the dress you are
wearing - polka dots, millions and billions of
them. You have no taste, even in clothes. Your feet
slop over the edges of your shoes. To put it simply
- you are a hideous mess. (Simplifying) But you do
need help. (Steering) I'm willing to give you this
help. I think you know now that I won't hesitate to
tell you the truth. You need to know the truth about
yourself before you can ever learn the things necessary to help yourself. (Haley 1973, p.93).

A third and simpler version would be the Corsini technique of freezing the group activity, and non-verbally
showing the main figure of the psychodrama out of the
room, just as the play of the problematic field comes to
a climax. Being alone, the main person then typically does
some active construing with regard to the theme treated,
though without direct steering (Corsini, 1966 p.106,
pp.126-7).

Construction of Semi-emptiness (COS)

A SAC structure taking better care of static phenomena
than that of transition, is called construction of semi-
emptiness. It refers to a situation where one is constructionally active, while there is too little variation in
the field of construction. It would be like attentively
listening - to a boring speech, or actively trying to go
to sleep - by a negation of one's thought content. It
opens for automatic increase of activity (e.g. restless
movements when listening; thoughts from the day popping
up when one is trying to sleep).

This should not be called 'construction of emptiness';
this expression should be reserved for a mature Kellyian
construing of emptiness which in the sleep example could
mean that one is comparing some friends' negations with
one's own, a performance which is not available in the
construct arsenal of our culture (but which would possibly
give immediate and pleasurable sleep from the combined
emptiness and variation). Neither is emptiness the appropriate word, as the focused field could contain some elements. A suitable wording might be 'semi-construction of
semi-emptiness', or, in a more useable form, 'construction
of semi-emptiness'.

Anxiety

'Construction of semi-emptiness' can be used to describe
anxiety, as in the following example. When trying to
emphatically study the field of experience of friend, I
first built up a broad attention field of independent
parts while looking at a landscape (seeing the house, the
sky, the ground, the tree, and so on, simultaneously: as
the friend described seeing them). When holding this state,

the uninteresting parts of nearby walls were experienced
as dreadful. A fear of white walls was indeed a problem
my friend had. This would be an illustration of COS: one
is construing actively (broad attention field) while there
is not enough variation in the field (uninteresting walls).
This view could also be applied to other specific fields
of anxiety, such as dread in open spaces (Richards 1977),
in high places, and in darkness.

In personal construct theory anxiety is defined as the
awareness that the events with which one is confronted lie
mostly outside the range of convenience of one's construct
system (Kelly 1955, pp.495-565). In the framework of COS
the 'awareness' could be seen as active construing, and
the 'outside range of convenience' as emptiness.

In the example above, SAC seems to go its own way. The
experimenter's relaxed superordinate attitudes of curiosity and concentration, the familiarity of the elements
(well-known house, tree, etc.) and the occurrence of anxiety in specific time and space, do not automatically fall
into the Kellyian view of anxiety as a reaction to confrontation with phenomena which are not construed inside
the range of convenience. But Kelly's definition is des-
irable, for example in McCoy's sense (1977):

> Viewing anxiety in terms of an awareness of the
> inadequacy of a person's construction system, sugg-
> ests various ways the therapist may deal with it.
> It enables him to design a therapeutic programme
> around a series of validating and invalidating
> events which will normally lead to construct system
> revision. (McCoy 1977, p.98)

SAC and personal construct theory seem to overlap,
while also having their own fields of prediction. Perhaps
their relationship is more of a cross-relational one than
an incompatible one, at least at the present level of
differentiation.

Complexity

Before going on to describe another state, that of
guilt, the concept of complexity and its relation to the
contrast dimension will be presented.

Complexity refers to number of elements and the relationships between them in what is treated as a unit at
any given point in time. Its values range from 'simple'
(e.g. the thought: 'She eats because she is hungry'), to
'complex' (e.g. the thought: 'She eats because that is
what she expects the host to be expecting, not realizing
that the host expects her to expect there are no expectations towards her'). It would not correspond to complexity measures derived from sequences of constructional
acts, such as those of Crockett (1965 p.51), and Zajonc
(1960 p.160), and those derived from the use of the Grid-
form, (reviewed by Bonarius 1965, pp.15-16). A complex

construct should be differentiated from a comprehensive
one which 'cuts across many other construct lines' (Kelly
1955, p.478), as it could fulfil this function while being
simple. It would be more like the situation of a person
buried in a sequence of unsolved tasks while having no
opportunity to forget any of them. Such a situation would
create an all-active 'complex plan', a TOTE-hierarchy of
Miller, Galanter and Pribram (1960, pp.27, 37). Also, the
double negation ('I'm not not happy') could be regarded
as complex.

Complexity of any given element in a set could be seen
to be inversely related to contrast values between those
same elements. Simple values are therefore more easily
compared than complex ones. Watzlawick, Beavin and Jackson
(1967) propose in the following that there is a limit to
our thinking at the fourth 'level of knowledge' (p.262):
'This is how I see you seeing me seeing you seeing me'
(p.266). Comparing elements on that level of complexity
to build up Kellyian constructs is difficult, not only
because of limitations in immediate information processing
possibly coming into play, but also because our culture
does not have a ready arsenal of those kinds of elements.
So although one has built up a complex element, there are
no easily available elements to make for continuation.
Thus the element is likely to fade away, and soon be replaced by elements on lower levels. To make new ones on
the spot would be too difficult, and comparable to just
having read one of Laing's knots (1970) and immediately
having to create two more by oneself. The situation could
metaphorically be described as 'the loneliness of the
pyramidal tops'.

Guilt

Guilt as defined by personal construct theory is the
awareness of dislodgement of the self from one's core
role structure (Kelly 1955, pp.502, 565). Guilt can also
be seen as nearly related to the limitation in contrasting
which comes when one construes elements of high complexity
value. This could be exemplified by a young person fully
committed to doing homework, but who then nevertheless
follows the temptation to spend a night with the gang.
The dislodgement when downtown would be that of instructing
herself to be placed in the previous situation ('I should
have been at home') while at the same time construing her
present situation as being seen from the home-self's view
('In reality "I" don't think I should stay here'). When
some eager therapist asks her to consider whether she
should not go home and read instead of pursuing this
'regressive' life, it is not 'the defence of repression'
or 'isolation' which makes her give an evasive response.
On the contrary, it could be her attempt to follow the
advice of the therapist, that is, to compare two poles

both seen from a third (home and town seen in perspective),
and simultaneously try to see the perspective as from one
of the poles (home) while being placed in the other (downtown), which is constructional positioned in the view of
the first one. Given our socialization, this could be
rather difficult for both client and therapist.

More generally one could say that from SAC's complexity
view of guilt, the core role is difficult to reconstrue
as long as one stays continually in the new position,
without some moving back and forth between the new and
old position, and also between positions inside and outside that system, which could further the contrast making.

The pain of guilt is seen here as stemming from the
capacity-taxing situation of simultaneously having two
frames with too different activity features, that is, the
staticness of the aforementioned intricate constructions,
and the variation of the new role-situation at the moment.
There would then be the possibility of *glad guilt* made
through simplification and duplication of guilt themes,
one ending up as some kind of content actor in life's
entertaining drama. When both Lazarus (1971 p.168) using
his fact-discovering instruction on the client's 'dis-
belief system', and Tschudi (1977 p.327) using his ABC
model on guilt, report ease following construing of positive aspects of the 'badness', variation could be a factor. The Kellyian view that one can be guilty in taking
a 'good' role (1969 p.180) is to be differentiated from
glad guilt, though not necessarily to be seen as incompatible.

From his content-structure background, Kelly (1977) has
fruitful instructions to offer in dealing with guilt not
covered by SAC. An instance of this is when he warns
against regarding a mistake as a deviation from a blueprint laid down for us, and as something to be punished
(see p.17). Instead we are told to examine our mistakes
to provide grounds for trying out better ways. The guilt
is then 'harmful or helpful, depending upon what we think
should be done about it' (see p.18).

Position in One Pole

Meeuwen (1977) and Richards (1977) propose viewing the
obsessionally plagued person as one who tries to construe
the world with one pole only. Here some implications will
be drawn.

The unidimensional construing of one's actual self as
bad, and as generally different from other persons mostly
construed as good and like the ideal self, was a predomin-
ant result in a group of diagnosed 'obsessional neurotics'
when tested with the Role Construct Repertory Grid (Makhlouf-Norris and Norris 1972, p.280). Possible incidence
in the rest of the population is not discussed here. The
result is noted, and the tentative stance taken that to

be positioned in the submerged pole of a 'subdeveloped core-construct' is a possible working factor at the time of obsessional activity.

Possible Creation

A goal could be construed as being particularly important if its negation, or alternatives, are not made explicit. If, as life goes on, neither that goal nor new sub-goals are reached or given up, they could come to form a 'complex plan' (Miller et al. 1960, p.37) of unsolved tasks. 'To manage A, I must do B, which I don't seem to master. So let me in the meantine at least manage C. But for the time being I must do other tasks asked of me....' etc. Possible difficulties had from before in comparing the goal to alternatives ($A-1$, $A-2$, etc.) or to its negation (not A), could then increase because of limitations in comparing complex units (accumulated, multilevel, negated elements). According to Kelly, meaningful construing implies some negation of a third element. So 'not to manage A and 'not to manage B', is 'not to not manage C'. As that differentiation is too difficult, they merge to 'not to manage anything', or 'I am all bad', which is a vague construct not easily contrasted to the goal.

So one does not see oneself clearly in relation to the goal, as one who for the moment does not manage it. Instead one ends up with a subdeveloped core structure, where an isolated, vague, superordinate, negational one-pole ('I'm all bad') represents one's actual position.

This complexity view on unidimensional self-construing of 'badness' is different from that of Makhlouf-Norris and Norris (1972 p.285). They view the negative self-construing as a self-fulfilling prophecy which more certainly gives validation than construing which implies positive goals; goals which then have to be reached.

Eternal Quasi-important Elements

What would it be like to construe elements with one pole only? As a one-pole predictor one would have to use identical replicas, as there would be no different elements or relationships. So, one table is all tables or, rather, an unending row of tables (Meeuwen 1977; Richards 1977). When one applies this to the experience of time, events could easily take on eternal importance, paralleling some obsessional content. However, as the elements would have no clear status, relating to other values along one or more dimensions, they would as such have less importance. It would be not knowing the importance of the importance, that is, quasi-importance.

Seen from the unending sequence of equal items, there would also never be any news, any surprises and the not built in divisions would make for embracing too long sequences. So there would be emptiness, resembling Kelly's

paragraph: 'A construct which implied similarity without
contrast would represent....a chaotic undifferentiated
homogeneity', and would 'leave the person engulfed in a
sea with no landmarks to relieve the monotony' (1955,
p.51). On the other hand, the lack of clear placement in
relation to the next item on one or more dimensions would
make for repeated newness, surprise and absolute stop for
every element. So there would be quasi-newness (never
'really' surprised), and quasi-ending (never coming to an
all-embracing end).

When, in particular would the one-pole come into play?
That would be at the transitions when abrupt changes in
the subordinate stream calls for superordinate construing.
And as the unidimensionality of obsessional construing
would make for limited resources of easily available alternative activity at any given time, so would the obsessionally plagued person relatively often have to rely on superordinate constructs when passing transitions.

On the Use of SAC in Therapy

The bridges and the examples of use of transitions in
therapy hint at the possibility of teaching the client
how to manipulate her own SAC variables. This could open
up the way for comparison of activity structures across
content-defined situations, and thereby the building of
(Kellyian) constructs of SAC variables and constellations.
As the SAC variables operate much from moment to moment
in the person's functioning, bringing them under control
should also make personal experimentation more of a possibility.

The redefining of one's problems as value constellations in relation to a larger variable system, should
make for liberation. This would resemble Radley's description of the person who 'flies into a rage and desperately
pulls at the drawer which jams'. Instead he 'becomes part
of the larger system ("person plus drawer") which he is
instrumental in changing' (Radley 1977, p.241). Also, as
the SAC framework would further the control over the
activity aspect of construing, one should be able to reg-
ulate activity and content more independently, thereby
getting more freedom to fulfil wants in both areas.

The knowledge to construe activational features is in
our content-minded culture not only a possible therapy,
but also a question of cultural change. Dorothy Tennov
(1977) has made a fascinating start in this great field
of therapeutic and cultural change. She teaches women
how to chart their varying degrees of activation throughout the day, and to compare the curve to the one they
make from data on their more or less capacity taxing activities at different times. Thus one could have 'over-
employment', trying to manage demanding tasks (e.g. planning, writing difficult letters), while on a low activation

level, and 'underemployment', doing simple things (e.g.
preparing breakfast), while on a high activation level.
Women can reorganise their activities with the help of
the information they get through the use of these constructs.

PERSONAL CONSTRUCT THEORY, NONAUTONOMOUS FREEDOM AND THE ART OF CHOOSING

MARK B. MENDELSOHN

Department of Psychology, George Mason University,
4400 University Drive, Fairfax,
Virginia 22030, U.S.A.

American psychology has contributed enormously to
the literature of behaviour modification and instrumental conditioning. (Those) who see themselves as
humanistically inclined are likely to disparage
this contribution ... and are alarmed by it. They
see it as a giant technological effort to make mankind jump through hoops ... Remember that the psychologist who makes it possible for me to accomplish
a difficult leap has done me no disservice unless
I am endangered by my own impulses. He has shown
me how to realize one of my hidden potentialities ...
(which may) add a new dimension to my freedom and
make it all the more real. (Kelly 1969b, p.135).
In the first part of this paper, 'nonautonomous freedom' is applied to the concept of personal autonomy in an
attempt to understand shifts in personal behaviour from
the perspective of changing stimulus conditions. In the
second part a clinical model based on operant psychology
and personal construct theory is presented.

Part I

Nonautonomous freedom (Mendelsohn 1975) was proposed
as a framework for understanding the construction of private events and the implementation of public events; where
personal accountability is invoked by an injunction to
share in the outcome of one's own behaviour, and behavioural questions may be posed with reference to both
utility (effectiveness) and quality (adherence to ethical
injunctions). My intention in using the term, nonautonomous freedom, is to convey the view that determinism *and*
freedom are joint parts of any person-environment accomm-
odation. Traditionally human behaviour has been understood
as *either* free *or* determined, and certainly *not both*
simultaneously. The question of 'freedom versus determinism' is a long-standing theoretical dilemma. Though
behavioural scientists and clinicians may 'choose sides'
or proceed operationally without regard to this issue,
many investigators will eventually be faced with a more

rigorous theoretical accounting. Such an accounting may
be particularly in order for the thoughtful psychotherapist. The specific goals of this discussion are to: (1)
demonstrate the error in logic and limited utility of
posing freedom and determinism as antithetical; and (2)
to propose as the logical alternative freedom and determinism as reciprocal expressions of the process of ongoing
behaviour. The increased clinical utility suggested by
such an approach is discussed.

Freedom and Determinism as Antithetical

Freedom and determinism may be viewed as clearly incompatible when the autonomy of a human being is questioned in personal value terms, as in 'Is a given human
being free or determined?' When posed in this way a human
being becomes the object of evaluation. Probably no empirical gain would result from such an assessment beyond what
could be learned by evaluating behaviour in regard to its
effectiveness and adherence to ethical injunctions. Perhaps the meaning of freedom and determinism may be probed
more effectively by considering behaviour, per se, as
might be done with a question such as 'Is a given unit of
behaviour free or determined?' Though not yet readily
amenable to empirical investigation, this shift of focus
does permit specification of target behaviours.

'Freedom or determinism' may be investigated empiric-
ally, however, by inquiring whether behaviour is free or
determined in regard to a particular set of antecedents
and consequences. The specific environmental triggers for
the occurrence of a unit of behaviour may be discovered
by understanding which stimulus conditions are necessary
to predict the emission or omission of a given target
behaviour. With reference to such prediction, the following question is intended to direct the investigator in
the clinic towards an understanding of empirical determinants: 'In regard to which relevant stimulus conditions
is a given unit of behaviour free; and, in regard to which,
determined?' Freedom in regard to stimulus conditions is
considered stimulus neutrality; whereas determinism in
regard to other conditions is stimulus control. Every
unit of behaviour has its unique set of controlling stimuli. This view may be particularly valuable for the clinician as it strengthens the empirical side of the psychotherapeutic enterprise by accommodating the methods of
operant analysis. Such an analysis enables the clinician
to outline both the public and private stimulus events
participating in the origination, development, maintenance,
and future course of a dysfunctional pattern of behaviour.
One might speculate clinical intervention with maximum
therapeutic impact to involve the application of stimulus
control procedures before dysfunctional behaviour has had
its full effect on the environment and becomes stabilized.

Freedom and Determinism as Reciprocal

Freedom and determinism as reciprocal expressions of the process of ongoing behaviour may be explored in the context of developmental theory. Stage theories of behavioural development generally postulate a fixed sequence of organism-environment interaction and assume an optimal period for the acquisition of various skills. For instance, consider the expanding social radius of the individual in Erikson's psychosocial view of development. Here, social development involves mastery in a succession of environments which results in an ever expanding repertoire. Such a repertoire may be viewed as the product of an individual's interaction with a series of different salient stimulus conditions. Presumably each stage of development has its own unique set of environmental controls; and, at any given stage of development, a particular set of salient stimuli predominate in directing personal behaviour. For every stage it is important to ask if the appropriate stimulus controls are operating in order to maximise individual functioning.

A comprehensive view of stimulus control may supplement traditional developmental theories and hasten our discovering how states of psychological development 'lock-in' with particular environmental triggers. An additional benefit of understanding the interconnection between controlling stimuli and newly emerging behaviour may be increased participation in the direction of life changes. The next section of this paper describes a model for analysing such interconnections.

Part II

> A construct is like a reference axis, a basic dimension of appraisal ... it can be regarded as an open channel of movement ... serving both to limit and open up passages of freedom. (Kelly 1969c, p.199).

An individual construes events, behaves publicly and may change over time. This changed behaviour is assumed to occur lawfully and may be viewed as a contingency shift or movement from one set of influential consequences to another. The concept of nonautonomous freedom provides the backdrop for exploring change from the perspective of contingency shifting. In this section a model is proposed for clinical assessment. The attempt is made to proceed on two levels of phenomenal analysis: clearly visible behaviour change and less visible constructional shifts. Visible behaviour may be described by the process of shifting contingencies and straightforward operant analysis. The less visible constructions may become apparent upon their entry into the community of events which is publicly observable. Constructions of events shift just as behaviours change over time.

Behaviours may be understood in light of ongoing contingencies, and self-control conceived as the personal
arrangement of those consequences. Constructions may also
be understood in light of ongoing contingencies, and choice
conceived partially as the personal arrangement of those
consequences. The difference, however, is that constructional modification may be largely a function of other relevant constructions as can be determined by a constructional analysis. An operant analysis may be usefully employed by analogy in our discussion of constructional analysis; as private constructions may be antecedent and consequent stimuli as well as responses. One's view of events
as well as the ability to move along any given constructional dimension may be reinforcing or itself reinforced.
Constructional equivalents of discriminative stimuli may
serve as switching devices to move an individual from one
construction to another. Again, as in an operant analysis,
a constructional system may be viewed as a function of its
consequences.
    A behavioural analysis which attempts to accommodate
cognition may proceed by reference to the following model.

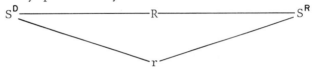

$$S^D \text{————————} R \text{————————} S^R$$
$$r$$

In this model the occurrence of the target behaviour (R)
is understood by reference to either a preceding stimulus
(S^D) and/or a consequent stimulus (S^R); both of which
would refer to overt behaviour. Cognition (r) is readily
viewed as a byproduct of observable behaviour and accordingly occupies a peripheral status. While an operant model
does offer considerable utility for analysing behaviour,
such an approach misses an essential feature of psychotherapy: a person's perception of his experience in the
world. Understanding an individual's perception of events
is crucial to conducting an accurate clinical assessment
upon which to base any therapy. This is no less the case
in a behavioural assessment, as the question: 'What does
this mean to you?' often reveals what is reinforcing to
a person.
    It seems a potent model for psychotherapy would do well
to include a method for understanding a person's perception
of events. Such a model is presented below.

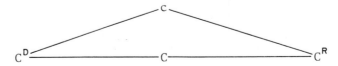

$$C$$
$$C^D \text{————————} C \text{————————} C^R$$

In this model the occurrence of the target construction
(C) is understood by reference to either a preceding construction (C^D) and/or consequent construction (C^R); both
of which would refer to covert behaviour. Behaviour (c)
is readily viewed as a byproduct of a person's organising
perceptions of the environment and accordingly occupies
a peripheral status. Now all this sounds rather familiar
as simply the 'underside' of an operant model. However,
just as an operant model did not permit satisfactory analysis of congnition, a constructional model of psychotherapy does not, by itself, permit an adequate focus for
behaviour change.

     An expanded S-R model including both constructional and
behavioural phenomena is presented below as an inter-
connected double tier. Though I might prefer to dub this
combined constructional-operant view, 'cooperant', I suspect the staunch behavioural evaluation of this operant-
constructional blend might be dubbed as 'opstructional'.

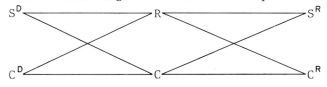

In addition to permitting a wider range of analysis, the
two-tiered model encourages the clinical investigator to
look at the application of private consequences as possible determinants of both public and private events. For
example, 'You did well'; 'Good job'; and 'Keep at it and
you will go far', may all serve as constructional positive
reinforcers. Constructional punishment may be presented
by, 'Give up; it is hopeless; you will never amount to
anything'. Private aversive control would also include
constructional negative reinforcers of the following sort:
'Maybe I am not as bad as I thought'; 'Perhaps it is not
futile'; 'All hope may not be lost'. Constructional extinc-
tion may be comprised of: 'I guess I blew it'; 'Maybe this
is not the way to succeed'; or 'That did not work out the
way I had thought'. These are a few examples of private
constructions that may influence thinking and experiencing
as well as having an effect on more readily observable
behaviour. (The reader is referred to Meichenbaum's (1974)
discussion of the effect of private events on public behaviour.)

     In the combined model public and private events may
exert reciprocal influence on each other. Additionally,
subanalyses may be performed as they are necessary without
loss of the overall perspective. The overall perspective
is one in which there is simultaneous movement along all
dimensions represented. Certainly both thought and action
and the various interconnections between them are relevant

to psychotherapy. Dividing a model into separate lines of
thought and action is not meant to imply that an organism
is divided in a similar fashion. The organism is viewed as
a unity which may sometimes be understood more clearly by
abstracting those features which seem characteristic of
the clinical enterprise. Therefore, while it is conceivable
to trace both constructions and behaviours simultaneously,
it is also possible to follow either one alone (i.e. to
do either a behavioural or constructional analysis), or
to follow a particular course of events across both behaviours and constructions.

CONSTRAINT AND FREEDOM: THE SOCIAL ORIGIN OF PERSONAL CONSTRUCTS

HARRY PROCTER* AND GLENYS PARRY[+]

* Tone Vale Hospital,   [+] MRC Social and Applied
  Norton Fitzwarren,   Psychology Unit,
  Taunton, Somerset.   The University,
                        Sheffield S10 2TN.

The Inadequacy of Individualist Psychology

Construct theory is a theory of meaning. It is committed to understanding the process by which we make sense of the world we live in. Psychology as a whole, because it makes the *individual* the focus of convenience, ignores the vital role of social processes. Indeed as construct theorists, we are forced to admit that our theory fails to take adequate account of the social nature of meanings and values.

Our concern is with the relationship between an individual's construct system and the ideology of the society in which she lives. Typically, social scientists have separated these, and concentrated on one to the exclusion of the other. By separating or ignoring the distinction between the personal and social worlds, any account of the relationship between them becomes impossible. In this paper we will argue that construct theory need not be sociologically naive, indeed it gives us an enlightening perspective on the interface between psychology and sociology.

Marx saw ideologies as reflecting social and economic interests of the different groups or classes in society. For example, Weber (1904) demonstrates that the Protestant ethic, with its emphasis on individual freedom and responsibility, is prevalent in capitalist societies. In contrast, Catholicism with its emphasis on destiny predominates in peasant societies. In each type of society the dominant ideology reflects the needs and concerns of the power-holding group. In this context, *any* action or statement is seen as having ideological implications. Thus, psychological theories which claim to be politically neutral are making an unwitting statement in support of the *status quo*.

Kelly himself seems almost entirely unaware of these issues. Where he does mention social class it is with a touching naivity about its importance in influencing an individual's view of the world. Thus he writes:

One of the most commonly used cultural groupings is

the socio-economic class.....From the standpoint of
the psychology of personal constructs this classification system has limited value only.....It throws
comparatively little light upon the way the people
of the different social classes strike off the dimensions along which living can be evaluated (1955,
p.694).
However, to be fair, one of the explicit philosophical
assumptions underlying construct theory is a materialist
one:
.....we attempt to make clear from the outset that
it is a real world we shall be talking about, not
a world composed solely of the flitting shadows of
people's thoughts (1955, p.6).
Therefore the criticism that Kelly is a naive idealist
is incorrect. Furthermore, he is clearly aware of a possible theoretical problem concerning the role of culture.
It may be difficult to follow this notion of culture as a validational system of events. And it may
be even more difficult to reconcile with the idea
of cultural control what we have said about man not
being the victim of his biography. The cultural control we see is one that is within the client's own
construct system, and it is imposed upon him only
in the sense that it limits the kinds of evidence
at his disposal. How he handles this evidence is
his own affair and clients manage it in a tremendous
variety of ways (1955, p.693).
Kelly's contribution is to show how cultural values
are not received passively but are built up anew by each
individual. Many sociologists are guilty of viewing the
individual merely as a passive occupant of socially determined roles.
The dialectic between the constraint of our culture
and our personal freedom is our fundamental concern and
one which we believe Kelly substantially resolved, although
he left the sociological aspect unelaborated. Kelly's
crucial discussion of free will and determinism will be
examined later.
At this point, a psychologist may argue that there is
no place in a psychological study of human behaviour for
sociological considerations. However, we believe that it
is impossible to give an adequate account of human behaviour whilst neglecting them. It is hard to see how a purely intrapsychic approach could handle epidemiological
studies of higher rates of psychiatric disturbance in
urban populations (Hollingshead and Redlich 1958; Brown
et al 1975), the influence of sex roles on attitudes and
behaviour (Mednick and Weissman 1975), the influence of
social class on linguistic styles (Bernstein 1961) or
indeed any anthropological study of cross-cultural differences in behaviour.

For a number of reasons construct theory is more able
to deal with such findings than any other major psychological theory. However, Marxists and sociologists have attempted to use a number of psychological theories to supplement their ideas. As construct theorists we find little
value in the various behaviourist approaches. Kelly himself has adequately criticised these theories for their
implicit assumption that the person is an inert being,
needing to be pushed or prodded into action. It is interesting to note at this point that the work of Vygotsky
was suppressed in the Soviet Union after the rise of
Stalin. The adoption of Pavlovian theory by Soviet psychologists accompanied the vulgarisation of Marxist theory.
Such reductionist and mechanistic theory has little in
common with the original thinking of Marx.
The recent popularity of cognitive approaches in Western psychology might appear to overcome the problems of
behaviourist theory. The basic notion here is of an internal representation of reality which is continuously corrected by reducing the mis-match between the inner and outer
worlds. Included here are for instance the theories of
Miller, Galanter and Pribram, Neisser, Mahoney, Piaget,
and possibly even Rogers. Although teleological, these
theories are nevertheless fundamentally reductionist, and
involve processes no more sophisticated than those of a
thermostat. Furthermore, their view of change as adjustment has potentially reactionary implications.
A number of radical thinkers have derived their theories
from psychoanalysis, most importantly Reich, Fromm and
Marcuse. Brown (1974) has argued that Freudianism is fundamentally incompatible with Marxism. This is too sweeping
a generalisation. Whilst we would agree that psychoanalysis
in its metapsychological aspects is incompatible, much of
the content provides us with a true understanding of many
human processes. It must be remembered however that this
is only so for the culture in which the theory was formulated. Reich has shown how much of Freud's early work
was genuinely revolutionary, but that when psychoanalysis
became an established discipline, the revolutionary implications of his work were destroyed. Thus Freud's early
view of the supression of the individual by society was
later replaced by the notion of sublimation of instinctual
drives in the interests of civilization. Society was ex-
cused for its repressive nature by the invention of the
concept of the superego, and political violence was traced
to the death instinct. From a Kellian point of view we
would part with Freud for his intrapsychic stance, and
also for his reliance on the concept of energy.
Reich, in his early work was an heroic figure in the
history of radical psychology. He had great insight into
the use of sexual repression as a political tool for the
preservation of the family. His analysis of the use of

the family in training children to conform to political
authority in later life is still relevant today. His work
on sexuality had many revolutionary implications, although
we find it difficult to espouse Reich as a sexual radical,
in that his theories are penis-centred, and are reactionary from the female and homosexual viewpoints. We also
part with Reich in his attribution of the rise of Fascism
in Germany in terms of the 'irrationality' of the masses,
thus ignoring the counter-revolutionary role of the German
Communist party, and exposing a contemptuous view of the
ordinary person. It is interesting in this context that
having committed himself to the core role construct of
'irrationality', he should personally live this out in
his delusional and bizarre theorising of later years. It
is noteworthy that in the current popularity of his work,
for example in bioenergetics, the middle class intelligen-
sia has latched on to these latter aspects, rather than
his earlier revolutionary contribution.

There are several reasons why Kelly's work is suitable
for our purpose in developing a psychology which is compatible with sociological theory. His fundamental view of
the person as a form of motion is compatible with dialectical views of change, human practice being seen as primary
in this; the philosophy of constructive alternativism
parallels the relativist requirement of sociology and,
finally, Kelly has a profound respect for ordinary people,
and a faith that change lies with them.

The Social Origin of Personal Constructs

Where do constructs come from? In examining this question we will look at some of the social structures and
processes whereby culture is transmitted from one generation to the next. Individual construct systems are constrained by the structure and ideology of the society.
However, this is only one aspect of a dialectical process,
and we will therefore also examine the important question
of how ideologies are continuously generated by material
from individual construct systems.

The family acts as mediator between society and the
individual. In our society it is the earliest important
arena in which the process of construct formation takes
place, although later the role of school, the work environment, the neighbourhood and reference groups increases.

Sociologists have shown how the family structure itself (nuclear, extended, matrilineal, patriarchal, gens,
etc.) is an integral part of the wider society. Family
structure and the wider social structure maintain each
other. The relationships within the family influence the
child's developing construct system. This is one important way in which construct systems are influenced by wider
social processes. In fact the family provides validational
evidence for a whole range of constructs; physical, psy-

chological and ideological.

An example may make this clear. The structure of our patriarchal society is dependent on a gender role system, maintained in every aspect of public life. The family structure not only reflects this system, but is essential in maintaining it. Little girls learn how to be women in the family, where mother and father act out the power relationship between men and women in general. 'Gender-appropriate' behaviours and attitudes are learned in this context, and it is not an accident that 'gender-inapprop-riate' behaviours, such as homosexuality, are seen as dangerous and are often labelled as pathological. For example, one establishment view of male homosexuality sees it as resulting from a deviant family pattern of dominating mother and passive retiring father. The patriarchal orthodoxy cannot afford such 'deviations', and homosexuality is rightly seen as a threat to its fundamental structures.

Recent research in developmental psychology has shown the vital role of the mother in selecting the salient aspects of the physical and social environment (Schaffer 1977). Videotape analysis of mother/child interaction shows the 'conversation' between them begins within the first days of life. Contrary to previous views, the child is an *active* participant in this dialogue, showing that the individual is not a passive recipient of socialisation, even at this early age.

It is ironic that psychology is only recently getting to grips with the idea of identity developing in a social context. This idea is at least 150 year old, starting with Hegel's dialectical argument that 'self' cannot exist without 'other'. Feuerbach put this concept on a material-ist basis:

  .....Man's being is contained only in community,
  in the unity which rests, however, only on the
  reality of the difference between I and Thou (Feuerbach 1843).

Psychologists have been surrounded by a host of workers in different disciplines who have elaborated this idea, including Buber, Erikson, the object relations theorists, Mead and the symbolic interactionists. Psychology though, blinkered by its individualistic stance, has until recently remained ignorant of this tradition.

What does construct theory have to offer developmental psychology? Kelly regards constructs as choices (not necessarily conscious) rather than merely as labels on a repertqry grid. This puts construct theory firmly in line with sociological approaches such as Marxism, symbolic interactionism and theories of action, which see practice as fundamental to change. At the core of all change Kelly sees a process of validation and invalidation of hyptheses. This begins at birth and continues throughout life. Con-

structs are gradually organised into a hierarchical system, through a continuous process of elaboration and revision. Kelly does justice to the complex dialectical
nature of development. Psychoanalysis views the basic personality structure as determined at an early age. Although
construct theorists would agree that a child of three
already has a well elaborated personal construct system,
it continues to change. Children's systems become more
hierarchical, their constructs increasing in complexity
with age, moving from using physical constructs to psychological ones (Livesley and Bromley 1973).

But personal construct theory, as it stands, is still
in danger of oversimplifying the effect of social factors
on development. We would argue that the psychoanalytic
notion of the latency period only contains some truth
because the child's social role does not change radically
in the nuclear family over these years. The later so-
called 'stormy' period of adolescence cannot be understood
in purely psychological terms. Adolescence is a phenomenon
specific to our culture, in which the person has reached
physical maturity, and yet is expected to remain dependent
on school and family.

The issue of education is also important in our discussion. The concept of 'education' is a relatively new
one, and should be distinguished from 'learning'. It
carries within it implications of the passive reception
of a body of knowledge, whereas as Kellyians we are anxious
to stress the active nature of learning. Illich (1971)
argues that the function of the school is not primarily
an educational one. He describes the 'hidden curriculum'
whereby the institution transmits the established ideology
and social structure. Heather (1976) writes:

> The school in our society is the primary, organised
> vehicle for the transmission of its dominant ideol-
> ogy.....Schools attempt little real education, in
> the sense of encouraging the child's natural curios-
> ity and confidence to think for herself, allowing
> her to develop her *own* abilities and providing the
> soil in which an awareness of personal morality and
> sensitivity to others can grow.....The school shores
> up the privilege of the middle classes, and teaches
> the working class child, at a very early age, to be
> a failure for whom the good things of life are not
> intended. In this way, the school services higher
> education and the job market without disturbing the
> existing boundaries of wealth, influence and power
> (Heather 1976, p.108).

But how do we, as construct theorists, reconcile this
view of schooling with our notion of the active nature of
learning? Here once more, we come face-to-face with the
constraint and freedom dichotomy. We must overcome this
by examining in more detail how society influences the

course of construct system development. It does this in two main ways. Firstly, it provides people with their validational experience, directly affecting the implications of their elaborative choices. Secondly, through this a construct system is developed which reflects the ideology, constraining a person to act in a *relatively* limited set of possible ways. This does not underestimate the enormous creative potential of the individual human being.

When one adopts the Kellyan view of learning as an active personal process, the concept of 'teaching' becomes problematic. What is it that teachers do? Vygotsky (1962) argues, for example, that scientific concepts cannot be taught. These have to be 'rediscovered'. Just as the mother selects aspects of the infant's environment, so the teacher draws one's attention to what she considers to be important, and away from what is considered irrelevant.

When being taught, we are being encouraged to make new choices. The teacher exhorts us: 'try this!', and if our relationship with the teacher is seen as elaborative, we will be 'motivated' to do so. But it is only by confronting the implications of this new choice in practice that learning really occurs.

Learning through *imitation* and *identification* may be seen in the same way. By no means is this an automatic process, but results from an active choice to be like the model. (Similarly, hypnosis should not be viewed as an active/passive relationship. The subject chooses to carry out the hypnotist's suggestions.) In imitating we are choosing to accept certain constraints in order to explore new possibilities.

Not all learning occurs in a social context; for example, solitary study or reading a book. Even in this situation we are making hypotheses and elaborative choices, construing our internal reality, 'playing a role with ourselves'. In this way the sociality corollary can be extended to our own construction processes.

The idea of *labelling* is an important one in understanding how ideology is internalised. The labelling theorists, deriving from Mead, show how a label applied by those holding authority can be made to stick. People so labelled can come to construe themselves in this light. This process is clearly seen in the way that a person in distress, once labelled as a psychiatric patient, comes to see herself as medically ill. In some circumstances, the person's attempt to remove the label may be seen as confirmation of the label itself. Labelling is a sociological process involving the maintainance of the social system, and cannot be understood in purely psychological terms.

The earliest constructs are behavioural discriminations in the physical environment. For example, a baby can discriminate warm from cold, and comes to associate this with

being in its mother's arms. But new constructs evolve
from earlier ones, and it is quite likely that the construct of 'warm personality' developed from this early
physical experience. This is a simple example of the use
of metaphor (Mair 1977a). Another interesting example of
the transfer of constructs from one range of elements to
another can be found in Levi-Strauss' study of totemism
(1962). Here the structure derived from one area of experience (e.g. different types of animals), is applied
to another (the rules of marriage between different tribes).
This is probably a universal phenomenon, and it is not
necessarily restricted to language. 'Behavioural' meta-
phors abound. Hysterical symptoms are a good example
(Szasz 1961). A patient recently referred to one of us
for severe chest pains, remarked quite unwittingly at the
end of the first session: 'It's good to be able to get
things off my chest'.

The role of behavioural metaphor in learning is well
demonstrated by the experience of Carlos Casteneda with
the sorcerer Don Juan (Casteneda 1968). In attempting to
teach him his view of the world, Don Juan put Castaneda
through a number of elaborate rituals, which could at best
only point towards the ideas he was trying to communicate.

Just as the ideology influences the individual's construct system, the reverse process takes place. The ideology is being continually fed by ideas generated by individuals in society. At any point in history, it is pregnant
with ideas waiting to be elaborated, and is posing a specific set of questions. This explains why the same important discovery is often made by independent workers at the
same time. In this way, only those ideas which accord with
the material and social relationships in the society are
selected. Thus ideas which are accepted at one time may
have been generated previously, although then society was
not 'ready' for them. For example, Freud's construct system changed the world, but if we can imagine his ideas
introduced in an earlier century, they would probably
have been ignored. There are many examples of genius before its time: Leonardo da Vinci's submarine, Hamilton's
wave mechanics, Mendel's peas, and Beethoven's late string
quartets.

The historical changes in ideology have their own logic
of development. This appears to offer a further subtle
constraint on what is conceivable at any one time. Ideologies develop through a progressive elaboration within
the current framework, until no further elaboration seems
possible. At this point a discontinuity in development
occurs. Some important aspect of the framework is changed
into its opposite, although this is not a total negation,
for the old is subsumed within the new. The term 'paradigm
shift' used by Kuhn, describes this process in the history
of science. It can perhaps be most elegantly illustrated

by the following example. The development of music from
mediaeval times consisted of combining sung melodies
(polyphony). The music was composed 'horizontally', that
is construed as notes arranged in series. This method
reached its zenith in the work of Bach, who would sometimes
compose music for eight or twelve independent parts. However, further elaboration along this road proved to be
increasingly cumbersome and at this point a shift to a
'vertical' way of construing occurred (harmony). However
the earlier fugal method was still included as is shown
in the work of Haydn and the classical school. Again har-
monic music became increasingly rich and complex (e.g.
the chromatic harmonies of Wagner) until a crisis again
occurred. Schoenberg, who had been composing with free
atonal harmonies, found it necessary to revert to a serial
method of composition once more.

This process cannot be fully understood without looking
at its material basis. The development of the orchestra
allowed wider possibilities than keyboard instruments just
as the latter were more versatile than singing voices.
Now the development of recording techniques and electronic
instruments have an important impact on musical development.

This example illustrates a dialectical process which
acts as a subtle constraint on an artist's creativity.
However it still leaves an infinite number of possibilities
within a given conceptual boundary. Kelly argues that
creativity is achieved by a cycle of loosening constructs
and tightening them into a new structure. Existing constructs are combined in new ways. This explains the creation of genuinely new work, even though the work of the
artist always bears the stamp of their personal style and
ideological heritage.

Constraint and Freedom

Chad Gordon has written:

> Autonomy.....constitutes one of the core dilemmas
> inherent in the individual's search for a viable
> personal identity that is at once unique *and* mean-
> ingfully connected to the ongoing social world.
> Analysis at this level of personal autonomy must
> consider both the 'objective' reality and the indiv-
> ual's subjective sense of the degree to which he is
> able freely and independently to direct the course
> of his own conduct so as to actualise as fully as
> possible his intellectual, emotional and interper-
> sonal objectives (Gordon 1969, p.350).

This 'search for a viable personal identity' has been
a major theme in the writing of the existentialists. For
example, when Frankl (1973) considers the constraint/
freedom problem, he sees freedom as lying in the stance
taken towards these constraints:

The freedom of a finite being such as man is a freedom within limits. Man is not free from conditions,
be they biological, psychological or sociological
in nature. But he is, and always remains, free to
take a stand towards these conditions; he always
retains the freedom to choose his attitude towards
them (Frankl 1973, p.14).

Kelly's work is consistent with this, but we believe
he has made a further contribution to the understanding
of this problem. Recognition of the constraint/freedom
dilemma is embedded in the formal exposition of his theory,
in the fundamental postulate and the choice corollary:

A person's processes are psychologically *channellised*
by the way in which he anticipates events. A person
chooses for himself that alternative in a dichotomised construct through which he anticipates the
greatest possibility of the elaboration of his system (our emphasis).

For Kelly, free will and determinism are two sides of
the same coin. It is nonsense to speak of something as
being determined without recognising that it is determined
by something else. Likewise it makes no sense to talk of
freedom without reference to what is being determined by
that freedom. Kelly is able to answer this problem by
arguing that constructs are organised in an hierarchical
system. Ideologies determine us to the extent to which we
internalise the values of the culture. Nevertheless we
are able to recognise this process, and in doing so, stand
above it. However the system that we use to construe *this*
fact is itself determined by a cultural context.

Pearce (1971) has invented a colourful metaphor of this
view with his 'crack in the cosmic egg'. It is possible
to break through the eggshell (conceptual boundaries) but
only to find ourselves in another larger egg.

Our position is strongly distinguished from Kant's in
which the world is fundamentally unknowable, a 'thing-in-
itself'. While we will never know more than the tiniest
fraction of possible knowledge, Kant's view is static and
takes no account of the historical development of knowledge. Antarctica was a 'thing-in-itself' before it was
discovered, but afterwards came into the range of convenience of our construct system.

The Kantian view logically leads to a position of mysticism in which the real issue of social practice is neg-
lected in favour of contemplation:

Social life is essentially *practical*. All mysteries
which mislead theory to mysticism find their rational solution in human practice, and the comprehen-
sion of this practice (Marx 1845 in Engels 1888
p.61).

We believe that it is possible to transcend conceptual
boundaries, but not without continuous conflict with the
prevailing social ideology which constrains us.

Implications for the Practice and Theory of Personal Construct Psychology

Construct theory is often seen as a radical alternative to empiricist and behavioural psychology. So it is, but without a proper consideration of the sociological arguments that we have discussed above, it is in danger of becoming just another individualist and static approach. It must be remembered that construct theory holds no implications for a politcal position, and this is shown by the wide variety of work within it.

Already we see a number of empiricists who find little use for construct theory and instead rely entirely on repertory grid technique. It is no coincidence that these works are involved in research which remains firmly within the given ideology ranging from studies of psychiatric disease entities, to the use of grids in market research. Even those who take construct theory seriously are not immune to this danger. Kelly's theory contains a number of interesting accounts of psychological change, but we would argue that these can only be a partial account. Such change is usually linked with a change in the individual's social role, for example when a new status position is entered. (We refer here to important concepts such as 'status passage' and 'career' discussed by Goffman. Thus in psychotherapy, it is often much more effective to intervene directly in the social role structure (strategic family therapy) than to focus on the patient's construction individually. A disregard of sociological issues is likely to accompany a lack of awareness of one's own role in society. So far, construct theorists have restricted their practice to individual psychotherapy and research into specific psychological problems. They have not paid attention, by and large, to wider issues.

The danger is that construct theory could become a merely contemplative system if its adherents ignore their own sociological and political positions. According to Engels, Feuerbach suffers from just this drawback:

> Feuerbachian theory.....is designed to suit all periods, all peoples and all conditions, and precisely for that reason it is never and nowhere applicable.....Feuerbach himself never contrives to escape from the realm of abstraction - for which he has a deadly hatred - into that of living reality. He clings fiercely to nature and man; but nature and man remain mere words with him (Engels 1888, p.36).

This is a personal matter for construct theorists, with our theory of change and practice. Do we sit in contemplation, or do we experiment and struggle with the living social reality which surrounds us?

Workshop Report

In the spirit of the ideas expressed in our paper, we did not read it at the Congress, but instead devised a number of experiential exercises which we hoped would give people the opportunity to explore the issues we raised. Twenty people participated. The structure of the day was arranged to move from games which explored the individuals' constructs, on to family systems, and then to larger group interaction. We had hoped to include a game which would explore societal construct systems, but lack of time prevented us from doing this. For those who are interested in using these techniques, we have included information about the latter 'tribal' game.

Exercise I. Biographical Constructs

People worked in pairs. One person in the pair elicited three constructs from the other, and laddered them (Hinkle 1965) until the person was satisfied that she had obtained one or more superordinate constructs. The person was then asked to think back in her life to the point at which this construct first emerged. She then examined this construct's 'ancestor' by asking the question: 'From what earlier construct did this one evolve at that time?' When the earlier construct had been obtained, the biography of this one was traced backwards in the same way, until the earliest superordinate construct was obtained. Life experiences associated with the construct's development were discussed. The earliest construct was examined in the light of family construct systems and parental influences.

Exercise II. Constructs in Families

Five 'families' were formed, each of four people. Everyone in these families at this stage wrote down three constructs to describe each of the other three family members. The members of the families were then asked to take on the role of either mother, father, daughter or son. Cards had been prepared beforehand describing these roles in each five different types of family. The ones used in the workshop were as follows:

(a) Child-centred family Middle-class family where the parents are genuinely interested in their children, and are involved with their friends. There are many activities in which the family take part as a group, e.g. picnics at weekends.

(b) Guilt-inducing family Family members are devious manipulators who do not express their needs explicitly but tend to use emotional blackmail instead.

(c) Fragmented family Family members have little contact with each other, they each have their own door-key, cook their own meals, etc. When things are discussed as a group, there are often loud arguments, people do not listen to others' point of view.

(d) Sexist family A family in which stereotyped sex roles are played. Dominant father throws his weight around, mother passive but undermines his authority in covert ways.

(e) Conflict avoiding family Disagreements are seen as dangerous in this family, which will avoid open conflict, although many non-verbal messages are given. The traditionally 'schizophrenogenic' family.

Each family was given a problem to solve as follows: the 15-year old daughter is staying out late, and the 17-year old son is very untidy and slovenly around the house. The family members, using the information given on the cards, role-played the discussion about this problem.

Everyone found this game very compelling, giving a powerful insight into the ways in which family structures affect construct formation and development.

Exercise III. The Labelling Game

The extent to which a label applied by others affects one's behaviour and core role constructs was explored in this game. The scenario was a social occasion in which a group of people who have previously met formally on a committee or jury, now meet socially for the first time. Everyone is given a label, which everyone else knows, but of which the individual concerned is ignorant. The rule is to behave towards everyone in the group in accordance with their label, and at the same time to try to discover what one's own label is. The labels were prepared in advance and pinned on the participants' backs. Examples of the types of label used are as follows: the appointed leader; the actual leader; the would-be leader; the pompous bore; the joker; the rebel; the self-righteous prude; the confuser; the silent one; etc., etc.

Following the game, a group discussion revealed that people quickly perceived the pressure to behave in ways consistent with their label, even before they had discovered their role identity.

Exercise IV. The Tribal Game

We were unable to use this game due to lack of time, but the structure is described as follows:

In this game we were going to simulate two mini-societies and watch how the role-structures affected and were affected by the individuals in them. Two tribes were to meet together to discuss an intended inter-marriage. One tribe was to have its roles prescribed in the usual way (leader, adviser, etc.). In the other, all members, unknown to each other, were to be designated

leader, although leaders in this tribe were to be
diffident (acknowledgements to George Walker for this
idea), in order that it would not be immediately obvious. The game represents a controlled experiment
investigating the interaction of given role and individual construct system.

HOW TO WIN FRIENDS AND ELICIT CONSTRUCTS

A. J. MURPHY

*Centre for the Study of Organizational
Change and Development,
University of Bath, Claverton Down,
Bath BA2 7AY.*

The issue of 'alienation' in the design and implementation of social science research is beginning to receive
a broad discussion (e.g. Rosenthal 1966; Friedlander 1968;
Harre and Secord 1972). Maruyama (1968), referring to the
advantages of inculture research, argues that much research is initiated, conducted and concluded from the perspective of the researcher without involving the client
and his epistemology in the research process. The same
conclusion might be drawn from any broad analysis of research methodologies in the social sciences.

In the organizational context, the client or subject
may often perceive the activities of the change agent, the
internal consultant, the researcher or the management
trainer as alien to his own needs, values and goals. This
alienation is often concretized in the utilization of
theories and methods which appear to the client as mysterious or meaningless. The primary source of this alienation is the exclusion of the client, or subject, from
both the problem definition and problem solution stages
of the intervention process. 'In this sense the more eso-
teric and sophisticated the specialisation, the more vulnerable is its impotence due to the non-involvement of
those for whom its benefit is intended' (Friedlander 1968).
Low identification by the client with both the consultant's
definition and solutions results in passive affirmation
of the content and the eventual negation of whatever recommendations may be made.

The need to institute and conduct interventions which
evolve from within the client's epistemology is therefore
particularly salient in the organizational context. Valid
entry by the interventionist is grounded in the client's
perception of the event as the contribution of a relevant
resource with which he, the client, may choose to reflect
on and ultimately change his world. The emphasis on the
identification of problems or issues as a collaborative
exercise is essential to the 'success' of many interventions. ('Success' in this context is defined as not only
the ownership of issues by the client but also the clear

commitment to action.)

The application of personal construct theory and repertory grid technique is receiving increasing attention from researchers, management trainers and, to some extent, from organizational development specialists. However, the use of this theory and its associated methodology may be critically evaluated by the client in much the same way as any other intervention is assessed. While the use of personal construct theory may appear to have distinct advantages for interventionists, particularly because of its idiographic orientation, to those to whom the organization is more than a passing focus, the issues of credibility and authenticity are fundamentally present. The singular and unilateral application of repertory grid technique is assured of eliciting responses which testify to the client's alienation from the process of the intervention. Feeding back a series of constructs or a cognitive map derived from the repertory grid is unlikely to produce either identification or commitment to action if it has excluded from ownership the client/subject in the data gathering process. Personal construct theory and repertory grid methodology have no divine right in picturing the client's epistemology. Constructs elicited unilaterally are potentially more a reflection of the relationship between client and researcher than the elaboration of the client's construction of organizational events. In seeking to elaborate the contribution which personal construct theory may make to organizational interventions, it is necessary to begin where the client is rather than where the practitioner believes him to be, or would like him to be.

Defining the contexts within which personal construct theory and repertory grid technique may contribute to authentic interventions may itself be the function of many successive 'creativity cycles' (Kelly 1955). I wish to describe one such creativity cycle which occurred during a management training programme in which I attempted to employ personal construct theory and repertory grid technique in a 'collaborative' context. It is possible that some of the implications of this intervention may be of broader interest to many forms of intervention.

Background to the Case Study

A subsidiary of a large manufacturing enterprise had embarked on the institution of a number of functional planning roles as a response to anticipated changes in its marketing and technological environments. Line managers with considerable production orientated experience were recruited to these new roles in the belief that they would be aware of the cultural context within which planned changes were to be implemented. A training programme was initiated by the Organization Development Manager to enable

these planning consultants to negotiate and practise some
of the interpersonal skills central to their new role. As
an external consultant, I was invited to contribute as a
resource to the training programme and its development.
The client group of planning consultants decided to focus
initially on their own management style and the effects
of this style on their ability to effect change.

In their early sessions the client group expressed the
need to identify in concrete terms their style of relating
to others and the potential effects of these constructions
upon their interventions. Although personal construct
theory and repertory grid technique appeared to be valuable approaches to facilitate this exercise, previous experience in organisations had demonstrated that their
application would require a considerable investment in
time and resources to first explain and then actively involve the client in the study. In this context, the need
at the beginning of such a training programme to gain
acceptance from the highly pragmatic line managers was
exacerbated by the constraints of time and consultant resources. As a consequence, I adopted an alternative approach in which the client group agreed to be individually
interviewed. Issues which they defined as salient to their
perceived style of managing, their relationships with
their own clients and the problem situations which they
were encountering were explored. These interviews, which
I wish to label Initial Construct Interviews, were hopefully a shared exploration of the client's epistemology
and, as it emerged, critical to the development of a relationship between client and interventionist. Subsequently
these interviews were independently content analysed by
myself and a colleague. Verbal labels which appeared to
identify the client's constructions were listed and disagreements on the labels were resolved by a re-examination
of the tape. Individual lists were thus prepared for each
client and also a general list of constructs, which appeared to be consistent through the client group, was also
produced.

At the subsequent training session, I presented a brief
summary of personal construct theory and attempted to discuss with the client group the ways in which it might provide a vehicle for their self learning. When I felt there
was some clear understanding of the theoretical approach
and some commitment to the analysis of their behaviour in
construct terms, the lists of individual constructs and
the summary list were distributed. In the ensuing discussion the individual verbal labels were explored, clarified and many times redefined. In focusing on their own
construction of events and comparing these initially to
the verbal labels and then to the explored meanings of
the lists, the client group appeared to be successfully
concretizing their perceived style of managing. Further,

the exploration of the shared meanings which individuals
attached to different verbal labels and, in the case of
the common list, the contrasting definitions applied to
a single construct label facilitated both the creation of
shared meanings within the group and increased communication between the clients and myself, the consultant.

Two of the planning consultants, for example, used the
verbal label 'technical expertise' to define some of the
skills required by their role; for one client its meaning
was construed as 'skills with people' while for the other
its meaning was defined as 'technical and analytical
skills'. The development of such a system of shared meanings became the vehicle for some of the client group to
begin to focus on the areas in which their construing of
events appeared to be limited. Thus the trainee planning
consultants who defined their new roles in task centred
terms attempted to reconstrue their activities in terms
of interpersonal issues and to practice the skills with
which to negotiate such situations. The concretization
and sharing of perspectives became the vehicle for self
analysis and growth. In Kelly's terms, the client group
was being asked to examine its own constructions, to loosen
tightly structured construct systems, to test out alternative constructions and to tighten those hypotheses,
which appeared to be validated in the training programme,
into a reformulated system of construing.

Subsequently, I attempted to provide the client group
with the opportunity to examine the structural aspects of
their construing. Were they construing events in terms of
one perspective, for example, that of a task centred perspective, or did they have a more differentiated system
of definitions? Individual repertory grids were constructed employing constructs which the client group had previously defined and elements, identifying levels of their
relationship within the organization, which had emerged
as salient during the Initial Construct Interviews.
Although most of the client group completed this grid
they did so only grudgingly. In the feedback session, the
immediate source of their rejection emerged in comments
directed at the numerical approach of the grid; the method
of measurement seemed artificial and inappropriate. Some
of the clients suggested alternative systems of classification to replace the choice of measurements which had
been presented. Ultimately the enterprise itself was seen
as illegitimate especially when compared to the earlier,
more successful, interventions. Possibly, I had failed to
adequately explain the purpose or mechanics of the grid
technique. A more probable reason emerged in discussion
comments which referred to their lack of control over the
data collection and analysis in this process. On reflection, I believe that these elements in the relationship
between myself and the client group defined the repertory

grid technique as an irrelevant mode of analysis; that is, the failure to develop an adequate exposition, the removal of control from the client, and also, perhaps significantly, the perceived inadequacy of the technique to represent the developing complexities of their cognitions: all these factors contributed to the failure of the repertory grid to be seen as useful and meaningful in this context.

At present, we are still employing the construct lists as a means of concretizing the changing perceptions within the group. The client group is now much clearer on the advantages of the process of data collection and the feedback session. The successive lists provide the internal consultants with the opportunity to reflect on their changing patterns of constructions. This approach to data collection and feedback has two clear advantages for the organizational intervention in that it tends to decrease the resource allocation required from both client and consultant when compared to more traditional forms of construct elicitation. Also, and perhaps more significantly, the interview process is initially seen as more authentic and in its exploratory context a vehicle for learning *per se*, in that it encourages the client to focus upon his own behaviour. Such approaches are clearly dependent on the skills of the consultant and the commitment of the client. However, it is probable that the client sees the exploration of personal issues in the Initial Construct Interview as an authentic and helpful exercise in itself. Consequently he may become more committed to its conduct and to act upon the outcomes of such a process. It also enables the consultant, client and client group to agree on a system of shared meanings, to appreciate alternative perspectives and to check out definitions. Thus such a process is both a learning goal in itself and a vehicle for future learning.

The conversational dialogue instituted by the Initial Construct Interview and subsequent sessions also enables the management trainer to be sensitive to the experience of stress in the client especially in the transitional stages of change; in this context, for example, a period in which a major change project was undertaken by the planning consultant. Such stress may be reflected in the lists of verbalised constructs, in their confusion, lack of change, or failure to construe the developing organizational changes in terms which adequately express their implications. For instance, the definition of a change event simply in task orientated constructs ignores their interpersonal effects.

I am not suggesting that such an approach is the panacea to the organizational intervention. In itself, it has a number of problems which will be discussed later. However, its limited success does reflect some of the factors which appear central to any organizational intervention. This is especially valid where we seek to employ personal construct theory or repertory grid technique which are, par excellence, idiographic, subject centered and humanistically orientated.

Firstly, the client needs to feel in control: to accept or reject particular methodologies, to seek out and identify his own issues and problems. Secondly, the interventionist is more likely to be seen as authentic by the client if he chooses to be identified as a facilitator, a resource to the client, rather than as an experimenter or trainer. Thirdly, where the client is encouraged to reflect upon his own experience he is more committed to action and to its implications. These elements characterise in several ways Kelly's (1955) description of the psychotherapeutic process. While the contextual pressures on the organizational interventionist are somewhat greater than in the psychotherapeutic situation, the definition of the interventionist's orientation is fundamentally the same. Indeed, as Kelly observes, to the degree that the organizational practitioner perceives himself as facilitator, as coparticipant in the process, he will be open to the same learning environment as the client.

Learning in the interventionist is a problematic process to advocate within an organizational context as it requires that the practitioner be as vulnerable as the client. For example, the external consultant is often assessed by his ability to 'sell' outcomes rather than to participate in their creation. A number of academic enterprises involving personal construct theory and repertory grid technique involve elements which strongly resemble this 'selling' dimension. In Argyris' (1975) terms, some of the research involving Kelly's theory and its associated methods falls within the definition of Model 1 behaviours rather than those of Model 2. Whether the subject is willing or not, he is often forced to construe triads, to produce constructs, to peruse Ingrid output (Slater 1972) with little apparent effort on the part of the interventionist to involve him in the choice of approach or the definition of contexts.

Discussion and Conclusion

Personal construct theory and repertory grid technique may be of considerable value in organizational interventions, whether in the context of change agency or management training. As Ronco and Schon (1977) observe, many actions are performed by individuals in organizations with little attempt or opportunity to reflect on the context of such events; that is, on the constructs with which these events are interpreted, the outcomes which are a consequence of such constructions and the ways in which one construct system succeeds, or fails, to integrate with the construct systems possessed by others. The elements of the

training programme described above present an attempt to
provide a vehicle for such reflection and a consequent
commitment to change and action. Indeed, in this context,
the success of the interventionist, be he researcher or
trainer, is defined by his ability to facilitate the client's reflection on his own theories of actions. Thus in
such training programmes the client is empowered to detach
himself from the organization, to disengage, to see himself as the arbitrator of his own activities and to commit
himself to action (Mangham 1978).

However, in employing personal construct theory in the
organizational context, several practical and theoretical
difficulties remain unaddressed. At the practical level
it is critical that the client identifies the context
within which he is construing his own behaviour. This is
perhaps achieved by the identification of concrete situations in which the client has, for example, actually
implemented a change programme or can clearly identify
and describe elements in a particular behavioural intervention. Often in varying the context of the construing,
the client's constructs themselves alternate. For instance,
the internal consultants in the training sessions tended
to define some situations as task-type issues which required problem solving skills while other situations were
more readily construed as involving inter-personal issues.
This focus of interpretation did not appear to be related
to intrinsic elements in the problem but rather to be a
function of the client's developing cognitions and the
sophistication in his differentiation of the organizational
environment.

Associated with these difficulties, there is the ever
present theoretical issue of distinguishing between the
client's espoused theory and his theory-in-use (Argyris
and Schon 1974). The espoused theory of the client constitutes the content of the Initial Construct Interview.
By focusing on actual behaviours the consultant has the
opportunity to explore and test out with the client the
reality of his constructions and their implications for
outcomes. Unfortunately the client, for whatever reasons,
may often seek to reinterpret such behavioural data in
terms which confirm the application of the espoused theory.
Learning which is based on the exploration of such espoused
theories tends to be, in Argyris' (1975) terms, single
loop learning: that is, a non-creative, homeostatic form
of change. To test out the relationship between elicited
constructions and theories-in-use the client and the
interventionist are required to focus on actual behaviour
and its construing. In the training programme the opportunity arises in role play and other techniques to check
out the congruences between the construction of events
and their verbalisation.

Unfortunately the training programme can never simulate

the reality of the organizational environment. The organizational context which is permeated with many, often conflicting, forces (for example, the power to allocate resources, the constraints of time) may preclude the construction of events which appeared appropriate in the training environment. For instance, in a recent Construct Interview the consultant, in describing his attempts 'to involve the client' and 'to facilitate rather than direct', was compelled to admit, when asked to reflect on a recent concrete example, that because 'the stakes were high' his behaviour could only be construed as 'directive' and 'task centred'.

Thus utilising personal construct theory and repertory grid technique in any intervention context, and especially in an organizational intervention, we face a series of problems. The question of authenticity is critical. If the researcher, trainer or change agent is not simply to parody the voyeur (Friedlander 1968) then a constant re-construing of his own role activity is required. As facilitator to the client he may need to sacrifice the repertory grid technique, to radically alter his process for eliciting constructs or to create an innovative means of enabling the client to reflect upon his own constructions. Such a philosophy is perhaps more in the spirit of Kelly's theory than some of the 'blind researcher' dominated applications which may presently be witnessed. By placing himself in the learning situation, as Kelly (1969b) suggests the psychotherapist should, the interventionist is more likely to experience and develop the reformulations in construct theory and its methodology which Kelly envisaged.

Further, the difficulty of clarifying the relationship between the theories we espouse and our theories-in-practice suggests that the focus of construct elicitation may be more accurately grounded in the construing of concrete behavioural events. This creates a series of new problems, especially in the organizational context, which may be associated with limits to the freedom of access and to cultural forces within the organization or within the society generally. The double loop learning which Argyris associates with authentic change and growth is ultimately grounded in the construing of theories-in-use. Thus for the organizational practitioner the goal of such intervention remains to be operationalised in short term gains, principally as a function of the relationships he can create and develop with his clients. Ultimately, the commitment to action central to the process of loosening, testing and retightening, which Kelly terms the Creativity cycle, is the intended outcome of most interventions. In the training programme described above, by reflecting directly on organizational contexts I sought to influence 'back home behaviour', not often successfully. However

personal construct theory does provide a valuable means
of disengagement, the opportunity to loosen constructions
and to test out new hypotheses. To validate these alternative constructions in a training context, or to elicit
constructs with repertory grids and feed back cognitive
maps in the accepting atmosphere of the training programme,
is never to simulate adequately the behaviour in an organizational reality. It provides simply the opportunity for
constructive re-assessment in posing questions, allowing
for appraisal and encouraging reconstruction.

In conclusion, if we begin to formulate our interventions in more facilitative terms, whether we are acting
as organizational consultants, management trainers, clinical practitioners or sociological researchers, we may
create for ourselves the opportunity to reconstrue our own
activities, to explore with the client the shared meanings
from which actions are derived. If we limit our subjects
we limit our own learning. Indeed to the extent that the
client or subject is excluded from the research process
so also is the interventionist (Friedlander 1968). As
Kelly observes: 'If the experimenter sees himself exploring only one of the many alternative constructions of
man, with the best ones yet to be devised, he will be on
a continual lookout for fresh perspectives emerging out
of his research experience' (1968, p.139).

Acknowledgement

I am indebted to Professor Iain Mangham for his help
in the preparation of this paper.

CONSTRUING INTERPERSONAL CONSTRUCTION SYSTEMS: CONJECTURES ON SOCIALITY

WILLIAM R. PERRY

*Division of Mental Health,
State of Hawaii Department of Health,
Honolulu, Hawaii 96813, U.S.A.*

What is offered in this paper is a somewhat loose configuration of personal reflections and speculations on
interpersonal misunderstanding, disappointment, and alienation and how aspects of these human experiences may be
understood in the light of George Kelly's psychology of
personal constructs. We will consider, in the main, two
topical areas which may help elaborate our appreciation
of the Sociality Corollary* - frustrations in transcult-
ural contacts; and important conflicts between persons
who otherwise enjoy familiar or intimate relationships.
If some generalizations can be ventured and tentatively
supported regarding the apparently wide span between these
two seemingly distant areas - one characterized by interaction between relative strangers, the other by that between persons more or less familiar to each other - then
perhaps another modest step has been taken in our science
of construing the construction processes of people.
    Kelly (1955, p.95) is quite clear in his insistence
that a 'social psychology must be a psychology of interpersonal understandings, not merely a psychology of common
understandings'. Thus, a kind of reciprocal intelligibility
or mutual comprehensibility is firmly set down as a prerequisite for role relationships - for sociality - rather
than an emphasis placed on mere similarity of outlook.
    The present paper addresses itself to aspects of *mis*-
understanding and does not concern itself with total *non*-
understanding between people. Upon careful reflection, we
may conclude that those hypothetical situations in which
one person views another's total frame of reference as so
strange or foreign as to be utterly unintelligible, may
not in fact exist. What follows, then, is rather more
closely attuned to relationships wherein at one point in
time the participants believe they understand each other,
then later come to doubt that they do or even conclude
they do not; exchanges or series of exchanges within which
some issues seem comprehensible, but others not; and interactions wherein persons may construe either agreement or
disagreement between them, yet another look suggests the

contrary to be the case.

The Misconstrual of Constructural Implication

As an introductory device, let us use the words 'to
provisionally share a construct' to indicate that state
of affairs whereby A has communicated to B at least one
pole of a personal construct. That is, A has communicated
to B a term or some other such sign, as well as a referent - at least one element to which that pole applies.
A may even communicate one or more implications which he
personally associates with that construct. The communication of some implications is almost always the case,
but this is not essential in establishing a temporary
working definition. At this minimal level, 'provisionally
sharing a construct' means that two persons have begun to
negotiate a common culture, in the sense that B now presumably 'knows about' A's construct. B need not embrace
A's construct as his very own, although he *may* hold a more
or less similar one in his own personal scheme of things.
Nor does the phrase, 'provisionally sharing a construct'
mean to include instances of B's simply attributing constructs to A without A's having supplied a minimal context
of a term and at least one referent. At the very least
then, 'provisionally sharing a construct' means that A
and B can now more or less refer to the same event and
employ a common, manifest designation for that event.
Since we are here considering matters of interpersonal
relationships, the 'events' referred to are more often
than not behavioral ones.

Now no one familiar with general semantics, cultural
anthropology, or personal construct theory - or even life
- will be stunned to hear that persons can 'provisionally
share a construct'; yet envision vitally different implications for that construct or as regards its applications.
A non-directive therapist may construe his behavior toward his client as warm and open, intending these qualities to facilitate exploration of feelings and personal
growth, but if that client happens to be an immigrant
freshly arrived from the Philippines, that 'warmth' and
'openness' may be taken as frank weakness and downright
incompetence. A youthful, athletic father may construe
his skate-boarding with his adolescent son and the latter's
peers as 'sharing' and as demonstrating camaraderie, but
that lad may view his father's conduct not only as intru-
sive, but embarassing.

So, there are no intended surprises here, to note that
certain behaviors regarding which both parties *might be
expected to share some degree of understanding* - a provisionally shared construct - may have different implications for the persons involved, and that some of these
implicative differences might make the role relationships
between the two a bit rocky.

Naive or timid discussions of such personal misunder-
standings as the two cited often stop short in *explaining*
the divergences between the outlooks people create for
themselves by merely *reaffirming* or *describing* the differences that exist. Even an occasional psychologist or an-
thropologist has been known to cop out with, 'They've just
got totally different ways of seeing things'. *Period.*
This is very much like the posture of the befuddled physician who, facing a difficult diagnostic situation, says
to his client, 'Have you ever had this symptom before?
You have? Well, you've got it again!'

It does not suffice in explaining interpersonal misunderstanding - any more than it is a 'passing' undergrad-
uate summary of personal construct theory - to simply aver
that 'everyone sees the world differently' or 'people
attach different meanings to different things'.

An ostensible step forward in coming to grips with the
manifold implicative differences found in the human community can be seen in the proliferation of relatively atheoretical and non-specific instructions and interventions
which purport to address increased 'sensitivity' or
'communication' - send that counselor to a workshop on
psychological stress in Filipino immigrants; help that
father and son develop 'relationship' skills! But there
are two dangers in such generic, relatively undifferentiated constructions of and approaches to human (mis)
understanding. First, they run the risk of adding to our
armamentarium of hackneyed techniques. Second, they often
seem to somehow increase our proficiency at name-calling,
in that now we are 'aware' that people place different
meanings upon things because, of course, they are third-
generation Chinese - or female - or poor - or gay - or,
horrible dictu, personal construct psychologists.

What is required in our grappling with the problem of
misunderstanding is a more clear statement of relevant
theory which can guide us in directions of more constructive action. Perhaps personal construct theory, or some
elaborative application of that theory, can be of help
in this regard.

Misconstrual and the Centrality or Peripherality of Constructs

Personal construct psychology incorporates certain
concepts which can be brought to bear in a fairly precise
way upon the problem of two persons' mismatched or incongruous implications for a seemingly or provisionally
shared construct. Of particular theoretical interest and,
hopefully, of some clinical utility here might be the
dimension of the relative *centrality* or *peripherality* of
the construct under consideration.

The first time the author became interested in the
theoretical distinction between *core* and *peripheral* con-

structs was on the occasion of his making a serendipitous
discovery while analyzing the data for his doctural dissertation. Subjects for the study had been selected on the
basis of extreme responses to a single questionnaire item
assessing their attitudes toward the use of the derogation
of naive subjects as an intervention in formal psychological research. A secondary analysis of the data indicated
that, of those who strongly disapproved of such techniques,
a large subset showed high scores on a 'guilt over hostility' scale; another subgroup who rejected this research
strategy did so within an attitudinal context of placing
a low value on psychological research in general. The two
groups - previously viewed as homogeneous in terms of
item-endorsement - showed significantly different responses
on some dependent measures, with some of the change measures for the two groups going in opposite directions.
Comparisons of several score variances on the two sets of
subjects suggested that, for those subjects who showed
little enthusiasm for research, the rejection of derogation as a research technique was relatively incidental
or *peripheral*; for those who registered a high degree of
guilt over hostility, the rejection was relative central
to their values, or *core*. This was an exciting, albeit
accidental, demonstration of people assuming the same
manifest posture, but for different reasons, and with
different personal implications for *action*.

If we postulate a contrast or a continuum, then, with
centrality denoting the quality of a construct's being
more closely implicated with a person's *core* constructs
(i.e. more closely involved with the person's maintenance
processes and his sense of identity), and *peripherality*
being less so implicated (i.e. more amenable to change),
then a great many instances of interpersonal dissonance
and communication screw-ups promise to come into sharper
focus.

Over and over again, counselors working in the cross-
cultural context report being mystified that they may
share a common language with their clients, and that they
can agree with them on 'lists' of topical concerns, only
to find that the clients dig in their heels, grow taciturn
and resistant, or terminate the contacts when the counselor proceeds to focus on what, by his lights, is a natural starting place. Yet, with a conceptualization of what
each party to that enterprise respectively holds as con-
structurally central or peripheral, it can be seen that
problems such as the following are cast in a different
light: A Euramerican counselor may assume that, for example, a somewhat reserved and reticent Asian client will
be able to reverse her family's weakening approval of her
by formulating more clear-cut academic plans and by growing more economically independent. Yet that client may be
puzzled and distraught that this counselor seems to be

pushing her to make such momentous decisions *on her own*,
without the counsel and direction of her family. It is
not claimed here that the client and counselor disagree
on explicit objectives, but rather that they treat the
superordinacy-subordinacy of these objectives differently,
that is, they *ordinate* them differently in their frames of
reference. Moreover, neither of them is aware of the exact
nature of the problem they are having with each other.
This particular situation is confounded by the likelihood
that, even if the client *could* formulate some impression
of the differences between herself and her counselor, the
situation may not be so easy to set right, since - if what
is said about Asians is true! - she may find it hard to
voice any strong disagreement, especially to one who is
seen as a high-status authority figure.

The hypothesis being developed here would hold that
therapeutic 'resistances' such as described may best be
conceived not merely as related to the different *implications* of a construct for the two participants, but even
more exactly, to certain *qualitative aspects* of these
implications. In other words, some instances of therapeutic 'resistance' may be firmly based on important differences in the perceived *centrality* of the issue being pursued or ignored at any point in time, which differences,
in turn, bespeak differences in the *assigning of priorities*, the *timing*, or even the simple *seriation* of the issues as presumably agreed upon by the two parties.

A husband may choose to establish himself both as a
good provider by working long hours and as an eager lover
by racing from shower to boudoir, but how can his wife
believe that he *really* loves her, when he persists in
leaving his sweaty socks on the bathroom floor?

'First things first', then, is an aphorism which does
not augur much for constructive change in a relationship
unless there is some thoughtful consideration of the cen-
trality-peripherality dimension as it respectively applies
to both (or all) involved persons' constructions of a
given issue or bone of contention. Much 'dead' or counter-
productive interpersonal or clinical time is expended not
attending to this very important 'construct about constructs'.

Motivational Analysis and the Attribution of Hostility

Many of the highly charged interpersonal hassles occurring in intimate or cross-cultural relationships are com-
pounded,or further obfuscated by one person's focussing
on a certain implicated issue and presuming not only that
the other person clearly understands - or 'should' understand - that the matter is a highly important one; but
that the other knows - or 'should' know - exactly *how* or
in what sense the item is of core significance. As has
already been suggested, the second party, in terms of *his*

implicative network, may in fact not be able to apprehend the centrality of the issue at all. *A*'s apparently exclusive focus on his own central implication - one perhaps looking irrelevant, incidental, or even silly to *B* - may even lead *B* to the unhappy conclusion that *A* is not attending to *B*'s needs - his more core considerations - either.

The American tourist who is startled and perhaps angered when he perceives the French shopkeeper as treating him coldly and rudely, and who then grows doubly indignant to subsequently learn that the Frenchman was *refusing* to speak an English he actually knew quite well, probably is unaware that the Frenchman himself had felt offended *first* - a relatively core consideration had been treated lightly - by what he saw as a *demand* to speak a tongue not his own. Had that tourist made a small gesture by way of asking the national's leave to speak English, or even had he pantomimed his needs, he might have found himself caught up in a much more congenial interchange - possibly even in English.

When one person in a relationship mistakenly assumes that the other person shares an appreciation of the construed centrality of the event under consideration; and when the first individual furthermore perceives the second as wilfully declining to attend to or validate that centrality, two social consequences frequently ensue: First, the invalidating or non-validating behavior is seen as maliciously motivated, that is, *A*'s embarassment, anxiety, or hurt is seen as *B*'s specific intent. Here pertinent scripts might read, 'you only said that to put me down', or 'you are deliberately *refusing* to understand what I am saying!' Second, the first, 'offended' party declines to discuss, *in the elaborative sense*, the respective significances of the invalidation or non-validation. There may be either accusation and complaining or withdrawal and sulking. But the point is, is that *constructive elaboration* is not the most typical initiative struck up in the face of disappointment by a person who makes the leading assumptions cited above. 'She knows how I feel when she acts that way with other men. What's the use of talking it over with her?'

People's temptations to 'motivational analysis', then, are often found to be an artifact of those kinds of disagreements in which the participants provisionally share a construct, that is, there is some specifiable range of common construction, but also wherein the constructural implications are more 'deep' for one person and more 'incidental' for the other. For the individual holding to the more peripheral implication, the other person may be construed in terms roughly analogous to *neurosis* - uptight, fussy, rigid, hypersensitive, and the like. For the one who embraces the event more centrally, the other person way be viewed in *moral* terms - cruel, insensitive, lacking appreciation, and so forth.

It is probably in moments of the most extreme disappointment with a familiar person, when one's deepest, most central values are not confirmed by a significant other, that some semblance of psychopathy or some other extreme moral deficiency is ascribed to the disappointing other. And perhaps *every* assignation of the psychopathic diagnosis reflects the feeling of having been betrayed, or the fear of being betrayed.

Motivational Analysis as an Act of Hostility

People not only treat behavioral events as relatively 'deep' or 'incidental' with respect to their own values and frames of reference - and do so differently, from one person to another - but they also construe the constructs of the other as relatively central or peripheral with respect to *what they imagine the total structure of that other person's values and outlooks to be*. The 'goodness of fit' between the degree of centrality *A* ascribes to one of *B*'s constructs in *B*'s total constructural system on the one hand; and the relative centrality of the construct for *B* himself, on the other, is but another phrasing or measure of sociality, of our 'construing the construction processes of the other'. If the fit is not good, then we have a social picture of persons going about construing what is 'deep' or 'superficial', 'real' or 'illusory', 'basic' or 'incidental' *about each other*, but with no necessary reference to how the persons construed may distribute these qualities amidst their *own* construct systems.

In this important regard, it is not only the psychoanalyst who plays the *I-know-you-better-than-you-do* game. In the parlance of domestic relationships, and as is often heard from clients in the conjoint therapies, the litanies of attributions and incredulities are extensive: 'Oh, she *thinks* she means it, Doctor, but she *really* doesn't'.... 'Yes, he's trying, but wait, it won't last - it's not really his *nature*, you see'....'Of course, I *know* they're doing the right thing, but for the *wrong reason*'....'The change isn't a *real* change - he's made a few adjustments, so I can't complain too much, but there's still something about his *attitude*....'

The complaint of *superficial compliance* is appropriately addressed here, and it is a construct which is monopolized by neither our informal social relations nor our agencies of coercive social control. Consider the prison inmate who is transferred into a maximum control cellblock with the admonishment that this move is intended to 'teach him a lesson' about his violating institutional rules. After many months of exemplary conduct living under his more severe circumstances, he is several times denied his original privileges on the grounds that 'the *only* (sic)

reason he's been good is because he wants to get *out*'. Or
take the example of the young wife who made considerable
efforts to improve her troubled marriage by spending more
time discussing her husband's business with him and in
demonstrating more visible friendliness toward her mother-
in-law, only to have her husband belittle these efforts
as 'insincere': the *real* (sic) reason she has recently
behaved in these wifely ways, he asserts, is because he
had complained that she previously had *not* been. She should
behave in these ways not because he had comlained, but
because she, herself, *wants to*.

Construct theorists might begin to reformulate what
other theorists have described as the paradoxical 'demand
for the spontaneous' by casting these traditional double-
bind transactions into terms of how the participants may
differentially construe what is incidental, peripheral or
superficial as constrasted to what is seen as central,
deep, basic, or core.

In sum, the inclinations of persons to engage in motivational analyses of others seems to be exacerbated when
there are important disparities in persons' respective
constructions of an issue (a 'provisionally shared construct') as being either *central* or *peripheral* in personal
implicative value. Such disparities in construing the core
from the incidental may be conceived as common roots of
many everyday experiences of misunderstanding, disappointment, and alienation. In relationships typified by these
experiences, active *hostility* is often read into the intentions of others for whom the issue at hand is not - at
least at the outset - of any central significance. Motivational analyses as such tend to take the form of construing, in the face of at least some information to the
contrary, what is more *central* (real, basic, deep) about
the construct systems of others. These ascriptions run a
high risk themselves of being *hostile*, in the exact construct psychology sense of 'extorting validational evidence in favor of a type of social prediction which already has proved itself a failure' (Kelly 1955, p.510).

Steps Toward a Triadic Psychology

Obviously, the dissonances and miscontruals found between members of a dyad who have their central and peripheral constructions all mixed up are not to be summarily
set aright by a third party who steps in in the role of,
say, Grand Master of Reality or Final Judge and Arbiter.
The best a third party can do - presuming that a better
understanding between the pair remains as an objective
for them - is to make suggestions as to how to proceed
and to encourage and perhaps facilitate experiments in
dialogue whereby the two might devise new and more promising ways of construing each other's construction processes. Even at this level of a third party's possible

helpfulness, however, the thrust and spirit of personal
construct psychology would have it that, in the final
analysis, that pair of people had worked out their *own*
understandings *themselves* - through venturing, risking,
testing, confirming, and revising their outlooks on each
other.

But while in a strict sense two people create their
own understandings of each other, there are important ways
in which any two people are *never* alone, psychologically.
One support for this generalization can be fixed theoretically. In personal construct theory terms, persons are
constantly construing reality, and the basic act of construal is a simultaneous sorting out of the similarities
and differences seen to obtain among a minimal context of
three elements. Providing that a person's construing at
any moment in time is a *social* one, for example, 'you and
I' - then any person actively engaged in an ongoing relationship with another will have, however vaguely, at
least *one* other person somewhere in mind as that relationship unfolds. This, of course, is reminiscent of Kelly's
observation that all social relationships are in some
fashion 'transference' relationships; that the other person is seen - even if only implicitly - as like or unlike
some other figure.

A considerably more mundane approach to elaborating
the view that a person populates his dyads beyond the two
figures visibly present is to invoke more impressionistic
and introspective examples: 'What if my father finds out?'
....'Do I remind her of her husband?'....'I want to tell
my brother about us'....'You put me in mind of a teacher
I once had'. It seems likely that even when a pair of
people are not discussing other people, there are other
'presences' there in the relationship, being sifted and
sorted, compared and contrasted - reminding, soothing,
warning, encouraging, criticizing, instructing.

The notion that 'we are not alone' enjoys certain loose
clinical applications, as can be seen in the many role-
playing methodologies, including the often dramatic 'two
chairs' technique of Gestalt therapy, wherein the client
addresses and 'works through' conflicts with significant
but physically absent others. In individual therapy, this
writer has employed analagous 'techniques' in spontaneous,
sometimes seemingly abrupt ways: to a Hawaiian client
whose outlook encompassed a belief in *noho* (visions), he
once interjected: 'Who just entered the room? We seemed
to be alone just a minute ago, but now there's someone
else here. Who is it?'; and to a rather constricted,
guilt-oriented middle-class client: 'Wait, say that again,
exactly the same way....Now, whose voice was that? Whom
does it sound like to you?'

The 'logic' of three persons is intriguing to the
author from yet another, phenomenological perspective, in

particular when cast in the sequence of one, two, three,
four or more persons. In solitude there is a subjective
quality of privacy such that certain acts (e.g. peeking
through keyholes, masturbation, picking one's nose) can
be effected with neither shame nor the necessity to negotiate a social construction of reality. The physical introduction of a *second person* noticeably changes the quality
of one's experience, as is perhaps most dramatically illustrated by a person's being suddenly espied, *in flagrante
delicto*, in any of the private acts just mentioned. Cast
in more positive terms, the quality of 'two' is probably
best indicated by the many forms of social validation
excitement, agreement, comfort, challenge, and the like -
upon which most persons, each in his way, are so dependent. Folk wisdom and studies in social psychology show
that the tangible presence of a *third person* engenders
yet even another change in possible phenomenology and
social parameters, for example, the concept of a witness
to a transaction; things with which one person will allow
another to confront him, but only if the two are alone;
'saving face'; addressing a person by a familiar name
when alone with him, but protocol demanding his being
addressed by title if another person is present; 'what
will the neighbors think?'; the choice as to sending a
straight carbon-copy or a 'blind' copy; 'not in front of
the children'. It seems abundantly clear to this writer
that the logic, the rules, the problem, and the experiences change markedly as one proceeds from a position of
solitude to the presence of another person, then to the
presence of a third. Yet, in terms of the phenomenology
just outlined - *all of which is predicated on construing
the construals of others and having one's own construals
construed* - the introduction of a fourth person, *in principle*, and *in a sheerly structural sense* - generates no
new issues, problems or considerations not already met
and dealt with at the level of *three*. The appearance of
the third person, then, appears to pose a certain psycho-
logical-mathematical limit, in that the presence of that
third person, within the parameters suggested, is indistinguishable from the subsequent appearance of any higher
number of others.
    These conjectures on a possible social psychology of
three persons are admittedly sketchy and certainly require
more careful definition. Yet it may not be premature to
draw a relevance between certain triadic issues and problems of the dyad, from a personal construct theory perspective. The author acknowledges and concurs with the
prevailing view that construct theory research is only
now beginning to scratch the surface regarding ways of
conceptualizing dyadic interactions. Yet that truth should
not prevent us from looking a little farther ahead.
    There is a way of framing a tentative statement - nay,

a *question* - about the psychological relevance of triads
to dyads which could, if reasonably pursued, satisfy three
conditions which the writer sees as elegant and which the
reader may find satisfying. The proper framing of that
question, first, will bear directly back upon the central
concern of this paper, *viz.* the construing of centrality
and peripherality of construction; second, will stimulate
fresh appreciation for the reflexivity of personal construct theory itself; and third, will not allow the individual person to be lost in the constructural shuffle.

The question is: *What can personal construct psychol-*
ogists say about one person's construing of two other
person's construing of each other's construction pro-
cesses?

There are two kinds of psychological situation which
abound in real life and which can be subsumed under the
question proposed. One is that state of affairs whereby
two persons construe their constructural processes as
similar, while a third person construes them as different.
In the other, the reverse, two persons construe their constructural processes as different, while a third sees them
as similar. These situations are at their most interesting
when the three persons engage in dialogue on their respective views of the situation, and, sure enough, the discussion quickly turns, not to just *any* old similarity or
difference, but to the *important* ones, the really *signif-*
icant ones, of course.

We shall leave it to the reader's own musings to decide
to what extent this question may, in fact, meet the three
conditions mentioned. *Caveat lector.*

Footnote

*The sociality corollary states that 'to the extent
that one person construes the construction process of
another he may play a role in a social process involving
the other person'.

DISCUSSION OF UNIVERSALITY AND RELATIVITY IN PERSONAL CONSTRUCT THEORY

DEREK E. BOLTON

*Department of Psychology,
Institute of Psychiatry, de Crespigny Road,
London, S.E.5.*

Preamble

The following talk was intended to open a discussion, and consequently its style is conversational and lacks the scholarship and some of the rigour of a more formal paper. But the informal style suits the points I wanted to raise, and to change it would misrepresent too much what was actually said, so that I have kept it for publication. For similar reasons I have included details of the discussion that followed my talk with little changed, though inevitably points have been shortened (by memory and by editing) and some brief contributions have been omitted. This published report of the group discussion has been prepared in consultation with the participants, but I am responsible for the final version.

The Talk

I should like to raise for discussion several problems which concern personal construct theory, and which have been troubling me for some time now. The problems are linked together more or less directly, the main theme running through them being an apparent tension between two aspects of personal construct theory, which could be called 'universality' and 'relativity'. Particularly I shall try to explore the implications of the Individuality Corollary - that people differ from each other in their construction of events - for our own attitudes towards the various theories and approaches in psychology, and towards the people who believe in them.

It will probably be agreed that the Grid methods are the outstanding practical contribution which personal construct theory has made to working psychologists, but while acknowledging the strong points of these methods, I think we need to remind ourselves that they (like any other single method of investigation) are very limited. For example, they seem best suited to measure conscious or readily-available constructs; they reveal little of the historical development of constructs; they are not designed

to investigate certain processes which are of central concern to psychology, such as memory, or the relation between speech and action; and so on.

On the other hand, it is natural that the home-grown
Grid methods should have received most attention from personal construct theorists: but, it might be argued, on
principle there is no reason why many and various other
techniques of investigation should not be wedded to the
theory - on the contrary, a major strength of personal
construct theory is just that it need not be limited in
its range and methods of enquiry. Personal construct theory
tries to give a general account of men's psychological
processes, for which purpose the empirical basis of the
theory seems at present too slender - but perhaps in the
future the theory can be put to work increasingly in diverse activities, in experimental research and in other
kinds of practice. A similar reply can be made to the
charge that the theoretical power of personal construct
theory falls short of its own aspirations. One frequent
objection being, for example, that the theory makes too
little of the distinction between conscious and unconscious
processes; here the reply is that personal construct theory
can incorporate various concepts and minor 'theories' in
psychology, and so need leave nothing of importance out.

The underlying claim here is, I think, that personal
construct theory is - or better, can be made into - a
metatheory for psychology. Personal construct theory contains statements of great generality about its subject-
matter, man and his psychological processes. These statements are not, for the most part, empirical generalizations, but they can be used in combination with certain
other assumptions, particularly with a theory and practice
of measurement (such as the Grid methods) to deduce empirical consequences. Thus personal construct theory contains
little empirical method or content of its own, but its
function is rather to supply a system of concepts for
formulating empirical results. The argument continues: the
propositions of personal construct theory lie on the res-
pectable borderline between philosophy or metaphysics and
empirical science. They can be the inner core of contemporary psychological science, influencing and being influenced by what we find out, but in complicated ways which
probably cannot be circumscribed in advance, but which
will need to be constructed with ingenuity. (This brief
description of the role to which personal construct theory
might aspire owes much to the account of the dynamic
structure of scientific theory given by Lakatos in his
paper 'Falsificationism and the Methodology of Scientific
Research Programmes' (1970). I should say that in making this reference I do not mean to suggest that psychology should emulate the physical sciences which are Lakatos' concern in this paper. Psychology may share with

the physical sciences, and indeed with, say, the historical sciences, certain structural features, in that each contains a core of quasi-philosophical assumptions, theories of observation of different levels, various methods of collecting data, and so on; but in other respects they may be very different, particularly, the empirical methods of physics do not, I think, provide an adequate model for the whole of psychology).

One of the central implications of personal construct theory is, I think, that life is activity, that activity by its nature constructs a reality, which we call experience, that as we act in different ways we anticipate and realize different possibilities, and it is by common action that we are held together. These ideas may seem a far cry from the psychological laboratory or clinic, but there is much theory and practice in contemporary psychology which fits in with them well, and which is based firmly on empirical findings. Briefly, for example: in cognitive psychology it has become clear that stimuli are genuinely processed and transformed in perception and memory, and in ways dependent upon individual differences; it is acknowledged in developmental psychology that the beginnings of thought are wholly involved with the child's activity, and that this activity is largely and increasingly social in nature; and so on. Further, not only could particular discoveries give empirical confirmation to personal construct theory, but apparently also whole theories and their techniques could be rewritten in the language of the theory; for example, treatment by behaviour therapy can be described as an experiment (by the patient), therapeutic transference can be described as based upon role constructs; and so on.

It would seem that the logical end of this line of thought is that personal construct theory should subsume a large part of the empirical basis of psychology, and should take its place as the representative of psychology among grand contemporary theories in science and philosophy. (And personal construct theory does have strong connections with them - as I have suggested in a paper 'Two Concepts of Man' (1975)).

It is all very well to say (as I often do to myself) that this or that fact or theory 'fits in well' with the kind of general scheme expressed by personal construct theory, but clearly there are enormous problems in the way between day-dream and reality. Will the connections between the almost philosophical language of personal construct theory and experimental details be too often too vague - important to those who are already convinced, but of little practical value to anybody else? Will the meaning of concepts and propositions of personal construct theory need to be stretched so far from the original in order to incorporate the various phenomena, that it would

be at best only in name (and likely not in that either)
that personal construct theory would approach being a universal psychology? If the propositions of personal construct theory can be tied down to a wide range of experimental procedures, will they after all, especially the
ones with more specific content, turn out to be true? Are
there not whole essential areas of psychology (such as
neuropsychology) which will be left entirely out of account?

But it is not these problems which I intend to discuss
now. It is obvious that they are enormous (perhaps absurdly
so) and can be tackled only by long and detailed study of
various areas in contemporary psychology. The problem I
have in mind is not whether many and various aspects of
psychology could be subsumed under personal construct
theory, but rather: what is the point of having (or want-
ing to have) a psychological metatheory with such wide
application? And this question leads to another: what
stands in the way of a psychology, such as personal construct theory, gaining general acceptance in the community?

Given that certain procedures and theories are used
more or less successfully by working scientists and therapists, what is the purpose of casting them into a very
general, almost philosophical, mode? One answer would be
to say: 'Look, psychology abounds with very wrong-headed
conceptions about what happens and what we are doing, so
that one aim of personal construct theory is to replace
these mistaken views about man, and to show that what is
right about them can be expressed in a better way'. If
this reply be given, it seems that personal construct
theory is joining a tradition among personality theories:
psychoanalysis studies the deepest psychological processes,
learning theory the fundamental scientific laws of learning, personal construct theory then the best constructs -
and each theory will rule out the others as respectively
superficial, non-scientific, and subordinate. But compelling though this position may be for a construct theorist,
it is likely to feel also uncomfortable - for personal
construct theory is meant to be epistemologically liberal.

This brings us to a problem which, in one form or
another, confronts all 'relativity' theories. The problem
was first raised (to my knowledge) by Plato in the *Theaet-
etus* in connexion with the doctrine of Protagoras, according to which 'man is the measure of all things', so that,
things are to me such as they appear to me, and are to
you such as they appear to you (152). Socrates observes
that according to this doctrine each man is to have his
own beliefs, and they are all right and true, and then
asks: 'Where, then, is the wisdom of Protagoras, to justify his setting up to teach others and to be handsomely
paid for it, and where is our comparative ignorance or

the need for us to go and sit at his feet, when each of
us is himself the measure of his own wisdom?' (161C-E).
There is one reply to this objection, and Plato understood
it so well that he could speak for Protagoras:

> But there is all the difference in the world between
> one man and another just in the very fact that what
> is and appears to one is different from what is and
> appears to the other. And as for wisdom and the wise
> man, I am very far from saying that they do not ex-
> ist. By a wise man I mean precisely a man who can
> change any one of us, when what is bad appears and
> is to him, and make what is good appear and be to
> him. (166D)

Protagoras gives examples, and concludes his reply:

> And as for the wise....I call them, when they have
> to do with the body, physicians, and when they have
> to do with plants, husbandmen. For I assert that
> husbandmen too, when plants are sickly and have
> depraved sensations, substitute sensations that are
> sound and healthy; and moreover that wise and honest
> public speakers substitute in the community sound
> for unsound views of what is right. For I hold that
> whatever practices seem right and laudable to any
> particular State are so, for that State, so long
> as it holds by them. Only, when the practices are,
> in any particular case, unsound for them, the wise
> man substitutes others that are and appear sound.
> On the same principle the sophist, since he can in
> the same manner guide his pupils in the way they
> should go, is wise and worth a considerable fee to
> them when their education is completed. In this way
> it is true both that some men are wiser than others
> and that no one thinks falsely; and you, whether
> you like it or not, must put up with being a measure,
> since by these considerations my doctrine is saved
> from shipwreck. (167B-D; these translations are from
> Cornford 1970).

It seems then, that we might dispense with an absolute
standard of truth without being forced into subjective
relativism, if we can make a pragmatic standard instead.
Truth would then not be static correspondence with a given
state of affairs, but would rather be dynamic correspondence between activity and the world. And wisdom consists
in preserving and cultivating action, in making grow.

It might be claimed: personal construct theory works
better than other theories, it makes more sense of personal experience, of different kinds of psychotherapy, it
would lead to more experiment and prediction - generally,
it is more useful. But is this true? Or, to go deeper:
for whom is this true? I think I know people who could
not use personal construct theory at all (and the same
would apply in the case of any other personality theory).

Some people might find that they could not get on with
Kelly's style and language, or that his books were too
long, others are preoccupied with different matters. There
are many kinds of reason why a person would not find the
theory useful, from banal but still effective reasons
such as these, to deeper incompatibilities between the
person and what personal construct theory wants to say.
This is connected with the fact, known well by Kelly,
that theories are essentially theories *of men*, that people
have and need different theories. There are personal differences between advocates of different theories, and why
should we suppose this would be any the less true in the
case of personality theories?

What has impressed me continuously since I have worked
in clinical psychology is that different personalities
are attracted to different kinds of theoretical position
with their accompanying techniques of therapy. And I think
it is important that these differences can be grasped
without commitment to a particular personality theory,
just by seeing what goes on. Behaviour therapists tend to
be, for example, interested in the application of traditional scientific methods to the study of living organisms
(as in physiology, say). They take simple views of people's
activity and difficulties they get into, they seem to take
less interest in non-scientific descriptions of man, which
presumably obscure what they see as the essential principles of behaviour and its modification, and they are
less involved with what is less suited to experimental
investigation, such as long and involved patterns of interpersonal relations. Psychoanalysts and psycho-dynamically
orientated therapists live with non-rational, semi-consc-
ious processes and influences, their life seeming to be,
as it were, filled with intimate personal relations and
their vagaries, wholly involved with mother father lover
and child. In the case of these two personality theories,
the likely personality of the theorist is clearly linked
with the theory.

Probably so it is also with less well-established
theories or approaches. For example, the transactional
analyst is drawn to the theory which talks about what
interests him most - the games people play - and which
underplays what, for whatever reason, interests him least,
the experience of being inside the 'game'. Or, perhaps,
the client-centred therapist wants a theory which says
what he or she already feels, that we do not know what
to do for the best, so we should be as decent as we can
be, and hope for it. People are drawn to a theory which
emphasizes what for them, in their lives, seems and therefore is most important to them - though this may or may
not be what troubles them most. And if a person does
accept a theory, original inclination and emphasis may
be exaggerated, because the theory selectively represents

reality. For example, a therapist works with those patients who respond well to his method, and inevitably spends less time with patients with different needs.

I should suggest that a man's personality or character matters in his choice of what personality theory to work with as much as, say, the experimental evidence which supports the theory. Or a better way of putting it would be this: only particular kinds of men can rely on experimentation as the major criterion for deciding what to believe and consequently how to act - this reliance is itself possible only in connection with certain other temperaments, abilities, dispositions and interests. The view being opposed is that scientific rationality constitutes an absolute (or logical) standard of practical reason which a man fails to recognize only at the expense of being an idiot or a scoundrel. For alternatively, we might accept that a man be of sound heart and mind even though he does not acknowledge or use scientific methods. In this sense a particular kind of theory, together with its own rules of evidence and rationality - whether scientific or otherwise - is taken in or rejected by a man, according to his whole personality. Choosing scientific evidence (of the kind we now have in psychology) as the guide, for practical action will seem right to one kind of man, but impossible for another. For another psychologist might say: experimental studies are generally so far removed from what I know from my own case and from what in fact goes on when a patient comes to see me, that it would be foolish for me to try to guide my action by that evidence - indeed I would not know how to go about it, I need to depend on my own experience and imagination, and frankly, not a little on 'intuition'. This psychologist might regard the experimentalist as the one who has failed, in that he is emotionally underdeveloped. Plain insults are avoided only if it is acknowledged that different ways are right for different men.

Faced with this diversity of needs and beliefs - a diversity highlighted by his own theory - how can the personal construct theorist claim that his theory is better than others? For is not the point that for some people (such as himself) personal construct theory does indeed work better than other theories, but for other people, going by what they say and do, different theories work better? And it also seems questionable whether all or most people *would* find that personal construct theory worked better than other theories of personality *if* they gave it a try. For if we consider what it means for a theory to 'work better' we find again, I think, a deep relativity to individual men. Someone who has enormous difficulties defining himself in the family, and who has resolved to tackle them, would be likely to find that a theory which dwells on just that kind of issue is the one

that 'works best' *for him*. Someone who always was and is
still, while working as a clinical psychologist, struck
by the connections between lower animals and man, will
likely be drawn to the experimental life sciences and
their methods, and they will serve his purpose better, I
should think, than personal construct theory. But are
there not universal needs that we all acknowledge as such?
Water, for example? Perhaps friends? For the rest, what
works for a man means only what makes it possible for him
to live - and this varies from person to person, since
our lives are and are made different.

But it might be replied now that this kind of objection
entirely misses the point that personal construct theory
is practically content-free, that it is not just another
personality theory alongside others; it can be, as it
were, all things to all men. Let us consider this reply.
Personal construct theory speaks of 'constructs' in general, and it is true that no one construct is introduced
at the start. It is important that in a Grid procedure
the person under test produces his own constructs for
study. But does this mean that personal construct theory
has no prejudice? Surely not; there is already an emphasis
on classification and the rules of classification - an
emphasis of course already manifest in the *name* 'personal
construct theory'. And in this sense one construct is
introduced at the start, the construct 'construct', with
all that this means.

This brings us to an issue which, you may have noticed,
I have avoided until now, namely: what kind of person is
attracted towards personal construct theory? There would
seem to be in him or her the desire (not unusual among
psychologists) for a systematic and all-encompassing
understanding of man, but particularly, for a rational
and deductive kind of understanding, even applied to
admittedly non-rational processes. Indeed the orderly
structure and systematic definitions of personal construct
theory already exemplify what the theory itself says is
(or can be construed as) the most significant feature of
our life. In an important sense, then, personal construct
theory is not content-less, and while its content does
have strong appeal for some people, we may expect that it
will not have the same effect on others. We can imagine
someone saying: 'What matters most to people is that they
should become able really to accept their relationship
with father and mother - the kind of classifying and sys-
tematizing you emphasize seems a minor consideration, at
least to me'. Another man would resist theories saying
what is essential to people, in the belief that there is
no telling this in advance.

Would the fact that different aspects of life matter
to different people go so far as to prevent any psychology
gaining general acceptance? How could there be a consensus

on a theory for psychology, when different people are capable of such diverse views of the phenomena? And how much
agreement can we expect even on the empirical basis of
psychology, when there are so many conflicting opinions
on what counts as finding out something worthwhile about
man's psyche and its logic? These seem to me open issues.
Of course we should not neglect what we do have in common,
or rather, at least what large groups have in common.
There are methods of experiment and investigation in psychology which command near universal respect; and there
are various treatment procedures whose validity is accepted at least by the clinical psychologists who can use
them. At the theoretical level, are there any concepts
which are universally accepted? There seem to be few at
present; but it may be that certain concepts will come
increasingly into common use in psychology, particularly
perhaps, those which will be needed to replace the old
dualistic ways of thinking.

It is relevant to our present concerns that Cartesian
dualism provided the basic framework for describing man
and the other animals for several hundred years, and this
despite there being so many different schools of thought
on the subject suited, I should say, to different kinds
of temperament - they included positivism and material-
istic physiology, introspectionism and idealism, and so
on. In other words: the fundamental categories of thought
were shared, notwithstanding their use in formulating
opposed doctrines. For example, at the crudest level,
there were the conflicting views on which of the two sub-
stances, mind or matter, was primary. The need for new
ways of thinking has been and will continue to be felt in
all areas and styles of psychology, and it may be that
new concepts will become common currency to approaches
which are otherwise, at one level or another, incompatible.

Kelly was aware of the historical movements in thought,
and knew that his own theorizing was modern. So one way
in which personal construct theory could expect general
recognition is by playing a part in the very difficult
task of identifying new concepts, problems and methods
for psychology. For example, Kelly makes a point of assert-
ing that human life is activity - which is just the opposite of what characterizes Cartesian dualism, with its
crude conception of the body, and its separation of mind
from body. Subsequently Kelly takes hold of ideas which
could have no central importance in a Cartesian system,
namely, that different people lead different lives, but
there are ways we are held together as a community.

On the other hand, I think some aspects of personal
construct theory are at present too weak: particularly
relevent to our present consideration is that they key
terms, 'construct' and its cognates 'construe' and 'construction', may need further explanation and elaboration,

of various kinds. I must admit that, at a very simple
level, I often do not understand the way these words are
used - the grammar of the sentence in which one of them
occurs puzzles me, or I cannot see how to substitute another word with roughly the same meaning, or both. (For
me the trouble starts already in the Construction corollary, but occurs then in less formal contexts also). Of
course I mention my difficulty here in the belief it is
not unique. Of course part of the problem is that the
ideas we are trying to express with these words are very
hard to grasp - if only because we are unfamiliar with
them. All the more necessary then to think through these
technical terms, and not to allow them to obscure the
issues. It may be useful in this task, and also in making
personal construct theory more accessible to the newcomer,
if the language of the theory could be explained in terms
of ordinary language, so that we can see, for example,
the connections between having a construct and, say, having a mental image or representation, or behaving in a
certain way, or using language. And also, if the constructs
of personal construct theory are to become generally accepted in psychology, in the sense indicated above, constant
attention would need to be paid to the different areas of
psychology investigating the nature and basis of human
activity, and continuing attempts made to relate the language of personal construct theory to these many and various investigations.

As things stand, however, at least in clinical psychology, we have a multiplicity of theoretical orientations.
Faced with one phenomenon, say a man's problematic way of
behaving towards anyone who employs him, one theory describes it as a habit, another says it is likely a re-living
of family dynamics, another that the man is using a certain
construct to anticipate (and bring about) what will happen.

Of course the temptation here familiar to all of us
is to see how very similar all these theories are, and
then to wonder whether the best theory might be simply
the distillation of what they have in common. But it may
be that the different personality theories derive what
power they have from what is unique to them, say a particular focus of interest, or particular links to some other
field of enquiry, and that this will be lost if we focus
only on what they have in common. In the present kind of
case, for example, what they have in common is likely very
dull, something like: people do the same thing over and
over (probably starting in the family) until they do something else. But the various personality theories bring
entirely different systems to bear on this one truth, and
they lead to equally different treatment procedures. The
behaviour therapist says to the man: Do something else -
and perhaps shows him what to do. The psychodynamic therapist will want to say: think and feel about your family,

recognize your fears, see if you can come to terms with
them now and so do things differently, perhaps starting
with me now. And the construct therapist: see the expectations you have in these situations that trouble you, are
they realistic, have you tested out what would happen if
you behaved differently - did you notice what really happened?

An alternative response is eclecticism, the method of
combining various parts of different doctrines, adding a
strength in one to a gap in another, with the aim of building a grand synthesis. One point about this method is that
it lends itself more readily to incantation than to practice. But another criticism is that it mistakenly still
dreams of the one theory. For in my view, the conclusion
to be drawn from the diversity of schools in psychology,
is not that they must all in the end be the same, nor
that some synthesis should be made of them all (though
this is not to exclude combination of some theories for
some purpose), but is rather that this diversity reflects
genuine multiplicity in human life and in what we make of
it, so that there is no 'single truth' about us.

This recognition that there is something to be said
for most of the many and different beliefs that men seriously hold and can use, does not mean that one accepts those
beliefs as one's own - clearly in most cases they will not
be one's own - it means rather that one sees that they are
right, at least for the time being, for others. In fact
on the contrary, there is a sense in which one believes
little, only in the need to let experience speak for itself, and to let another man speak for himself. This is
important in therapy, for example, since there is a limit
to the discrepency a client can and will tolerate between
the treatment being offered and his own natural way of
understanding and behaving. For although we have spoken
mostly about differences in the temperament and in the
personal needs of therapists, such differences are to be
found among clients too. Individual needs and methods may
be less obvious in a client, generally he comes with no
theory about them, and all the more important it is to
watch for his potential, going by signs such as his symptoms, and what he says or does not say about them.

Awareness of the client's strengths and weaknesses,
and the ability to help the client use the one to overcome
or to come to terms with the other, is the characteristic
of a successful clinician, regardless of his theoretical
orientation and technique. The relation between therapist
and patient, in which the therapist encourages one of the
natural ways in which the other person can work towards
health, and discourages or blocks his ways of staying still
or returning to his symptom, seems to me what is essential
to therapy. And it may be this relation or process which
constitutes the proper 'empirical basis' of clinical

psychology, which, as we mentioned earlier, seems problematic while we focus on the bewildering array of clinical
techniques now in use. For in this one respect at least
there may be something in common between different methods: that the therapist is aware of the client's potential
for change, and can use his method to help the client realize that potential. But of course, written down, this
is only vacuous! And I'm not sure that refining our language here would help. Because what this process comes to,
in particular cases, is many different things, and cannot
be defined in advance. The ability to see the way forward
for clients (and indeed for oneself) can perhaps be learnt
only through experience, and by being taught in particular
cases what it means. In this case, therapy will remain in
significant part atheoretical, for the practice will always be richer than our theories about it. It will depend
on our sense of direction. When a therapist has a technique
backed by a theory, still he needs to know what the theory
cannot tell him, namely, how to use the technique in a
particular case: how to begin with a particular patient,
when to be demanding, when to hold back and wait, when to
change tack, how much and for how long; and so on. This
kind of practical knowledge is surely needed in all of
the various treatment methods, and it depends upon what
men can have in common, the ability to recognize what is
right for each other.

Perhaps what different treatment procedures have in
common is no more and no less than that they can help
people get better. This does not mean that the different
procedures are all essentially the same, as though there
were one form of therapy wearing (for some queer reason)
many disguises. The so-called 'non-specific- variables,
such as the reliability of sessions, kindness from the
therapist, increased motivation and expectation, do apparently effect change in clients, but equally important must
be (I assume) the specific ways in which the different
techniques promote and practise change, for example, the
use of role-play, or of the therapeutic transference, or
discussion of experiments with new ways of acting in daily
life.

The many and various methods of treatment are in important respects genuinely different. Hence, for example, it
is usually a genuine decision which approach would be best
to adopt towards a particular problem. In making such a
decision, it should be borne in mind that the success of
a particular kind of therapy depends partly on the therapist - a fact often obscured in various ways; for example,
therapists naturally gravitate towards the method they
can use best, and then infer (by typical psychologic)
that the others are unusable, that they are not methods
at all, for anyone. And the outcome depends also on the
client, on whether or not he finds that the method offered

to him provides a possible way for him to change.

I have argued that the temperament, personality, abilities, interests and inclinations of the therapist will decide in large part which treatment method he can work with best; similarly those same kinds of factor will help determine the ways in which the client can work. Of course these terms 'temperament' and the rest are vague, but I can think of no better ones; particularly it seems questionable whether the typologies now used are sufficiently widely-based, or sufficiently detailed, to be useful in understanding and working with the variety and subtlety of the individual differences which matter in therapy (whether these typologies be psychiatric diagnostic categories, applied to patients, or from general personality theories).

At a practical level then, insofar as a clinician believes that people construe their lives differently, he will try to understand different methods of treatment, and to be able to use as many of them as is possible and right for him, so that he can the better judge which approach would best suit a particular client; and insofar as he has the power of referral, he should also be conscious of the particular strengths and weaknesses of those therapists whose services he can request. The skill required in these decisions of policy, along with the skills needed to solve the problems which continually arise during therapy itself, seem for various reasons to defy complete capture in rules and theories.

It is one of the main advantages of personal construct theory that it does not obscure or ignore the differences in the ways people construe their lives, but on the contrary, makes them axiomatic. A consequence of acknowledging these differences, I have tried to show, is that we accept a fundamental relativity in human affairs, and that we abandon the idea that there is one essential truth about us, which would, if we knew it, take care of our actions in advance. Instead we would need adopt a liberal and vigilant attitude to others, and to what they believe and must do. But it should be said that if these attitudes are what personal construct theory recommends to people, then again much stands in the way of its general acceptance - there is much resistance in us to giving up the belief that our own reality is more real than others.

Discussion

Peter Weinreich   I would like to take up one of your points where I disagree. A professional person's choice of personality theory is not just a matter of personality, a view which appears to imply that there is no validity in any theoretical orientation to personality. The development of personality theory is also a matter of clarification of concepts through (relatively) objective methods, that is, the adoption of a particular theoretical orientation is not wholly subjective.

Fay Fransella No, it is not *just* a matter of personality, but personality *is* vitally important. One has only to look at the kind of people drawn, for example, to Maudsley psychology compared with those who have escaped from it.

Harry Procter I am not happy about explaining the choice of a personality theory on the basis of an individual's 'personality'. A personality theory fulfills a function for someone in a given role in a social power structure.

Derek Bolton Yes, but there are also individual differences within a given social system - these are the personality differences I was referring to.

Glenys Parry To raise another point - I think you are wrong in your interpretation of what a metatheory is. It is not a matter of taking over other theories; it is rather that personal construct theory is a theory *about* theory-making.

Peter Weinreich Agreed. Consider physics for example: one could describe in personal construct theory terms the organization of the physicists' theory, and what they do with it. But clearly there is no question of construct theory 'subsuming' physics. In principle, the methods of personal construct theory allow one to examine the constructs used by physicists, but the theory has had no part in developing these concepts which physicists have done over the generations in order to elucidate their subject matter. Construct theory shows us how we might investigate other theories.

Miller Mair Yes, but I should like to express a worry that I do not see this happening very often. Some construct theorists do not seem to take interest in other people's views. And further, I am concerned that personal construct theory can encourage in people an unscientific attitude, in this sense, that we can believe we already have a theory without paying due regard to the phenomena.

Derek Bolton Taking up Peter's example of describing the theory of physics - it was a very helpful one. But surely there are differences when it comes to, for example, describing what the psychoanalyst does. The construct theorist would not simply describe the construct system used by psychoanalysts, he would also want to translate it into personal construct theory terms - he wants to redescribe the phenomena in a preferred way.

Peter Weinreich Yes, it's possible to do this, but it is more complicated than a straight translation; it requires a clarification and redefinition of, say, specific psychodynamic concepts (the psychodynamic concepts of 'identity', 'identification with another', and 'conflicts in

identification with others' are examples which I consider
in my paper to the Congress).

Brenda Morris   It is important though that some concepts
of Freudian theory cannot be translated into personal construct theory, for example the concept of death instinct.
This is because personal construct theory is not wholly
content-free; it of course contains a definite picture of
man.

Glenys Parry   In any case there is no paradox in using
other theories while accepting personal construct theory.
For example, when faced with problems of clinical depression, I use what Freud wrote, but without believing his
whole theory - that is nothing to worry about.

Kay Frost   But it does worry me - perhaps it ought to you.
I also use Freudian theory for some clinical work, and
the fact that I need to makes me wonder whether the personal construct theory I have is adequate.

Derek Bolton   Time has run out, I'm afraid, so we must
leave these many issues for future discussion.

CONFUSION AND THE CLOCK

GEORGE KELLY

Some Things I would Like to Know, But Not Yet

It has often occurred to me, as I am sure it has to you too, that it would be amusing to have a peek through the curtain of night at what tomorrow has in store. Suppose I could observe what I would be doing at this time tomorrow night. It might be interesting to watch the goings on from this present vantage point of the evening before, yet not to participate in them, nor to be concerned with whether I was doing what I was supposed to be doing, nor even to be in any danger of being recognized as an intruder. Such a thing would have to be done surreptitiously, however, for I am sure if I were to be caught at my eavesdropping, my tomorrow's I (How do you say that?) would become self-conscious about the arrangement and start acting in an unnatural manner. He might not even do things the way he was destined to do them, and the whole affair might fall apart in a shambles of irreality.

But if I could manage to keep out of sight, so that all the performers in tomorrow evening's episode would act the way the sum-total of their previous experiences supposedly required them to act, that is, would act naturally, the affair might come off pretty well. Now that I think of it, the other people, other than myself-tomorrow and myself-today, ought to be easy enough to fool, even if they did get a glimpse of me eavesdropping. They would probably no more than mistake me for myself-tomorrow, and think it quite natural that I should be there - unless, of course, I was wearing a different colored shirt, or hadn't shined my shoes, as I haven't tonight. So that part of the arrangement has a reasonable chance of being worked out, in spite of what some of my more skeptical readers - not you; I didn't mean you! - are likely to think.

Where I would get into trouble, if I weren't extremely careful, is with myself. Perhaps if I arrived in some kind of disguise, it would keep me from finding myself out. Now, let's see: I could go as my Cousin Leander. I don't know him very well, and if I looked a little familiar to myself, there would be a perfectly logical explanation.

Leander, however, if I remember correctly, is a little
nearsighted, and, unless his nearsightedness has been off-
set by presbyopia during the last ten years, he might miss
a good deal of what was going on. Besides, I doubt if
Cousin Leander would be very much interested in what I am
going to do tomorrow night. That wouldn't be a real obstacle, of course, since I would only be pretending to myself that I was Cousin Leander.

Still, the performance would have to be pretty good -
pretty realistic, I mean - to fool me, because I am sure
that I would know right off that the real Cousin Leander
was not genuinely interested enough to be acting so alert
to all the things that would need watching. So, if I let
myself get too closely involved with the events of the
evening, I am sure that my tomorrow's self would suspect
that something unusual was up and start asking pointed
questions. And, whenever that happens, I mean when I start
to ask myself pointed questions, I get confused and my
stories don't hang together.

Before the evening was over I am sure I would be found
out and I would have to come back to today, if it weren't
too late, which is where I am now. Then, I would simply
have to wait it out until tomorrow came around and I found
out what I want to know by the time-honored method of living through it. While this wait-and-see approach to the
problem seems unnecessarily conservative - even reactionary
- I doubt I shall be able to do much in the way of improv-
ing it, at least until I have given the matter a great
deal more thought.

Still, I don't like to give up on this project too
quickly; people who give up too quickly are apt to earn
the reputation of being unwise; like my grandfather who
once bought a thousand acres of rice land in Texas. He
sold it a year or two later, just before oil was discovered
on it; which was *unwise*. He did not know that he was selling a part of the fabulously rich Beaumont Field.

Then, on the other hand, there is my neighbor, I mean
there was my neighbor - that is to say, he is now a neighbor to where I used to live - who has been convinced for
years and years that there is oil underneath his farm.
He thinks there is oil under mine, too, but only the edge
of the oil deposit is under mine. The center of it, where
the gushers are going to be, is under his.

Now some people think he is being a little fanciful
about the matter, but if he holds on year after year, and
some day they do find oil on his place, he will, unlike
my grandfather, be acclaimed as a very wise man, if he is
still alive; and if he isn't still alive, they will probably acclaim him as an even wiser man. On the other hand,
if they don't find oil, all he has to do is to sit and
wait until something else turns up - maybe a new market

for sandburrs - and after that he will be considered
almost as wise as if it had turned out to be oil.

So, let me try again. While I probably will not succeed
this time either, I can at least establish the reputation
of being a person of vision. Then, if something does turn
up later and people can tell what is going to happen to
them twenty-four hours in advance, I can put in my claim
to wisdom.

Since writing the paragraphs above, I have been thinking very hard and I believe I have reached a conclusion.
The real sticker in this business of predicting the future
is the danger of my remembering in the midst of tomorrow
night's activities that I have already been there, and
who that fellow over there who claims to be Cousin Leander
really is. Now I think, at last, we have got to the nub
of the matter, like isolating the schizococcus, and it
should only be a matter of time until we achieve a major
break-through and the whole thing will seem as simple as
A-B-C.

We shall need funds, of course, to achieve this break-
through. Perhaps someone will organise a *Tomorrow Research
Fund* and put on campaigns with the neighbors around the
block collecting coins from each other. Or a *March of
Times* might do the trick. Now that we know what the problem is - our discovery that the human mind takes account
of what it has foreseen - our research will have a wholly
different emphasis.

The task will be to help forget what they foresaw just
before it happens. This would enable them to step across
the threshold of any new situation with a freshly opened
mind, completely emptied of its expectations. In a word,
we would replace memory with foresight. Thus, we would
always know in advance what was going to happen, but we
would not be hampered at the instant of occurrence by
looking for it or remembering what it was.

My! My! We could predict events faithfully, right down
to the last sneeze, even down to the sneeze that doesn't
quite come off, but we would be just as pleasantly surprised as ever at the final ka-choo! Sneezes would appear
to have slipped up on us unawares, just as they do now.
And, while we would know that the next sneeze that fails
to come off was not really supposed to come off anyway,
we could enjoy the suspense and the tingling sensation
that precedes sneezes that don't come off. The sneeze
that doesn't happen is an event, too, you know, or didn't
you realize that?

This brings me to an obstacle. I know that wise men
always surmount obstacles, so I suppose I should try to
be wise enough to climb over this one too, just as I have
been scrambling over a good many others during the past

few minutes - *your* minutes, *my* hours - that some of you
might have considered insurmountable. The obstacle is
this: If something like a sneeze doesn't happen, and you
already knew in advance that it wasn't going to happen,
why is its failure to explode into reality *an event*? Are
all the things that don't happen events, just like the
things that do? Can something be an event without ever
happening, or something happen without being an event?

Looked at this way, our little peeks into the future
are going to be very complicated, because we will have
to see displayed before us all the things that are not
going to happen as well as the one thing that will. Sorting out the one from all the others will be like finding
a needle in a haystack. It may not even be worth the
trouble it would take. My grandfather, for example, would
have had to paw through an awfully big clutter of things
that were not going to happen to his land before coming
across the one thing that was *not* not-going-to-happen -
discovery of oil. Even he, though he was a prodigiously
energetic man, might not have felt it was worth the bother.

There is one possibility that I have not considered.
Now that I think of it, it seems so obvious that I wonder
why it did not occur to me before. Perhaps man already
knows how to anticipate the future and the reason he
thinks he doesn't is that he always forgets what he has
predicted just before it happens. Or, just before it
doesn't happen, whichever is the case - I mean if he predicts that it will not happen and, sure enough, it doesn't,
then, instead of saying, 'This is just what I expected',
he forgets, and finds himself just as surprised as he
would be if he hadn't ever known. This is just what we
were talking about, isn't it - forgetting our predictions
so as not to spoil the taste of things when they actually
happen?

Now take me. The night before last I was wondering
what would happen the next night - remember? So I wrote
about it, and if you have been reading this chapter
straight through, you must have come across what I had
to say. Well, now, that next night has come and gone -
the night I wanted to foresee. There was nothing very
unusual about it, nothing that I noticed, anyway. Nothing
seemed incongruous with what had happened the night before,
and I don't remember thinking of anything that was expected to come off and didn't Cousin Leander didn't show up
and even the TV show turned out the way it was supposed
to, as far as I could tell.

Now, while I may have forgotten what it was I predicted,
let us suppose that when I wrote about forecasting, I could
actually tell just what was going to happen, and that when
last night rolled around, I promptly forget what I had
predicted. Would that not explain why I felt that I was
experiencing things for the first time?

A curious thing! I had the feeling that everything was going along reasonably enough, even though I couldn't think what was supposed to happen. I wonder if that was because, while I had forgotten what was supposed to happen, I had not forgotten the fact that I had been expecting it. This kept me from being flabbergasted at everything my wife said, although I had no idea of what it was to be. Thus, the whole evening went by pretty much as if I were being reminded of something. Altogether, it was a very pleasant experience - not a bit shocking - just a series of interesting reminders. There is even the fact that I didn't get very much written yesterday. That is always a source of minor annoyance. But even that did not surprise me very much. You know, I don't think I expected to, anyway!

In a way, I wish that I could remember what I must have known I was going to do this afternoon. In particular, I wish I could remember - but, of course, I can't - what it was I was destined to write this afternoon. Especially I would like to remember how it was going to be said. It seems like such a long ways from the kind of discourse in which I am now involved to the point where I will be saying anything you can agree with, or that will make the whole passage come together, coherent and reasonable. If I could only remember now, then I would have nothing to do except type it off in a hurry and use the extra time before supper to putter around in the basement shop. Somehow, I have the feeling that puttering around in the shop is not in the cards for me this afternoon.

It has doubtless occurred to you that we could check up on this hunch about forgetting one's infallible predictions if we simply wrote down our predictions at the time we made them, and then came back to see if things had turned out the way the writing said they would. This assumes that we would remember having written something down. But, in any case, my wife would probably find the manuscript and ask if I was ready to have it burned with the trash; and if I had already started to forget I would probably tell her to go ahead.

I must confess this bothers me, and casts some doubt on my entire line of reasoning. A while ago, I thought it was going to turn out all right, but now I am not so sure. It must be that ever-present forgetting process again; it has just now erased my prophesy of what I was going to say.

Thirteen months and an ocean now separate me from the time and place at which the last of the sentences above were written. As it happens, the manuscript was not burned with the trash. Yet, as I re-read it, I find that at no point did I do what I was talking about doing and make specific predictions of what would occur during the ensuing

days. Perhaps the part of the manuscript containing the
predictions was destroyed, though I doubt it. It would
be especially interesting to read what I might have said
was not going to happen. But nothing like that was put
down and I cannot be sure how much of what did go on was
anticipated. This I know: Nothing that came about was
wholly expected and nothing was wholly unexpected. This
raises a question of whether one is ever capable of being
completely surprised, either by the things that happen
or those that don't. But, that is something we can take
up later.

What took place, among other things, was this. I was
writing during the weekend, and on Saturday had a rather
good day of it, probably because I was letting my mind
wander unhampered into all kinds of logical traps without
concerning myself with how I was going to reason my way
out of them. Then came Sunday; as usual, a lazy day. That
was the day I was to disguise myself as Cousin Leander.
Perhaps I was waiting for something special to happen,
and rather proving to myself that nothing special actually
would.

On Monday the going was tortuous, as it usually is even
when I pretend that I am typing out a message to the most
fascinated and wide-eyed listener my imagination can dream
up. I remarked to you in that day's manuscript that there
wasn't anything particularly special about the evening
before. As the writing shows, I even wished on Monday
that the conjured fates would take over and tell me what
to say, so I could get on with it.

Tuesday and Wednesday my muse deserted me altogether.
This was no great surprise. She often leaves me like this,
without warning, and, while I don't like it and I occasionally complain to her about her fickleness, I have decided
that she must find herself cramped by my efforts to put
her soft breath into precise psychological terms, and she
must slip away to recover her composure, or perhaps to
avoid quarreling with me openly. If so, it is better that
way, for I would not want matters between her and me to
come to such a state that we would break up permanently.

If you have a few moments to spare, perhaps you wouldn't
mind my trying to describe our relationship a little more
fully. If you are in a hurry, just skip ahead, since the
following passage has very little to do with what I set
out to tell you.

BEMUSED

Whose muse are youse?

Last night, the cushioned hours
Piled deep and soft,
You whispered close.
Your voice was in my ear.

"You're mine", I thought.

"All mine!"

So I set down
The throbbing syllables.
And then, at dawn,
I read those lines
I'd written in your spell
And -. What-th'hell!

No sign!

No trace of all
Those sentient moments we
Alone had shared.
You'd slipped away
And stealthily closed the door
And where we lay -

See!

The pillows there,
Each one puffed smooth and bare.
And where, where
Are you? Just where
Are you? And look! In my hands
These incoherent words!

So!

Today, I played
The game a different way.
Within my den,
The hours stacked high
With books upon the floor,
I read from men

Of yore.

I sought only words
That meant just what they said,
And nothing more.
Then twilight came.
The print began to fade,
And there, instead -!

You jade!

You wench! You whore!
Our secrets of the night before
You'd been whispering into others' ears
A thousand years

Or more!

Tonight, recluse,
I sit. No man nor muse
Dares pass that door!

In dark silence sit,
Until, across the room,
I hear a sigh.

She's here!

Already here,
She sits as lone as I;
Ten thousand years
Without a love.
Of all the consorts she
Has had, none wooed

Her true!

Each one pressed close
The eager lips to snatch
Some precious words,
As dowry pay
From her supply, to shout
Themselves, all day.

Hard gold!

And so had I;
Just so had failed to clasp
My lonely wraith

In love!

From now I woos m'muse!

Well, that's that.

Thursday, with some reluctance, I went to see my doctor about a pain I had in a certain place where I had always supposed my stomach to be. It's not that I have ever taken much interest in anatomy - internal anatomy, that is. It's rather, that in a general sort of way I like to know where my vital possessions are. I remember distinctly that my seventh grade physiology book at Pleasant Valley School had a picture in it that showed precisely where the things I swallowed got formally admitted to the stomach. Moreover, I know from experience that on those rare occasions when admission is denied, or recinded, this is the spot where the rumpus starts.

Perhaps I had better explain my reluctance. It's not that I don't like to talk to my friend, the doctor. I do like to talk to him. He happens to be a scholar, and is therefore both humble and fascinated by a variety of things. Medicine, of course, is one of them, though I doubt if he recognizes the vital relationship between it and country club membership. Indeed, I would be surprised if it should turn out that he ever belonged to a country club. No, the reason for my reluctance was that I always felt rather embarrassed in going to him about a furtive pain, or a persistent wart, or an ambulent itchy spot that has developed in the inaccessible reaches of my back.

I know he finds medicine just as puzzling as I find psychology, and it seems a little unfair to keep presenting
him with problems like these that may trip him up.

But still, he is a man who has faced up to the vagaries
of medical practice, and, therefore, has sense enough to
make me share some of the responsibility for the decisions
that are made. Moreover, he seems to recognize my inalien-
able and constitutional right to manage my own insides,
and would never think of giving me 'doctor's orders'. Nor
has he ever audibly invoked 'The Medical Profession' in
my presence. Instead, when I turn up with something pretty
vague or obscure we are both likely to be embarrassed, so
we sit there and look at each other and try to think of
something to say that will relieve the other's discomfort.

As a physician he has his more enterprising moments,
just as I have, and on these occasions he shows great
ingenuity in thinking of places that can be looked into.
This is the way he was on this particular Thursday. In no
time at all he had wangled an appointment for a series of
tests in a laboratory the next day.

None of this seemed particularly surprising, nor, on
the other hand, was it anything I could have precisely
predicted. It was all, more or less, within the pattern
of life according to which I lived day by day. I felt no
more than the usual relief that something systematic could
be done, the usual annoyance at further intrusions on an
already unproductive week, and the usual undertone of
curiosity about how much of this life I would be privileged
to see.

That evening the Thursday Nighters gathered. These are
the patient souls who accept the standing invitation my
wife and I extend to all those who are willing to listen
and comment on whatever manuscript I have produced during
the preceding week. Needless to say, I often greet them
with apprehension, an apprehension I try to hide beneath
my role as host.

This evening I read the latest installment of this
manuscript - right up to the end. They were puzzled, as
they had been with the previous installments of this particular undertaking, and not particularly pleased with
what I was doing. What literary reputation I have among
them is that of an expository writer with a commitment
to a certain amount of scientific discipline, and, while
they knew I was off on a different track this time, they
did not see that I was going anywhere. But they were
momentarily interested in the propositions conjured up by
my whimsy and, somewhat to my relief, turned the discussion
to such questions as whether *anticipation* was a posture
one assumed toward the future and if it should be distinguished from *prediction*, the latter being something which
may be better understood as a probability statement about
events. And, too, they raised the question of 'phenomenal

time' and wondered if anticipation were bounded by that.
According to my notes, we did not, on this occasion, get
into a discussion of anxiety, the central topic of this
chapter.

Early the following morning I had an acute coronary
attack - my first. Some years ago I watched my mother die
from a coronary. It took two weeks of agony. It has seemed
to me, particularly since that experience, that mankind
ought to find a better way to go about this business. I'm
all for putting it off as long as it is decently possible,
of course, but when the time comes it should be possible
for a person to pass on with a little more dignity. I have
in mind that one ought to be able to think noble thoughts
on such an occasion, or, if he finds it hard to think
noble thoughts on his own, he ought to have a chance to
recall the lines of Thanatopsis, which are pretty noble,
I think, or something like that.

While I have noticed that death often does give other
people in the vicinity a certain amount of inspiration -
particularly those whose lives are not too intimately tied
up in the deceased - it is apt to be a very distracting
and messy business for the person who is doing the dying
and for those who lose part of their own lives along with
him. The fact that death, in many cases, is preceded by
months or years of physical and mental deterioration adds
to the indignity.

In this case, of course, I didn't die. Moreover, I
managed, I think, to retain a certain amount of dignity,
though not as much as one might wish, and I kept it until
I got to the hospital. There, in spite of my best efforts,
professionals who are highly trained in such techniques,
took most of what I had left away from me.

The pain, at first, was terribly distracting and, when
I realized what was going on inside me, which was within
an hour or so after the commotion started, I supposed
that the odds were pretty much against me - a mistaken
conception, as I was to discover later. So, here I was,
with a Fire Department inhalator over my face, and, so I
thought, on the brink of one of life's greatest ventures.
I was facing for myself the one thing in the world that
has most stirred mankind's imagination, yet has offered
him the least literal verification of his outflung hypotheses. I remember thinking of this, in the split seconds
between cramps, retches, and gasps.

I remember thinking, and being somewhat relieved to
discover, that there was nothing particularly frightening
about it. I even thought about one of the allegorical
tales of Sir Garth, I believe it was, from the Idylls of
the King in which the same theme was expressed, and I
thought to myself how true it was. It might have been
interesting to mention this point to some of the people
close to me, later on when I could talk. But it was a

thought not particularly appropriate to the kind of torture
they were going through and it seemed in rather bad taste
to bring it up at the time. No, there was nothing frightening, as far as I was concerned about the imminent prospect
of dying. Nor was the climactic experience I was having
utterly strange or confused.

I remember thinking, while we were waiting for the
ambulance, that, since this had developed into a nip-and-
tuck affair, I was going to put up the fight of my life.
I felt, strangely enough, that I was ready to put up such
a fight. I had been in a similar spot before, holding on
by my teeth against losing consciousness, and I had won.
Besides, if this was to be my last fight, I wanted it to
be a good one. And I remember thinking, too, that in the
months I might be able to hang on, even if I survived this
first attack, there would probably be some everyday things
to be done in order to make the transition as easy as possible for my family. But this was about as far as my planning went. I was much too involved with immediate matters
to try to go into these speculations in any detail.

Again, let me come back to the theme of this chapter,
which is really the only excuse for talking about these
rather personal matters. Was all this that happened something that was, in some measure, anticipated? Had I seen
them behind my Cousin Leander's mask? Yes, I think so. I
had indeed eavesdropped on myself in this moment many
times before, but had never been clear as to what I saw
going on or as to when it was happening. Perhaps this was
because of Cousin Leander's nearsightedness, or perhaps
his tendency not to be greatly interested in my personal
affairs.

And, another question: Was the experience itself characterized by further anticipations? I think it was that,
too! I have already mentioned my fleeting glimpses of
what the future might be. But there was more of anticipation in the experience than that. Even among the tortured
moments each gasping pain was a preview of the next, telling me what to expect moment by moment, and the contor-
tions into which I twisted myself were as much postures
against the next onslaught as they were reactions to the
last. Nor did I, before undertaking each spasm, have to
reason to myself that the next stab was coming; my prep-
aratory efforts were as spontaneous as life itself. As
life itself!

In general, then, was it not, on the one hand, a passage
of human experience whose strange unprecedented notes
derived significance that early morning from the underlying theme of my life, which they so sharply embellished,
and, on the other, one whose meaning stemmed less from
the repetitive familiarity of its details than from what
it seemed to foretell.

But now I am arguing, I suspect, and this book is not

intended to prove anything; only to be an adventure in
human feelings, one in which I have asked you to join me,
so that, when we are finished, we can each ask the other
where we have been and what we have found out.

So far, in talking about this experience, I have reported only those feelings that had to do with my direct
personal relationship to the events. There were also other
things that crossed my mind. Like those I have already
mentioned, one-half these were experienced both in their
reassuring and in their disquieting dimensions. In fact,
I am not sure I can always tell the difference between
what is reassuring and what is not, or between what is
pleasant and what is not. Such qualities often seem not
to be so much properties of the things that happen as
there are ways of coping with them.

There are some things, I grant, that I would find
terribly difficult to regard as pleasant. The pain I had
was an example. I didn't like that, not one bit! The knack
of enjoying it was an art I had not mastered at all, possibly because I've never really tried. But I am not sure
that there aren't some people who would be delighted by
such misery. I'll go even further; I know that there are
people who are thrilled by such experiences. I have seen
them at it. And, now that I think of it, I can remember
there have been times when I have myself enjoyed sharp
pains, as in playing football, for example. But that was
'sport' and, so far, I have not taken up coronaries as a
form of sport.

As for regarding some of my experiences as intrinsically
disquieting, that, too, is hard to pin down. I have referred to the pain as 'distracting'. It turned my attention away from what I was doing; got me away from this
manuscript for a whole year, as you can see. But this
flat label may be a misnomer. During the months when I
was trying to get caught up with other things, so I could
get back to writing, I thought many times about the discussion in which I was engaged when my work was interrup-
ted. In a sense, then, the effect has been quite the opposite of distraction; instead of being turned from what I
was doing, I have found myself preoccupied with it. Moreover, this is not a reaction against - a turning away
from - the illness, in some sort of counter-play, but
actually a viewing of it in a new perspective. As one can
see, I am now turning out page after page of manuscript,
splashing the events of last year across the outlines of
this chapter. So, as I say, even my cautious adjective,
'distracting', may be too arbitrary a term for what happened.

And as for what is inherently disquieting or reassuring,
or whether the feelings I have described so far were
essentially calm or turbulent; that, too, I cannot set

down definitively. I can talk about those feelings from the standpoint of the calmness I perceived. And, I can talk also about turbulance - as I have, in some degree! But what were the feelings, really? I don't think I can answer that question. And, I think I would be very skeptical of anyone who tried to answer for me.

There are some scholars who make a big to-do about getting down to the genuineness of human experience - the existentialists, for example, whoever they may be (I have never been quite able to identify them). Or, the followers of Carl Rogers who concentrate upon the full acceptance of feelings as they naturally are (these folks are easier to identify)! I can't say I disapprove of such efforts to reach a terminal point in human inquiry; it is only when someone claims to have arrived that I get that restless feeling again.

So now, as I start to talk about the other things I found in the experience - the ones I did not mention in the paragraphs above - I want to enter an advance protest. I still do not know whether the events were of themselves good or bad, painful or pleasant, reassuring or disquieting. All I can do is report what I made of them; that is to say, what I thought, or what I remember thinking. To do this I have to align my perspective along various preconceived axes, else it would be practically impossible to have any sense of ever having been there at all. The dimensions I use are the dimensions I have myself devised, both for description of such events in general and for the fullest possible appreciation of the particular experience itself. Who knows how adequate these terms of reference are! This is what I do about such matters, and the best I can do about this special matter, and probably something of the sort is the best anyone can do in coming to grips with such affairs.

I remember looking at my wife and thinking of the chilling shock she must be experiencing at that moment. Yet there was no outward sign, only an alertness and a quick efficiency, as she turned here and there to do the things that had to be done. It crossed my mind that I was very proud of her, that she was probably stronger than I was accustomed to give her credit for being, and that there are great resources in the human personality which one can easily overlook in day-by-day casual living. But there, inside, there was none-the-less the icy grip of reality; I knew that for sure, in spite of all the resources she might be mobilizing against it. And there I was, sprawled and twisting on the bed, making a shameful spectacle of myself, and, moment by moment, making matters all the worse for her. All these were scarcely more than fleeting thoughts, of course.

There was also a dimension of reprehensibility that ran through these feelings. That is to say, I could not

escape thinking that I was responsible for the mess we
all were in. If I had listened to the experts and heeded
their dire warnings, I might have been able to live the
life of a healthy organism. In that case, I would have
been waking up just about then, bouncing into a cold
shower, eating a hearty but leisurely breakfast of prunes
and yoghurt, and getting ready for a snappy day at the
office, during which I would delegate responsibility right
and left, make clear-cut simple-minded decisions, clear
my desk promptly, and - with never a backward glance at
the inanities I had perpetrated - arrive on time for three
o'clock golf, followed by an inspirational dinner meeting
on the subject of 'Why isn't *everybody* smart and successful'. I cannot say that I thought in exactly these terms,
but this was the gist of it.

While I felt uncomfortably responsible for the confused
state of affairs into which it appeared I had plunged us
all, I remember I still felt rebellious against doing the
things that people say would have avoided it. So, not only
did I feel ashamed, responsible, and stupid; I also felt
unrepentant. And, then a whole new round of thought threatened to start; I was beginning to feel ashamed of being
unrepentant. As long as I was on this track, I was caught
between being a virtuous vegetable and an independent
corpse. Stretched out along this axis of appraisal - this
yardstick - I found myself confused, disorganised, put
upon, and, as if I were trying to go two ways at once.

Now let's have no misunderstanding about this. I know
perfectly well, and I knew then, that the way to avoid
this kind of feeling is to conform to some ready-made
doctrine. And if you get caught and find that you have
already slipped up, you start kicking yourself in the
shins and make some special display of your eagerness to
conform. In some cultures this is called 'repentence', in
others, 'self-criticism'. Of course, nobody claims that
self-abnegation will keep unpleasant things from happening to you - well, *almost* nobody these days - but there
is ample evidence to indicate that it keeps you from being
upset over the messes you stumble into.

There are still other people who take the view that the
sort of confusion I experienced at this point constitutes
bed-rock realistic thinking. Things actually are in a
mess - all over - everywhere! They say we are all inclined
to ignore the trouble we are in and we go blithely about
making it worse by engaging in such diversions as watching TV, whistling, dressing up to go places, and being
polite to each other. Finally, when we are all alone and
it is too late to do anything about it, there is nothing
left to do but look at the nightmare that has been shad-
owing the backs of our minds all the time.

To subscribe to this kind of notion takes a bit of
preliminary thinking. You have to start out by assuming

that the stark naked truth of man's existence is to be
seen just by turning around and looking at it. We just
open our eyes, stare in the right direction, and the whole
thing stands there perfectly clear. You don't understand
things by experimenting with interpretations of them -
you understand them directly, by confronting them. Just
around the corner of your facade you can face up to what's
what.

Well, this is one way to go at it. When we start out
with such a notion in mind, it happens that each time we
turn a corner and see something rather grim we are likely
to think, 'This is it. We have arrived. This is the end'.
Still, there always seem to be more corners to turn and a
starker nakeder truth that someone claims to have glimpsed
in the dusk just ahead. It's awfully hard to settle on
something grim enough to suit everybody.

So, while I was quite miserable, in some ways, about
the goings-on that Friday morning, I was not then, nor am
I now, convinced that I was face to face with the ultimate
meaning of my life - or even very close to it, for that
matter. Almost anybody - certainly any of my readers -
could think up something a great deal more stark than
what I have described. As a matter of fact, if I may address myself to you personally, haven't you already done
so while reading this? As for me, if there was a nightmare catching up with me, I was well aware that it was
the one I had personally manufactured and not the ultimate
logos.

It seems to me that it must make a considerable difference whether one assumes that the ultimate facts of life
are close at hand or that there are vast remote truths
towards which we progress but slowly. The former view often
seems quite practical - quite workable. You figure something out, and you believe it's there, and you believe in
it, and you cling to it, and its everyday workability
seems to support your feeling of having hit upon something
solid. Like money, for example: there are so many things
you can do with money, and, day after day, quite consistently, money gets results. So most of us put a lot of
faith in it. Moreover, if we were smart enough, we could
probably do a good deal more with money than we do.

But now consider the latter view, the view that there
are vast remote truths towards which we progress but slowly. That is the kind of outlook that can encourage mysticism. You are always expecting tomorrow to be different,
and you get fooled because it turns out to be the same,
thousands of times in succession. Pretty soon you begin
to look like an utter nincompoop. So you go through life
half believing that anything is possible, no matter how
unlikely it may be.

If every day were under a firm contract to duplicate
every other day the bed rock realism of the former view

should be the more comfortable of the two. The vast majority of one's days are indeed pretty much alike - at least
we can get by by construing them so - just as the Sunday
night about which I speculated in the first part of this
chapter could be interpreted as pretty much like any other
Sunday night. I wrote a remark - which I intend to retain
in the manuscript - about this on Monday, the day my muse
was packing up to leave. Having experienced a good many
thousand of such everyday appearing days I suppose one
could hardly blame himself for concluding that he had a
pretty realistic slant on life.

But then you come to a day, just one day out of all the
thousands, that does not fit the realistic way you cross
off your calendar. Perhaps it is the day you die. Then,
then if you try to cope with that day as just another
Sunday night, or Friday morning, you may very well get
the impression that you have been missing the truth of
things and it is too late to do anything about it.

So, I lay there, that one day that was different from
the thousands I had known before, that Friday morning,
and I felt twinges of anguish. The anguish was a mixture
of things: the ambiguity of my being - future, past, and
present - the disarray in the orderliness of mind and
body I had come to rely upon, and the unspeakable loneliness of guilt which threatened to cut me off from those
closest to me. In fact, I suspect if I had been a very
practical or exacting idealist I would have felt that
truth had played me false, and, from that point on, the
whole thing would have gotten badly out of hand. ('Practical Idealist!' No incompatibility of terms here, if we
take the view that an idealist is anyone who carries a
clear image of perfection around in his head!)

But, even in those moments, I could not honestly believe
that truth had played me false simply because I can't take
truth very literally. Of course, I believe in truth, believe in it very deeply, but not literally like some
people who hold up a book and say, 'This is it, the only
infallible rule of faith and practice', or who intone
some sonorous phrase, loaded with seventeen incompatible
implications, and then say, 'Ah!' or 'Amen!' or 'Court's
adjourned!' Why don't they say instead, 'This is the story
of men's quest of God. As you can see, they haven't got
very far. But it's a better guide to our further quests
than the pronouncements of any one man, no matter how
devout he may be'. Or, at least they could say, 'Ah, there
must be more there than I can understand; I'll go home
and think it over'. Or, when they rap the gavel, instead
of saying, 'Court's adjourned!' why don't they say, 'Sorry!
That's the best we can do today!'

Now that I think of it, I have never staked my existence wholly on the practical 'facts of life', though I
have repeatedly told myself that I should. But how can

one spend his whole life, the one and only life that is
given him, taking notes on things as they are, without
once using his pencil to make a little sketch in the margin
depicting things as they might be. Must we always pretend
that truth is only what is? Even on the one day, the one
that is different from the thousands before, must we still
pretend that?

All I need to say about keeping my anguish from envelop-
ing me with practical disruptions is that I am not very
practical anyway, and what idealism I carried over from
my youth still tends to be vaguely wistful and inexact.
I have never known beforehand precisely what I wanted or
what I wanted to be, unless it was to be so many things
that I could not decide what to eliminate. But this lack
of singular purpose does not mean I have altogether failed
to strive for what generally seemed worthwhile, or that
I did not, in the erratic course of this striving, often
find myself sitting with my arms around the very thing I
wanted most. Moreover, a gratifying proportion of this
striving I have managed, with a few annoying distortions
here and there, to piece together into a vocation - a
stroke of good fortune, in this vocation-oriented society
of ours, for which I frequently have feelings of profound
gratitude and amazement.

I hope, for Heaven's sake, it is clear that I am talking about my own experiences here, and not presuming to
utter some basic truth about how your life can be made to
conform to your most cherished expectations, or how your
expectations can be stretched to conform to your life.
You will have to figure out for yourself how to do that;
although what I have written may suggest either ways to
go about it or inadvertencies you will want to avoid.
Besides, there are plenty of occasions when I find myself
in circumstances I have not bargained for, and, while in
retrospect I am often able to speculate on where I have
made my mistakes, there are many outcomes that still have
me bamboozled. So, don't take my medicine unless you want
my headaches, too.

I must tell you, too, that as far as I can see, things
do not turn out in others' lives the way they have in mine.
To be sure, most people do not approach life the way I do,
but, even if they did, there is nothing to guarantee that
their experiences would add up the same way. There are
some people, for example, who have had a very bad time of
it - altogether too many people! And, of these, there are
those who are overwhelmed and there are those who write
successful books about their misfortunes and then contrive
to repeat the inspirational cycle. Each person has his
own entanglements and it is often convenient for him to
preserve them. I know this. Among those who have spent
long periods in psychotherapy with me, the cherished in-
tricacies are vastly different, and one has to rise to

very high levels of abstraction, indeed, if he is to formulate any simple over-arching principles that can be regarded, even tentatively, as inevitably governing all
men's lives.

But, it is still Friday morning. I remember the faces
of our daughter and son. There was deep concern there,
but not, as far as I could see, any sign of panic. My job
was cut out for me; it was to survive, if I could. But
what were they to do? They could not help but be aware,
even in that first hour, of the difficulties that my death
would plunge them into. How well had I managed to fore-
stall those difficulties? Not very well!

There were a thousand and one thoughts, intangible,
important, that I had long imagined myself sharing with
them, but always these had seemed to require a more pro-
pitious moment. So, not only was I lying there in a most
unfatherly exhibition of helplessness that must give them
none of the sense of security that children have a right
to expect of a father in times of emergency, not only was
I at the point of leaving them without having properly
planned for their future, but I was about to be cut off
from the last hope of ever saying to them what was always
in my heart. I felt all this, not in sentences, as it is
written down here, but altogether in one choking lump.

Then, there was this thought; it was a separate thought,
I believe: Here I was creating additional strain for our
pregnant daughter who, with her husband serving overseas,
was already under too much stress. And I thought of our
first grandchild, expected in a few weeks, whom I might
never see, and to whom I might never tell the wonderful
stories that all grandchildren should hear.

There were other moments, when I looked at our son and
realized how like him it would be to try to sacrifice his
own opportunities to make life easier for his widowed
mother. He would undertake the sacrifices I had failed
to make.

It occurred to me, too, how families always feel guilty
when one of them dies, and everyone is inwardly depressed
because he remembers how badly he treated the deceased.
I know how terrible the pain of this kind of guilt can
be, and how much one appreciates some sort of timely reassurance. So, I wanted to reassure the three members of
my family standing there - to tell them how perfectly
wonderful they had been. But how could I say that, without
dramatizing a 'death-bed' scene! So I thought the better
of it and kept my mouth shut. Besides, the doctor and the
Emergency Squad people were standing around, and it was
strictly none of their business.

The cruelest clutch of all came during those moments
when I thought of the window's loneliness I might be bringing down on my wife. There seemed to be nothing I could
do about this except to try desperately to stay alive.

How does this business of human relationships work out?
With one person you share too little, and when you go you
leave in his memory only the shreds of the legacy he might
have had; with another, you share too much, and when you
go you leave in his memory altogether too great an emptiness.

There were other thoughts during this day that was like
no other, many that do not lend themselves to words, and
many too intimate to mention here. What I have said ought
to be enough to indicate how, on such a day, things can
become a bit messy, and may even fall apart completely if
there is nothing to stop them. In my case, there was one
thing that helped immensely - I didn't die. So that is
something that comes later! But no matter; it seems clear
now that death was not itself the bugaboo I faced. The
pain: that was to be taken more seriously, and I must say
it occupied a lot of my attention. But pain is not the
worst; it can be helped, and, in my case, it soon was.

What is not so easy to help is the failure of those
'truths' that have served to make so many thousands of
days turn out as expected. We believe them because how
else is one to know what is really so, or how else to
bridge the chasm between past and future over which we
always find ourselves suspended, how else to find continuity and thus to live. These 'truths' - they can be little
tick-tock-tick-tock truths that keep repeating themselves
in the corner - and always so impersonal about what is
going on that you don't mind having them around - or they
can be big round shining truths - brittle as all perfect
things must be - that roll along majestically until they
crash against the day that was not meant for them, and
leave you with nothing but their fragments, a litter of
words - leave you shattered too.

I suppose one solution is to forge bigger, rounder,
fuller truths - really perfect truths this time, or, if
not perfect, so hard they will not be shattered by the
crash of single events. Then, when that one day comes
along, we can simply regard it as an exception to the rule,
a statistical improbability, or, if it is something nice,
as a miracle. The trouble with this is that once you come
face to face with this pesky statistical improbability you
have to be an awfully fast talker to keep yourself convinced that it is not genuine. But then, some of us are
awfully fast talkers, and quite ready to believe something
does not exist if we keep telling ourselves it is not there.

But how about grasping the perfect incontrovertible
truth, the frozen ultimate, the knowledge of the way things
really *really* are; would not that end the confusion of
having something happen unexpectedly, end it once and for
all? With such knowledge in our possession nothing could
possibly occur unexpectedly and our lives would be lived
out perfectly in peaceful contemplation of what was coming

next.

   This, it seems to me, is like a man teetering on what
he thinks is the edge of the universe and daring anyone
to push him off. He feels perfectly safe because he thinks
he knows what is what and there is obviously no such thing
as ever going beyond the limits of reality. Still, occasionally he makes a pretense of looking over the edge, just
for laughs, and he says, 'See, there really isn't anything
there - just a lot of nonsense'. Then, out of the corner
of his eye he does catch a glimpse of something moving out
there in the nothing; at first, perhaps, no more than the
shadows of his own imagination. All night long he wonders
what is the perfect truth about them, how much further out
their limits lie. So he secretly tests these shadows, tries
to see if he can make them move. Soon he is working with
his hands.

   In time, there arise out there in the nowhere whole new
cities, built outside the walls against which he once
leaned so confidently. Now his world is different. Now
his once 'perfect' truths tell him what he can see is not
so, and, faithful as he may try to be, he can offer no
more than lip service to them. Now, each time he looks up
from his work and peers beyond his latest achievement, he
wonders who he is to have imagined such things, and what
he is doing, and he shudders to think how much of his life
was spent behind the old barriers, or what unseen walls
may imprison him now. And then he wonders more; to what
destinies has he been false - and why has the evening
grown so late?

   This tail-spin of thinking starts as all tail-spins
do, from the stall that occurs when one tries to stand
still in mid-flight. From the moment we assume that truth
is a stationary achievement, rather than a stage in a
lively quest, it is only a matter of time until things
start spinning round and round. Truth is neither reality
nor phantasy. It needs to be understood, instead, as a
continually emerging relationship between reality and
ingenuity, and thus never something that can be skewered
by a phrase, a moment, or a place. But can man ever trust
himself aloft to such aerodynamics? Will he ever be able
to get his mind off the ground and fly?

   I looked at my family that morning and it occurred to
me that if I had wished for the most wonderful thing in
the world to happen it would turn out to be just such a
family. And I realized that while life had given me only
a small proportion of all the miscellany I had, at one
time or another, grasped for, it had generally ended up
supplying me with the very best that could be managed
under the circumstances, better than anything I could
claim to have deserved.

   There is a certain injustice in this kind of outcome.

Perhaps it would be more just for all of us to get exactly
what we demand; it might serve us right. This is a familiar theme that runs through our folklore. The moral usually
drawn is that we should not reach for anything at all,
that we should sit around waiting patiently for our just
reward. I must confess that I do not find the idea of living in a community of such deserving people very attractive. We would all be trying to out-deserve each other,
and such a public exhibition of deservingness could become obnoxiously unctious. What a way to live!

But, anyway, this is not the way things are. Instead,
the world is filled with injustices, heart-rendering injustices for the weak, disgusting injustices for the strong.
Added to these are a lot of outcomes that are hard to
appraise one way or the other, for our notions about what
constitutes justice, and whose job it is to see that it
happens, are still pretty foggy. I suppose we are inclined
to think that justice is something to be dispensed by
Providence or by incorruptible public officials, rather
than something that has to be figured out by all of us.
Thus, we tend to regard it like truth, something all packaged, rather than something continually in the process of
definition.

I suppose I could have treated this undeserved reward
so closely gathered around me as an insult to my sense of
true justice, and only further evidence that the world
was badly managed. Or, I could have held on to my proper
misery by claiming that the reward was illusory, that
only a little family-bound parochial mind would describe
these three dimwitted anthropoids as 'wonderful'. Thus
my Olympian sense of pure and perfect justice could be
kept intact, along with any long-standing complaints I
might have against God and man for their loose administra-
tion of such important matters.

None of this occurred to me that morning. What did
occur to me was that it was a shame to waste these precious
moments in self-recrimination when there before me was the
best that a man could want, and that simply their being
the kind of persons they were was the best of all the
things I could have wished for them. Whatever else I might
have provided, none would have been as valuable as what
they already possessed. Whether all this was a reward
intended for me, or whether it was deserved by me was
quite beside the point. If there was anything tragic about
my state that morning, it was my momentary failure to see
what was there before my very eyes. This is what I thought.

But what about my own reprehensibility? Did the fact
that I felt rewarded prove I was any less guilty? Of
course not! It was just as clear as ever that the role
I had enacted in life was not all it should have been.
How smug would I have had to be to claim otherwise! Certainly the more one scrutinizes his relations with his

fellow-man, the more he should be able to find wrong with
them. And the more he tinkers with those relationships to
make them better, the more practical faults will turn up.
So, it seems to me that a sense of wrong-doing is what
inevitably results from examining yourself and from making
efforts to do better.

Perhaps if one only sits around and rationalizes, he
may be able to set his house in apparent order, and keep
it that way. But that assumes that he neither examines the
facts critically nor experiments with improvements. Once
one starts experimenting, the bugs, as they say in manufacturing circles, are bound to show up. The more you try
to do right, the more you find wrong with yourself.

One way to assuage those horrible guilt feelings is to
regard a mistake as something to be punished rather than
an occasion for revision of outlook. This tends to keep
you from experimenting and hence from discovering new
faults. Such a view helps one stabilize himself, and, of
course, keeps him from making any genuine progress.

Closely allied with this view is the belief that a mistake is any deviation from the blueprint that has been
laid down for us. All one has to do, then, to slough off
the guilt is to get himself punished and thereafter keep
his finger more firmly on the blueprint. This is the view
a lot of people take toward sin, and it seems pretty superficial to me. To be frank about it, punishment and conformity usually work even harder for the perpetuation of
evil than for the achievement of goodness.

There are philosophers who agree that punishment and
conformity are not a cure for sin. That is good. So they
try to figure out what has gone wrong. That is good, too.
The more they think about it the more of a clutter they
discover in man's affairs. Naturally! But there they stop
the enterprise and start caterwauling. They generate a lot
of anguish in themselves, they are overwhelmed by their
guilt feelings, and they are often furiously angry at anyone who refuses to share their misery.

Suppose one takes the rather practical view that a mistake - or sin, if the point is to be made more dramatically
- is something to be examined and corrected. This is what
I think repentence means; but, then, most people don't
agree with me. Once you do this, you start turning up new
complexities, old values become shaky, new values begin
to shape themselves, and you find that you have been making a host of blunders that you had never recognized before. Moreover, the simple perfections on which you used
to pin your faith begin to look brutally primitive.

So far, there is really nothing dangerous about this
line of inference. But if you lose sight of your objective
at this point, and start telling yourself that punishment
is the cure for all these freshly revealed mistakes, and
that you are not fit to belong to society, then you are

immediately in trouble - deep trouble. So there is a real hazard in examining your mistakes, unless you keep firmly in mind that the sole object is to provide grounds for trying out better ways of doing your part. The sense of guilt, then, can be harmful or helpful, depending upon what we think should be done about it.

So when I looked up at the faces so dear to me and mustered sense enough to recognize what had really happened in spite of my shortcomings, I felt a great surge of reassurance. The moment is still very clear to me. As for my feelings of inadequacy, of wrong-doing, or of sin, it became clear that they were important to me only if I lived to do something about them.

It occurred to me, also, that most people were wise enough not to expect me to be perfect, that I had myself long since outgrown such an exalted image of my destiny, and even if I did make a flat-out attempt at here-and-now perfection, I would probably stiffen up into just as foolish a posture as have the other people I have seen make that attempt. Besides, I still could not put my finger on where all my mistakes had been - mostly I knew only where I had deviated from convention - or whether all of them had actually been mistakes; nor did I know what could readily be done even if they had been mistakes. Naturally, I had some clues, here and there, but, in the main, these were questions it would take years to work out, and, if I did well with them, they would be followed by further, more perspicacious questions.

So that was that! It was at this point in the proceedings that I found myself free to go single-mindedly about the immediate task of surviving and trying to restore to my family whatever composure my antics had destroyed.

Taken altogether, what happened that week at the beginning of which I asked you to join me in imagining what it would be like to look in on our tomorrows? I don't know what happened to you, but one thing for sure, a lot of me was thrown into disarray - my insides, my orientation toward my surroundings, the enactment of my role as a responsible person, and, to some extent, my dynamic and delicately balanced status as a human being. My insides could not get into step with my heart, my mind could not pace itself to the successive moments that tumbled down on me, my pattern of life failed to lead up smoothly to the new turns of events, and, to make a long story short, the whole system of anticipations - who expects what to happen when - got badly mixed up. The zigs stopped matching the zags.

Depending on the level at which we focus attention on this confusion, we can call it 'pain', 'anxiety', 'guilt', or - if you prefer an up-to-date soul-shaking term for chaos - call it 'anguish'. But the anxiety was not as devastating as I suspect it might have been if I had not,

in some generaly way, already envisioned such a state of
affairs. I had indeed eavesdropped on this moment, and I
was not altogether without some notion of how things might
be managed.

The part of the experience that more particularly might
be called 'guilt' - the sense of loss of role, the failure
to live up to my own expectations in relation to those
closest to me - was the most difficult part to get hold of.
It was to abate only when I looked more carefully at what
was there in front of me and when I was to realize that
guilt feelings are for the person who has some time to do
something about them.

Q. And what do I now think of the whole incident?
A. I can't say that I liked it.
Q. So?
A. I wonder what will happen next week.
Q. Haven't I learned not to wonder about such things?
A. Oh, No! Quite the contrary!
Q. But won't speculation about them tend to make them
   happen?
A. Perhaps, but I insist on having some continuity in
   my life.
Q. What am I going to write about next?
A. Joy and depression.
Q. Is that to be based on experience too?
A. I don't know - yet!

REFERENCES

Aaronson, B.S. (1968). *American Journal of Clinical Hypnosis* **10**, 160-166.

Adams, J., Hayes, J. and Hopson, B. (1976). Transition: Understanding and Managing Personal Change. Robertson, London.

Adams, M. and Moore, W.H. (1972). *Journal of Speech and Hearing Research* **15**, 572-578.

Adams-Webber, J. (1970). *In: Perspectives in Personal Construct Theory* (ed. Bannister, D.), Academic Press, London.

Ainsworth, S. (1945). *Journal of Speech Disorders* **10**, 205-210.

Argyris, C. (1975). Adult Learning and Leadership Education. Harvard University Press.

Argyris, C. and Schon, D. (1974). Theory in Practice. Jossey-Bass, New York.

Bakan, D. (1967). On Method. Jossey-Bass, San Francisco.

Bannister, D. and Fransella, F. (1971). Inquiring Man. Penguin Books, Harmondsworth.

Barker-Lunn, J.C. (1970). Streaming in the Primary School. National Federation of Educational Research, London.

Bartlett, F.C. (1932). Remembering. Cambridge University Press.

Bartlett, F.C. (1958). Thinking: an experimental and social study. Basic Books, New York.

Beech, H.R. and Fransella, F. (1968). Research and Experiment in Stuttering. Pergamon Press, Oxford.

Bergson, H. (1910). Time and Free Will: an essay on the immediate data of consciousness. Macmillan, New York.

Berlinsky, S.L. (1955). *Speech Monographs* **22**, 197.

Bernstein, B. (1961). *In: Education, Economy and Society* (ed. Helsey, A.H., Floud, J. and Anderson, A.C.), Free Press of Glencoe.

Berry, M.F. (1938). *Journal of Pediatrics* **12**, 209-217.

Biggs, B.E. and Sheehan, J.G. (1969). *Journal of Abnormal Psychology* **74**, 256-262.

Biggs, J.B. (1976). *Contemporary Educational Psychology* **1**, 274-284.

Blanton, S. (1930). *Proceedings of the American Speech Correction Association* **1**, 70-73.

Bloodstein, O. (1975). *In: Stuttering: a second symposium* (ed. Eisenson, J.), Harper and Row, New York.

Bloodstein, O. (1975a). A Handbook on Stuttering: revised edition. National Easter Seal Society for Crippled Children and Adults, Chicago.

Bloodstein, O. and Shogan, R.L. (1972). *Journal of Speech and Hearing Disorders* **37**, 177.186.

Boland, J.L. (1953). *Speech Monographs* **20**, 144.

Bolton, D. (1975). Proceedings of the Annual Conference of the British Psychological Society, Nottingham.

Bonarius, J. (1965). *In: Progress in Experimental Personality Research,* Vol. 2 (ed. Maher, B.A.), Academic Press, New York.

Bradley, F.H. (1883). The Principles of Logic. Routledge and Kegan Paul, London.

Brown, G.W., Bhrolchain, M. and Harris, T. (1975). *Sociology,* **9**, 225-254.

Brown, P. (1974). Towards a Marxist Psychology. Harper Colophon Books, New York.

Brutten, E.J. (1963). *Journal of Speech and Hearing Research* **6**, 40-48.

Buhler, C. (1971). *American Psychologist* **26**, 378-386.

Bullock, Sir A. (Ch.) (1975). A Language for Life. Her Majesty's Stationery Office, London.

Burleson, D.E. (1949). M.Sc. dissertation, University of Pittsburgh.

Carlson, J.J. (1946). *American Journal of Orthopsychiatry* **16**, 120-126.

Castaneda, C. (1968). The Teachings of Don Juan. University of California Press.

Cole, J.K. (ed.) (1976). Nebraska Symposium on Motivation 1975: Conceptual foundation of psychology, Vol. 23 University of Nebraska Press, Lincoln.

Conture, E.G. and Brayton, E.R. (1975). *Journal of Speech and Hearing Research* **18**, 381-384.

Cooper, E.B., Cady, B.B. and Robbins, C.J. (1970). *Journal of Speech and Hearing Research* **13**, 239-244.

Coriat, I. (1943). *The Nervous Child* **2**, 167-171.

Cornford, F.M. (1970). *In: Plato's Theory of Knowledge.* Routledge and Kegan Paul, London.

Corsini, R.J. (1966). Roleplaying in Psychotherapy: a manual. Aldine, Chicago.

Crockett, W.H. (1965). *In: Progress in Experimental Personality Research,* Vol. 2 (ed. Maher, B.A.), Academic Press, New York.

Dearden, R.F. (1972). *In: The Integrated Day in Theory and Practice* (ed. Walton, J.), Ward Lock Education, New York.

Deiffenbach, J.F. (1841). Die Heilung des Stotterns durch eine neue Chirugishche Operation, eine Sendschreiben an das Institut von Frankrech. A. Forstner, Berlin.

Dewey, J. (1884). *Andover Review,* 278-289.

Dreyfus, H.L. (1971). *Nous* **5**, 81-96.

Duncker, K. (1945). *Psychological Monographs* **58**, Whole No. 270.

Engels, F. (1888). Ludwig Feuerbach and the end of Classical German Philosophy. Progress Publishers, Moscow. English translation 1946.

Feuerbach, L. (1843). Principles of the Philosophy of the Future. Translated by M. Vogel (1966). Bobbs-Merrill, New York.

Flanagan, B., Goldiamond, L. and Azrin, N.H. (1958). *Journal of Experimental Analysis of Behavior* **1**, 173-177.

Flatten, Ø. (1965). *In: Referat fra. 8. psykoterapiseminar pa Modum Bads Nervesanatorium* 9-11. September 1965. *Mimeographed,* Modum Bads Nervesanatorium, Norway. Pp. 79-88.

Frankl, V.E. (1960). *American Journal of Psychotherapy* **14**, 520-535.

Frankl, V.E. (1969). The Will to Meaning. World Publishing, New York.

Frankl, V.E. (1973). Psychotherapy and Existentialism. Penguin Books,

Harmondsworth.

Frankl, V.E. (1975). *Psychotherapy: Theory, Research and Practice* **12**, 226-237.

Fransella, F. (1968). *British Journal of Psychiatry* **114**, 1531-1535.

Fransella, F. (1972). Personal Change and Reconstruction: research on a treatment of stuttering. Academic Press, London.

Fransella, F. (1977). *In: New Perspectives in Personal Construct Theory* (ed. Bannister, D.), Academic Press, London.

Freud, S. (1909). *In: Standard Edition of the Complete Psychological Works of Sigmund Freud* **10**, 151-318. Hogarth Press and the Institute of Psycho-analysis, London.

Friedlander, F. (1968). *In: The Research Society* (ed. Glatt, E. and Shelley, M.W.), Gordon and Breach, New York.

Gadelius, B. (1896). Om Tvangstankar och dermed Beslagtade Fenomen. Malmstrøms, Lund.

Galton, F. (1883). Inquiries into Human Faculty and its Development. Macmillan, London.

Giorgi, A. (1970). Psychology as a Human Science. Harper and Row, New York.

Giorgi, A. (1976). *In: Nebraska Symposium on Motivation 1975: Conceptual foundation of psychology* Vol. 23 (ed. Cole, J.K.), University of Nebraska Press, Lincoln.

Giorgi, A., Fischer, C.I. and Murray, E. (eds). (1975). Duquesne Studies in Phenomenological Psychology II. Duquesne University Press, Pittsburgh.

Glauber, I.P. (1958). *In: Stuttering: a symposium* (ed. Eisenson, J.), Harper and Row, New York.

Goffman, E. (1971). The Presentation of Self in Everday Life. Pelican Books, Harmondsworth.

Goldman-Eisler, F. (1958). *Quarterly Journal of Experimental Psychology* **10**, 96-106.

Goldman-Eisler, F. (1968). Psycholinguistics: experiments in spontaneous speech. Academic Press, London.

Gordon, C. (1969). *Journal of Nervous and Mental Disorders* **118**, 350.

Habermas, J. (1973). Theory and Practice. Beacon Press, Boston.

Hahn, L.E. (1972). *Philosophy Forum* **11**, 3-39.

Haley, J. (1973). Uncommon Therapy. Ballantine, New York.

Ham, R. and Steer, M.D. (1967). *Folia Phoniatrica* **19**, 53-62.

Harre, R. and Secord, P.F. (1972). The Explanation of Social Behaviour. Blackwell, Oxford.

Harri-Augstein, S. and Thomas, L.F. (1975). Towards a Theory of Learning Conversation and a Paradigm for Conversational Research. Centre for the Study of Human Learning Publications, Brunel University.

Heather, N. (1976). Radical Perspectives in Psychology. Methuen Essential Psychology Books, London.

Hinkle, D.N. (1965). Unpublished doctoral dissertation, Ohio State University.

Holland, R. (1970). *In: Perspectives in Personal Construct Theory* (ed. Bannister, D.), Academic Press, London.

Hollingshead, A.B. and Redlich, F.C. (1958). Social Class and Mental Illness: a community study. Wiley, New York.

Horney, K. (1945). Our Inner Conflicts. Norton, New York.

Hunt, J.McV. (1965). *In: Nebraska Symposium on Motivation* Vol. 13 (ed. Levine, D.), University of Nebraska Press, Lincoln.

Huttenlocher, J. and Presson, C.C. (1973). *Cognitive Psychology* **4**, 277-299.

Illich, I.D. (1971). Deschooling Society. Penguin Books, Harmondsworth.

Illich, I.D. (1973). Celebration of Awareness. Penguin Books, Harmondsworth.

Jenkins, J.J. (1974). *American Psychologist* **29**, 785-795.

Kahneman, D. (1973). Attention and Effort. Prentice-Hall, Englewood Cliffs.

Kelly, G.A. (1955). The Psychology of Personal Constructs Vols. I and II. Norton, New York.

Kelly, G.A. (1958). *In: Assessment of Human Motives* (ed. Lindzey, G.), Rinehart, New York.

Kelly, G.A. (1969). *In: Clinical Psychology and Personality: The selected papers of George Kelly* (ed. Maher, B.A.), Wiley, New York.

Kelly, G.A. (1969a). *In: Clinical Psychology and Personality: The selected papers of George Kelly* (ed. Maher, B.A.), Wiley, New York.

Kelly, G.A. (1969b). *In: Clinical Psychology and Personality: The selected papers of George Kelly* (ed. Maher, B.A.), Wiley, New York.

Kelly, G.A. (1969c). *In: Clinical Psychology and Personality: The selected papers of George Kelly* (ed. Maher, B.A.), Wiley, New York.

Kelly, G.A. (1970). *In: Perspectives in Personal Construct Theory* (ed. Bannister, D.), Academic Press, London.

Kelly, G.A. (1970a). *In: Perspectives in Personal Construct Theory* (ed. Bannister, D.), Academic Press, London.

Koch, S. (1964). *In: Behaviorism and Phenomenology* (ed. Wann, T.W.), University of Chicago Press.

Koch, S. (1969). *Psychology Today* **3**, 64-68.

Kuhn, T.S. (1970). The Structure of Scientific Revolution (2nd edition). University of Chicago Press.

Kvilhaug, B. (1965). *In: Referat fra 8. psykoterapiseminar pa Modum Bads Nervesanatorium 9-11*. September 1965. *Mimeographed* Modum Bads Nervesanatorium, Norway. Pp. 39-53.

Laing, R.D. (1970). Knots. Penguin Books, Harmondsworth.

Lakatos, I. (1970). *In: Criticism and the Growth of Knowledge* (ed. Lakatos, I. and Musgrave, A.), Cambridge University Press.

Landfield, A. (1977). Personal construct theory correspondence and reference list. University of Nebraska, Lincoln.

Lazarus, A.A. (1971). Behaviour Therapy and Beyond. McGraw-Hill, New York.

Levi-Strauss, C. (1962). Totemism. Penguin Books, Harmondsworth.

Livesly, W.J. and Bromley, D.B. (1973). Person Perception in Childhood and Adolescence. Wiley, London.

Loveday, T. and Forster, E.S. (1913). *In: The Works of Aristotle* Vol. VI 804b, 26-31 (ed. Ross, W.D.), Clarendon Press, Oxford.

Mair, J.M.M. (1977). *In: New Perspectives in Personal Construct Theory* (ed. Bannister, D.), Academic Press, London.

Mair, J.M.M. (1977a). *In: Nebraska Symposium on Motivation 1976* Vol. 24 (ed. Landfield, A.W.), University of Nebraska Press, Lincoln.

Maklouf-Norris, F. and Norris, H. (1972). *British Journal of Psychiatry*

121, 277-288.

Mancuso, J.C. (1974). Some comments on some recent publications. Unpublished manuscript. State University of New York at Albany.

Mancuso, J.C. (1977). *In: Nebraska Symposium on Motivation 1976* Vol. 24 (ed. Landfield, A.W.), University of Nebraska Press, Lincoln.

Mangham, I.L. (1978). Interactions, Organizations and Interventions. Wiley, New York (in press).

Martin, R.R. and Siegel, G.M. (1966). *Journal of Speech and Hearing Research* **9**, 340-352.

Martin, R.R. and Siegel, G.M. (1966a). *Journal of Speech and Hearing Research* **9**, 466-475.

Maruyama, M. (1969). *Dialectica* **23**, 229-280.

Marx, K. (1845). Theses on Feuerbach. Progress Publishers, Moscow.

McCoy, M.M. (1977). *In: New Perspectives in Personal Construct Theory* (ed. Bannister, D.), Academic Press, London.

McLeish, J. (1970). Student Attitudes and College Environments. Heffer, Cambridge.

Mednick, M.T. and Weismann, H.J. (1975). *Annual Review of Psychology* **26**, 1.

Meeuwen, R.V. (1977). Personal communication.

Meichenbaum, D. (1974). *In: Behavioral Approaches to Therapy* (ed. Spence, J., Carson, R. and Thibaut, J.), General Learning Press, New Jersey.

Mendelsohn, M. (1975). *Behaviorism* **3**, 117-119.

Meshoulam, U. (1977). Unpublished Ph.D. dissertation, State University of New York at Albany.

Miller, G.A., Galanter, E. and Pribam, K.H. (1960). Plans and the Structure of Behavior. Holt. New York.

Morris, B. (1972). Objectives and Perspectives in Education: studies in educational theory 1955-70. Routledge and Kegan Paul, New York.

Morrison, A. and McIntyre, D. (1974). Teachers and Teaching (2nd edition). Penguin Books, Harmondsworth.

Murphy, A.T. and Fitzsimons, R.M. (1960). Stuttering and Personality Dynamics. Ronald Press, New York.

Nash, R. (1973). Classrooms Observed. Routledge and Kegan Paul, New York.

Osgood, C.E., Suci, G.J. and Tannenbaum, P.H. (1957). The Measurement of Meaning. Univeristy of Illinois Press, Urbana.

Øst, L.G. (1974). Unpublished manuscript, Forskningskliniken pa Ullerakers Sjukhus, Uppsala.

Østerberg, D. (1966). Forstaelsesformer. Pax, Oslo.

Pask, G., Scott, B.C.E. and Kallikourdis, D. (1973). *International Journal of Man-Machine Studies* **5**, 443-566.

Pearce, J.C. (1971). The Crack in the Cosmic Egg. Julian Press, New York.

Pepper, S.C. (1948). World Hypotheses. University of California Press, Berkeley.

Perkins, W. (1970). *In: Stuttering: research and therapy* (ed. Sheehan, J.G.), Harper and Row, New York.

Perls, F.S. (1969). In and Out the Garbage Pail. Real People Press, Moab, Utah.

Perry, W.G. (1959). *In: Reading: Today and Tomorrow* (ed. Melnik, A.

and Merritt, J.), University of London Press.

Perry, W.R. (1965). Unpublished Ph.D. dissertation, Ohio State University.

Pirsig, R.M. (1976). Zen and the Art of Motorcycle Maintenance. Corgi Books.

Polanyi, M. (1958). Personal Knowledge. University of Chicago Press.

Polanyi, M. (1967). The Tacit Dimension. Anchor Books, New York.

Quist, R.W. and Martin, R.P. (1967). *Journal of Speech and Hearing Research* **10**, 795-800.

Radley, A.R. (1977). *In: New Perspectives in Personal Construct Theory* (ed. Bannister, D.), Academic Press, London.

Radley, A.R. (1978). *Journal of Phenomenological Psychology* (in press).

Radnitzky, G. (1970). Contemporary Schools of Metascience. Scandinavian University Books, Goteborg.

Rado, S. (1974). *In: American Handbook of Psychiatry* (ed. Arieti, S.), (2nd edition), Basic Books, New York.

Raymond, F. and Janet, P. (1903). Les Obsessions et la Psychasthenie. II. Alcan, Paris.

Reid, W.A. and Holley, B.J. (1972). *British Journal of Educational Psychology* **42**, 52-59.

Richards, B. (1977). Personal communication.

Richardson, L. (1944). *Psychological Monographs* **56**, 1-41.

Rickard, H.C. and Mundy, M.B. (1965). *In: Case Studies in Behavioral Modification* (ed. Ullman, L.P. and Krasner, L.), Holt, Rinehart and Winston, New York.

Rogers, C. (1973). *American Psychologist* **28**, 379-387.

Ronco, R. and Schon, D. (1977). Knowledge-in-practice: an inquiry into real-world cognition in professional practice. Unpublished manuscript, Massachusetts Institute of Technology.

Rosenthal, R. (1966). Experimental Effects on Behavioural Research Appleton-Century Crofts, New York.

Royce, J. (1976). *In: Nebraska Symposium on Motivation 1975: Conceptual foundation of psychology.* Vol. 23 (ed. Cole, J.K.), University of Nebraska Press, Lincoln.

Runkel, P.J. (1958). *In: Handbook for Research on Teaching* (ed. Gage, N.L.), Rand McNally, Chicago.

Runkel, P.J. and Damrin, D.E. (1961). *Journal of Educational Psychology* **52**, 354-361.

Santostefano, S. (1960). *Journal of Speech and Hearing Research* **3**, 337-347.

Sarbin, T.R. and Allen, V.L. (1968). *In: Handbook of Social Psychology* (ed. Lindzey, G. and Aronson), Addson-Wesley, Massachusetts.

Schaffer, H.R. (1977). Studies in Mother-Infant Interaction. Academic Press, London.

Schilling, A. von (1966). *In: Speech Pathology* (ed. Rieber, R. and Brubaker, R.), Lippincott, Philadelphia.

Schlesinger, I.M., Forte, M., Fried, B. and Melkman, R. (1965). *Journal of Speech and Hearing Disorders* **30**, 32-36.

Schneider, E. (1922). Ueberdas stuttern. Francke, Bern.

Schon, D.A. (1967). Invention and the Evolution of Ideas. Social Science Paperbacks, London.

Shames, G.H. and Sherrick, C.E. (1963). *Journal of Speech and Hearing*

Disorders **28**, 3-18.

Shannon, C.E. (1951). *The Bell System Technology Journal* **30**, 50-64.

Shaw, M.L.G. (1977). Notes on Computer Programs. Centre for the Study of Human Learning Publications, Brunel University.

Sheehan, J.G. (1970). Stuttering: research and therapy. Harper and Row, New York.

Slater, P. (1972). Notes on INGRID 22. Unpublished manuscript, St. George's Hospital, Tooting, London.

Staats, L.C. (1955). *In: Stuttering in Children and Adults* (ed. Johnson, W. and Leutenegger, R.), University of Minnesota Press, Minneapolis.

Stein, L. (1942). Speech and Voice: their evaluation, pathology, and therapy. Methuen, London.

Szasz, T. (1961). The Myth of Mental Illness. Hoeber, New York.

Tennov, D. (1977). Super Self: a woman's guide to self-management. Funk and Wagnalls, New York.

Thomas, L.F. and Harri-Augstein, E.S. (1976). The Self-Organised Learner and the Printed Word. Final Progress Report S.S.R.C. Further Development of Techniques for Studying and Influencing Reading as a Learning Skill. Centre for the Study of Human Learning Publications, Brunel University.

Thomas, L.F. and Harri-Augstein, E.S. (1977). *In: Adult Learning* (ed. Howe, M.), Wiley, London.

Thomas, L.F., McKnight, C. and Shaw, M.L.G. (1976). Grids and Group Structure. Centre for the Study of Human Learning Publications, Brunel University.

Thomas, L.F. and Shaw, M.L.G. (1976). FOCUS Manual. Centre for the Study of Human Learning Publications, Brunel University.

Thomas, L.F. and Shaw, M.L.G. (1977). PEGASUS Manual. Centre for the Study of Human Learning Publications, Brunel University.

Travis, L.E. (1931). Speech Pathology. Appleton-Century Crofts, New York.

Tschudi, F. (1977). *In: New Perspectives in Personal Construct Theory* (ed. Bannister, D.), Academic Press, London.

Vgotsky, L.S. (1962). Thought and Language. Massachusetts Institute of Technology Press.

Walker, V.J. and Beech, H.R. (1969). *British Journal of Psychiatry* **115**, 1261-1268.

Watson, R. (1967). *American Psychologist* **22**, 435-444.

Watzlawick, P., Beavin, J.H. and Jackson, D.D. (1967). Pragmatics of Human Communication: a study of interactional patterns, pathologies and paradoxes. Norton, New York.

Watzlawick, P., Weakland, J.H. and Fisch, R. (1974). Change: principle of problem formation and problem resolution. Norton, New York.

Weber, M. (1904). The Protestant Ethic and the Spirit of Capitalism. Translated by T. Parsons (1930). Schribner, New York.

Webster, R.L. and Dorman, M.F. (1970). *Journal of Speech and Hearing Research* **13**, 82-86.

Wertheimer, M. (1961). Productive Thinking. Tavistock, London.

West, R. (1958). *In: Stuttering: a symposium* (ed. Eisenson, J.), Harper and Row, New York.

Wilden, A. (1972). System and Structure: essays in communication and exchange. Tavistock, London.

Willey, F.T. and Maddison, R.E. (1971). An Enquiry into Teacher Training. University of London Press.

Wilson, R.J. (1968). *British Journal of Hospital Medicine* **1**, 134-135.

Zajonc, R.B. (1960). *Journal of Abnormal and Social Psychology* **61**, 159.167.

ABSTRACTS

1. ASSIMILATION AND CONTRAST IN DICHOTOMOUS CONSTRUCTION PROCESSES

JACK ADAMS-WEBBER

*Brock University, Ontario,
Canada*

In explicating the theoretical implications of his controversial *Dichotomy Corollary*, Kelly (1955, 1969) points out that the contrast pole of a personal construct is just as necessary as the similarity pole in defining its meaning. This paper/discussion session focuses on two related hypotheses concerning the contrast poles of constructs in personal judgement:

(1) people attempt to keep their usage of the similarity poles of constructs as consistent as possible with what they understand to be the commonly accepted 'lexical' meanings; however, they tend to employ the contrast poles more idiosyncratically in the light of their own personal experience;

(2) people tend to use the similarity pole to characterize events approximately 62%-63% of the time, rather than 50% of the time as Kelly assumed *a priori*, so that those events designated by the contrast poles will stand out maximally as 'figure' against a relatively undifferentiated background of diffuse similarities (cf. Benjafield and Adams-Webber, 1976).

References

1. Benjafield, J. and Adams-Webber, J. (1976). *British Journal of Psychology* **67**, 11-15.
2. Kelly, G. A. (1955). *The Psychology of Personal Constructs,* Norton, New York.
3. Kelly, G. A. (1969). *In: Clinical Psychology and Personality: The Selected Papers of George Kelly* (B. A. Maher, ed.), New York: Wiley.

2. PERSONAL CONSTRUCTS IN TRANSSEXUALS

J.M. ANNEAR

Guys Hospital, London

Personal Constructs are being investigated in a series

of transsexual patients as part of an assessment programme
toward consideration for gender reassignment.

In one inquiry the elements described included the Self
at Present, as viewed retrospectively at different ages,
and projected into the future after gender reassignment.
Other elements described include first degree and other
close relatives, figures of significance during upbringing
and career and own spouse and children or close personal
friends.

In another investigation the elements considered were
the subjects' own Body Parts. The Constructs used in these
investigations were supplied and elicited, with emphasis
on gender-related items.

Principal component analyses reveal a view at present
of lifetime movement of the Self through construct space
along or between component axes. Direction of movement of
Self as related to other elements is illuminating in certain instances with respect to identification and comple-
mentation in gender of Self and gender object choice.

Some of the lesser components are also considered.
Clinical vignettes will add significance to the personal
construct findings.

3. PERSONAL CONSTRUCT THEORY AND MULTIOPERATIONISM IN STUDIES OF ENVIRONMENTAL COGNITION AND SPATIAL CHOICE

JOHN F. BETAK

University of Texas at Austin,
U.S.A.

This presentation is concerned with two illustrations
of multi-operational studies which included personal construct theory as an essential component in eliciting the
cognitive dimensions underlying: (1) peoples' evaluation
and choice of residences in an urban area, and (2) peoples'
evaluation of the impact of proposed transportation investments in their community. Also discussed is a proposed research program to use personal construct theory as part
of a linked design to develop and evaluate a theory of
mode and destination choice.

The two studies and the proposed program illustrate
how personal construct theory may be effectively combined
with multidimensional scaling models, such as INDSCAL, to
provide insights and prototheoretical statements regarding
environmental cognition and spatial choice. The respective
designs are outlined for the three studies, and results
are summarised for the first two projects. Difficulties
encountered in these two projects are also discussed, as
well as the implications of the problems for such research.

4. AN EXPERIENTIAL SESSION ON THE ANALYSIS OF GRIDS ILLUSTRATING THE USE OF ON-LINE COMPUTER ANALYSES

JANE CHETWYND AND PAUL FELTON

*Institute for Advanced Study in Applied Psychology,
Christchurch, New Zealand*

This session will be devoted to explanations, demonstrations, and participations in the computer analyses of grid data. Building on INGRID and the other programs in Slater's Grid Analysis Package, a number of on-line advanced analyses of grids have been developed. The session will be devoted to explanations of the basic computer analyses in terms of what analyses are available, what each produces, and when each should be used. A small computer will be utilised in the session and will be available for demonstrations of the analyses and for participants to explore the possibilities of the programs with a variety of grids.

It can be argued that, particularly in the clinical field, the use of grid technique is hampered by the lack of fast, accessible analyses. In this session we hope to demonstrate that with a small computer (or with a computer terminal) feed-back on grid analyses can be practically instantaneous thus greatly enhancing the attraction of grid technique as a therapeutic tool.

5. NOTIONS OF PERSONAL CHANGE

DAVID CHILDS

Runwell Hospital, Essex

It is often hard for the clinical user of repertory grids, to know how to apply the results in treatment. In particular, there may be difficulty with the 'monolithic' grid which seems to consist of little more than a strong statement of self-dissatisfaction and isolation.

It is possible to elaborate the element 'myself at the moment' in such a way as to distinguish between those ways in which a person wants to change which are accessible (sometimes experienced) and those which are purely ideal (never experienced). Each of these changes (as either experienced or imagined) can be described and compared. A simple mapping of the results is made using axes of Cost (change entailing loss of valued attributes) and Benefit (desired personal change).

This procedure can help to decide on a particular aspect of a person's experience as a focus for intervention. It may also show how the construct system itself, as a set of linked assumptions about character and action, can restrict the individual's search for solutions.

The early results of work extending the use of this method to people who are not seeking psychological help suggests that this group have as many 'implicative dilemmas' in their thinking about change as do a psychologically distressed group. The feature which does distinguish the distressed group is their greater reliance on rigid concepts of how change might theoretically be experienced rather than on actual experience itself.

This theoretical notion of change presumably owes a good deal to the assumption of similarity in meaning between the personal constructs by which it is described. In contrast, a description of how patterns of change are actually experienced will owe less to such assumptions and more to the greater variety and flexibility of real life.

6. ZEN AND THE SCIENCE OF PERSONALLY CONSTRUING

GUY CLAXTON

University of London

Within psychology, personal construct theory stands out as the most general and the most elegant theory of how man sees himself and his actions, and how he sees his relationship to his environment. But we can ask whether man actually *is* the way he thinks; do his actions really come about in the way his common sense *as formalized by personal construct theory* says they do? There is another theory of man, just as general and just as sophisticated, that says our 'common sense' is, although very common, very unnatural, and that it is a socially-spun illusion which, at heart, undermines, rather than enhances, our effectiveness and our happiness. This radical psychology is found in the Eastern 'mystical' traditions of Buddhism, Taoism and Hinduism.

The purpose of this discussion group will be to explore side-by-side the notions of man-as-scientist and man-as-mystic to see where they overlap and where they contrast. We will work with our own intuitions about our selves, and compare these with the view of man as an integral part of a dynamic and interrelated universe that underlies the Eastern traditions - and is beginning to emerge in certain areas of Western Science.

7. CONSTRUCTION SYSTEMS FOR FREEDOM

J.A. EASTERBROOK

*University of New Brunswick,
Canada*

Abstraction, anticipation and constructive alternativism are the bases of free will. Emphasizing these features of human information processing, and being a meta theory, personal construct theory nicely accommodates a psychological analysis of freedom.

The concept of freedom refers to a relationship between an entity and its environment. The entity's freedom, like its responsibility, varies as a function of its ability to determine what it does and what happens to it. The actions of free persons are determined, as Kant said, in 'the world of understanding' - to the degree that understanding is correct - rather than in 'the world of sense'. They are determined by knowledge, not stimulation. They are shaped in 'construction systems'.

Instrumental construction systems depend on knowledge of processes. Some of them sometimes lose their systemic character, leaving a person's behavioural processes open to simple determination in reaction to environmental events. The critical difference is not a simple matter of initial cognitive complexity, quantitatively assessed. Researches into responsibility show it is related to consistency in validation of personal constructions.

Internal validation (or 'self reinforcement') is involved in the integrity of construction systems, in their resistance to alteration by contrary suggestion or insufficiently contradictory experience, and in the selectivity of changes that follow sufficient contradiction. It underlies an advanced form of Freedom, but it entails the risk that a system will lose fidelity as the practice is repeated. A suitable check against this danger may develop when a construction system includes a positive evaluation of objectivity in its own structure.

8. PERSONAL CONSTRUCT THEORY AND LEARNING IN ORGANISATIONS

MARK EASTERBY-SMITH

Durham University Business School, U.K.

This paper is presented from the perspective of a user of repertory grid technique. It is argued that the experience of applying the grid to solve novel problems may contribute towards the overall development of theory; essentially it is up to the theoretician to determine what is possible, and it is up to the practitioner to determine what is worthwhile.

The potential range of applications within work organisations is defined. Illustrations of these applications describing single states and changes in states are given in relation to individual and group development. These examples indicate that the grid has considerable potential for providing unanticipated insights into development needs and into the results of learning programmes. However, they highlight some of the weaknesses of construct theory and associated methodologies for monitoring change. Firstly, one of the most significant aspects of changing grids are the differences in *content* of the grids - and this cannot be adequately measured by existing methodologies, which concentrate on *structural* indices. Secondly, a more theoretical point is that changes in construct systems are normally assumed to be independent of the client's environment. However the case studies illustrate that changes in the individual and changes in the objective environment may be significantly inter-related, and therefore assessment of changes due to educational programmes may be extremely difficult. In most cases it is only the client who is able to differentiate between inner changes and outer changes. Therefore it is suggested that there is a need for fuller interaction with the client particularly when interpretations of changing grids are to be made.

9. CONSTRUCTIVE APPROACHES TO OPTIMAL FUNCTIONING

FRANZ EPTING

University of Florida, U.S.A.

The purpose of this paper is to examine some of the ways in which personal construct theory relates to personal growth and the general human potential movement. Presented first are a number of issues which must be understood from a personal construct point of view. These include the nature of human potentials, transendent experience, the full cycle of experience, the nature of obligation and responsibility, and the general social implications to name but a few. The second part of the paper describes five techniques and procedures that can be used with growth group and classes on personal growth. These include a completion of the self characterization technique, a description of a multiple role group, a perception of change techniques, a procedure for students to design their own growth experiments, and a group on developing loving behaviors.

10. ARCHITECTS' CONSTRUING OF SPACE

RANULPH GLANVILLE

*Architectural Association School of Architecture,
Bedford Square, London.*

The limitations of verbal labelling are highlighted in
an account of several attempts to use Kelly grids, both
manually administered and using PEGASUS, to elicit spatial
constructs from architecture students. Examples are given
of exceptional differences in meaning structures within an
experimental group handling common material, which are resolved using graphic representations. Further experiments
are recounted that suggest not only ways of extending techniques akin to the repertory grid in their range of usefulness, but also that the grid has clearly discernible limitations, and an outline is given of the mechanism for
distinguishing such limits.

11. SOCIAL NETWORKS AND *INTER*-PERSONAL CONSTRUCTS

COLIN HARGREAVES

Edinburgh University, U.K.

The cohesiveness and explanatory power of personal construct theory, as well as its own elusiveness, seem to
have restricted its theoretical development. Questions
upon the derivation of constructs and their inter-relation-
ship tend to be avoided with throw-away statements about
past experience and future designs.

From grid analysis it is very evident that different
verbal labels do not necessarily define independent constructs. Orderings of elements seem to have a certain
stability, independent of the particular construct. But
from what does this stability arise?

Furthermore, if the orderings are to any extent independent from the labels, from where do the labels arise? The
idea of 'project' may be helpful temporarily in explaining
them, but raises even more complex questions in the long
run. These problems are particularly poignant in the study
of interpersonal constructs.

Studies upon interpersonal perception have been generally very individualistic, for methodological reasons if
no others. But do people experience others as separate
individuals? An overtime study of new students' constructions of old and new social contacts shows how important
a knowledge of a person's social network is to the understanding and explanation of a construct system. It is also
hoped to show how existentialist concepts, such as 'being-
with-others', may after all be of great use for the theoretical development of personal construct theory.

12. INTERPERSONAL CONCEPTUAL STRUCTURES, PREDICTIVE ACCURACY AND SOCIAL ADJUSTMENT OF EMOTIONALLY DISTURBED BOYS

BRIAN HAYDEN

Brown University,
Rhode Island, U.S.A.

Thirty emotionally disturbed boys in residential treatment were evaluated in terms of their level of social adjustment, predictive accuracy in sequencing social behavior, and structural characteristics of their interpersonal conceptual systems. Findings indicate that among emotionally disturbed boys the degree of their construct differentiation is associated with their level of social adjustment. Also, the greater accuracy of a boy in predicting the sequence of another person's behavior, the more appropriate is his interpersonal behavior. Thus, when a child's person perceptions are limited or deficient, the social predictions facilitating effective social encounters suffer. The mediating link between the interpersonal conceptual system and social behavior appears to be the extent to which a child reduces the social environment into a few functionally equivalent events. Theoretical, methodological, and practical implications are discussed.

13. LEARNING ABOUT RULES

ROBIN HODGKIN

University of Oxford, U.K.

Four items of material were presented:
(1) A commonplace school situation in which a student had infringed a time/place/hierarchy boundary (commonly called 'being late for a lesson' and 'colliding with a teacher').
(2) A review of the current Dworkin versus Hart debate on the nature of law. Hart (1960) took a positivist view of law; Dworkin (1976) sees laws as being rooted in widely accepted but tacit, principles.
(3) The first half of the film *Signals for Survival* - Tinbergen's study of 'seagull city' was shown.
(4) An apologia and warning about the importance of, and dangers of, making extrapolations from animal to human societies.
Various concepts were defined, explored or discussed.
Boundaries. These need to be thought of as marking more than space - time for instance or a level in a developing process or in a hierarchy. A person who faces such boundaries from within a process will often do so with a considerable charge of feeling. An external observer may dis-

cover the component constructs in such a confrontation but the person involved will give an account of the situation which can be seen as lying somewhere along a spectrum between a high degree of fantasy and considerable rationality.

What is a norm? Sociologists never seem quite clear about this. But our model helps. A norm is a negotiated boundary which has been generated by a dialectical system, for example, the male and female animal moving from aggression to mating.

What is a rule? An observed and verbally articulated regularity. If this regularity is a social norm it generally becomes a rule. It may become prescriptive - how to play a game or the procedure for getting married (= crossing the threshold of family life) or it may have a conditional quality. If the rule is sufficiently important and enduring it may be given institutional backing which may involve code, custom or sanction and then the rule becomes a law. But the roots of both laws and social rules are negotiated boundaries of various kinds.

What then are *principles?* According to Dworkin these are the partly explicit tensions and orientations in which all laws have their roots. But what does construct theory say? (Several people came up with helpful suggestions here but specific references would be appreciated.) Presumably a principle is a value-laden construct and one which I am sufficiently aware of to be able to articulate in words. If it is quite inarticulable it is likely to be termed a prejudice or, in the case of a seagull, an instinct.

If I am on one side of a hierarchical, social boundary - under the law say, or on the upper side, administering, much will depend on how I understand the process of boundary negotiation and control in which I am involved. There are important questions about how I construe the situation. But there are also questions about the accounts I give or the fantasies I weave in this situation. Richard Gregory's suggestion that we should define psychology as "the science of fiction" has relevance here and points to an area of feeling and symbolism about which construct theory has little to say. Gregory Bateson's distinction between *ethos*, the feeling texture of a group, and *eidos*, the shared, cognitive *problematique* of a group is also highly relevant. But there is a lot of work to do in pegging out conceptual domains here.

14. CHILDREN'S PERCEPTIONS OF THEIR PEERS: A DEVELOPMENTAL ANALYSIS USING THE IMPLICATION GRID TECHNIQUE

TERRY HONESS

University of Aston in Birmingham, U.K.

Kelly and Werner are particularly concerned with the individual's attempts to represent the world through the medium of language. This common interest allows Werner's description of development to be readily translated into a number of predictions concerning the development of children's construct organisation. The hypotheses received excellent support from an analysis of children's perceptions of their same age, same sex peers as a function of their own age (8-16 years), sex and verbal intelligence.

Construct organisation was inferred from the children's perceptions using a new form of the 'implication grid' which was evolved in the context of Kellian and Wernerian theory. The children's grid responses were shown to be reliable, and consistent with an external criterion: their written descriptions of liked and disliked same sex peers.

The potential of the implication grid is stressed by reference to its capacity for measuring construct system 'differentiation', construct 'superordinacy', and pinpointing 'contradiction' in construing.

15. TECHNIQUE-FREE AND NONPRESCRIPTIVE THEORIES OF PSYCHOTHERAPY: PROMISCUITY OR PROMISE?

THOMAS O. KARST

Medical College of Ohio at Toledo, U.S.A.

The qualities of psychotherapeutic systems that allow means/ends differentiation were explored. Behavioral systems illustrate one approach: stating treatment goals in specific, concrete, observable terms and thus allowing flexibility of treatment method. Personal construct theory illustrates a second approach: generating a series of abstract, theoretically meaningful propositions pertaining to psychological change which can be operationalized in various ways to yield a variety of treatment methods. The 'non-rational' aspects of such movement from the general to the specific were noted as an indication that personal construct theory views such translations from theory to method as a creative process.

Systems of psychotherapeutic change which permit means/ends differentiation were characterized as more mature and developed in a logical sense. Theories which are tied to a single, prescriptive treatment method were seen as tautological, and in such cases, either the treatment theory or treatment method is redundant. It was concluded, then, that technique-free and nonprescriptive systems of psychotherapy were not promiscuous but, rather, could be considered robust.

To illustrate this point, two techniques that seem on their face to be too directive, non-humanistic, and, therefore, antithetical to PCT - operant conditioning and hypnosis - were discussed. It was stated that personal construct theory could sanction such treatment methods if certain requirements are met: (1) The treatment must be meaningfully related to one or more personal construct theory propositions regarding psychological change. (2) The technique is presented to the client as an experiment that may lead to change. (3) The client is fully informed regarding the procedures. (4) The decision to use such techniques is cooperatively arrived at by the client and therapist and not dictated by the therapist.

The ability to incorporate such diverse techniques and ideas is a further demonstration of the nature of personal construct theory as a 'theory of theories'.

16. TEACHING APPRAISAL BY REPERTORY GRID TECHNIQUE

TERENCE R. KEEN

Plymouth Polytechnic, Devon

TARGET (Teaching Appraisal using Repertory Grid Elicitation Techniques) is a system of teaching appraisal designed to provide a service to teachers. Research results suggest applicability of the system in the discipline of Physics and it is now being developed in other subject areas. By means of TARGET techniques, a teacher is able to establish profiles of effective (and ineffective) teaching as he perceives it, and he is able to see the extent to which these profiles match his intuitive perception of his own teaching style.

TARGET, therefore, does not depend upon a comparison of individual teaching styles with models of 'good' or 'bad' teaching which are often derived from externally specified criteria. Nevertheless, the TARGET system will, eventually, provide standards of comparison. These, however, will emerge as profiles of peer, or student, perceptions of effective teaching, enabling a teacher to compare his own teaching style with these profiles.

17. CONSTRUCT THEORY AND DELINQUENCY

DOUGLAS KELLY

Surrey Probation and After-Care Service, U.K.

An essential part of the treatment of offender clients
is an appreciation of the way in which they see the behaviour that has earned them this label. In seeking to
understand this I have often found that they employ constructions which not only neutralise the criminality of
the act, but actually re-interpret it as virtuous behavior. The Robin Hood syndrome is well known. Theft may be
seen as a rightful protest against social inequality. By
construing the victim as wealthy there may be a denial of
injury, or as an evil profiteer, using what Sykes and
Matza call 'condemning the condemners', the focus of attention is shifted from the deviant act to those who disapprove of it. Fransella and Adams have related how an
arsonist construed his firesetting as the meting out of
just retribution. Unless such constructions are recognised
the thief, for example, who has re-interpreted his devi-
ance as virtue will readily agree on the demerits of theft
while not relating this to his own behaviour. By using
case illustrations it is hoped that the usefulness of PCT
in revealing the offender's construction of his offence
and the place that his offending occupies in his self
image will be demonstrated and how this can be utilised
both in treatment and assessment of risk of re-offending.

Reference

1. Fransella, F. and Adams, B. (1966). *British Journal of social and
   clinical Psychology*, **5**, 51-62.

18. WORKSHOP ON INTERPERSONAL TRANSATION WITH ROTATION DYADS, A METHODOLOGY RELATED TO KELLY'S SOCIALITY COROLLARY

ALVIN W. LANDFIELD AND MARY ANN BARR

University of Nebraska, U.S.A.

The history, research and applications of the Interpersonal Transaction (IT) group will be presented along
with demonstrations of the procedure. Demonstrations which
provide direct, although limited, experience for the workshop participants will be interspersed with brief lecture-
discussion periods. The IT method, a laboratory for the
construct researcher, may be tailored to many research
and clinical purposes.

The workshop format will accommodate from 2 to 20 participants. Demonstrations focus on groups of four within
which persons interact in pairs. All persons will partici-

pate in the groups at the same time. One or both of the
leaders will interact in the groups to fill out the groups
of four.

It would be helpful, but not necessary, to read the
article by Landfield and Rivers, 'An Introduction to Interpersonal Transaction and Rotating Dyads', *Psychotherapy:
Theory, Research and Practice*, 1975, **12**, 4 (winter) 365-
373.

19. CHILDREN'S CONSTRUCT SYSTEM AND OVERT BEHAVIOR

MICHAELA LIFSHITZ

Haifa University, Israel

Implicit in personal construct theory is the notion
that an individual's construct system directs his overt
behavior. The present paper reviews several studies which
investigate the nature of the relationship between degree
of perceptual differentiation and social behavior with
reference to: (a) area of perceptual differentiation (sensori-motor vs. verbal-conceptual; neutral vs. significant
persons in one's life); (b) age (kindergarten to adolescence); (c) culture (authoritarian vs. democratic); (d)
social organization (city vs. kibbutz; stable vs. diver-
gent communal experience), and (e) family structure (intact vs. fatherless).

Findings suggest that: (a) cognitive differentiation
and variability of overt behavior are both influenced by
cultural socialization practices, mainly those practices
pertaining to freedom of self-experimenting; (b) degree
of perceptual differentiation and integration of neutral
sensori-motor elements is consistently related (for all
age groups investigated) to diversity of positive social
behavior; however (c) the relationship between social
behavior and differentiation of the constructs of significant persons varies according to the child's family structure and the amount of change in his life. During times of
relative disorganization (e.g. adolescence, loss of father,
social mobility), tightening of perceptual structures of
significant others, especially those related to the mother,
seem to be a prerequisite for adaptive social behavior.

20. WHAT DO PEOPLE KNOW ABOUT REPRIMAND?: THE CHOICE COROLLARY IN EVERDAY IMPLICIT PERSONALITY THEORY

J. MANCUSO

State University of New York at Albany, U.S.A.

Much of our daily activity is devoted to having others

'see things our way'. (In discussing children we talk
about 'getting them to do the right things'.) It's clear
that violence, coercion, and reinforcement have been explored as effective (or non-effective) accompaniment to
reprimand. Other conceptions deserve our attention!

We advocate exploring the proposition that people work
from a day-to-day implicit personality theory which states
that behavior will be efficiently altered in the prescribed
direction under those conditions where the reprimand successfully induces the transgressor to adopt the perspective which guided the generation of the rule being advocated by the reprimander. In other words people implicitly
know the essences of Kelly's *Choice Corollary*. Reprimand
does not work unless the person already accepts the validity of a large portion of the construction which the
reprimander intends to affirm.

We would like to discuss children's development of an
understanding of this principle, and to venture an explanation of why people advocate coercive reprimand, even
though they understand the Choice Corollary.

21. LIKING AND DISLIKING

MILDRED McCOY

University of Hong Kong

A new model of cognitive structure which accounts for
the relationship between evaluation and the descriptive
basis of judgement is offered. The model has evolved from
personal construct theory in consideration of issues
associated with understanding liking and disliking. Its
special feature is that it reverses the commonly held
view (in Psychology) of the direction of causality between
attribution of evaluative and descriptive aspects in interpersonal judgements. Whereas the halo effect holds that
liking or disliking unduly influence one's judgements of
other characteristics, this model proposes that people
are judged on descriptive dimensions which may eventuate
in liking or disliking. Additionally, according to the
model, the most personally significant descriptive dimensions tend to be involved in a network of related dimensions which may, but does not necessarily, include a relatively superordinate construction such as liked versus
disliked. The tendency to include evaluation is limited.
Variations in it are both individual and cultural.

A number of useful applications of the model are presented. Of particular interest are the applications in
counselling and psychotherapy which are illustrated with
graphical presentations of research data. Likewise, the
model illuminates the role of 'feelings' with regard to
effecting desired behaviour change. The relationship of

this latter topic to several theories of psychotherapy is identified.

22. CONSTRUING OTHERS: A NEW APPROACH TO THE STUDY OF ROLE AND ROLE CONFLICT

CLIFF McKNGHT

Goldsmith's College, University of London

The paper aims to offer some tentative solutions to the problems surrounding the concepts of 'role' and 'role conflict'. These problems are taken to revolve around the lack of operational definitions.

From a personal construct theory point of view, a person's behaviour is mediated by his construing. There is no apparent reason why role behaviour should be any different. Hence, in order to understand what a role means to a person, we must look at his construing - not at the expectations of everybody else!

Since role behaviour is not a special case, a general model of choice behaviour is presented which combines personal construct theory and Multi-Attributed Utility theory. The notion underlying the model is that not only are a particular set of constructs relevant for an individual in a situation, but within this set some constructs are more salient than others. It is the combination of construing and differential salience which results in choice behaviour.

The concept of role is then explored from within the general model, using data from a single subject. A method of predicting role conflict from within the model is also outlined.

One advantage of the proposed approach is that both role and role conflict are defined operationally in the person's own terms. It is also suggested that the general model provides an important link between construing and action.

23. KELLY'S 'MATRIX OF DECISION' AND THE POLITICS· OF IDENTITY

PETER DU PREEZ

University of Cape Town, South Africa

Kelly's classic paper, *Europe's Matrix of Decision* (1962), proposes that decisions are made in a network of construed alternatives. The important feature of his theory is that decisions are not examined on their own, but in relation to contrasted possibilities. What I shall be examining is the choice of political identity in a group which is caught between more powerful groups. Identity is a commitment: it implies one set of choices rather than another. Political identity is systematically related to position in a connected system of exchange of rights and obligations and the exact choice which is made depends on exchanges with other groups in the system. Exchanges occur in the economic, educational, entertainment, political and kinship systems of society. In each of these systems, participants negotiate specific identities which relate systematically to the exchanges in that system. In this discussion, the focus will be on the negotiations of identity in the political system.

Reference

1. Kelly, G.A. (1962). Europe's matrix of decision. *In: Nebraska Symposium* (M.R. Jones, ed.), University of Nebraska Press, Lincoln.

24. WAYS TO LEARN

ALAN RADLEY

Loughborough University of Technology, Leicestershire

This paper argues that the way in which student and teacher work with the material at hand is an expression of the system of relationships in which they participate. Two modes of relating are described, and these are compared within the framework of personal construct psychology in an attempt to elucidate some factors giving rise to these different forms of learning. This makes possible a critical discussion of the limits of psychological (e.g. personal construct) theory in educational practice.

25. CHILDREN'S SELF DESCRIPTION GRID: THEME AND VARIATIONS

A.T. RAVENETTE

London Borough of Newham

In the self description grid the child is invited to stand in the shoes of people who are significant to him and say how they see him both qualitatively (psychological attributes) and quantitatively (through grid procedures). This leads to the making of inferences as to how the child sees his validators and how he judges his inter-personal relationships.

There are three variations of the self description grid - in the first, the child indicates where, on an eleven spaced continuum, various people would place him; in the second the child rank orders psychological attributes as he thinks other people would describe him; in

the third he rank orders people according to the likelihood that they would describe him with each attribute.
    The three variants provide different forms of constraint
for the individual in making his judgements and a different
level of inference for the psychologist. These differences
are important both clinically and theoretically.

26. SOCIAL AND PERSONAL CONSTRUCTIONS

FRASER REID

Plymouth Polytechnic, Devon

    The need to establish the situational determinants of
human conduct has directed the attention of social psychologists to conversation as the fundamental social activity. One distinctive feature of conversation is the capacity for interactants to monitor their encounters and to
construct novel and imaginative role-relationships. A
decisive factor in role-making is the manner in which
interactants gather, utilise and release social feedback
in the construction and reconstruction of role models.
This concern represents a point of contact between clinical
and social enquiry. Whilst the clinician seeks to enhance
his client's competence in managing social feedback, the
social psychologist attempts to exhibit the principles
underlying its control and utilisation. The ethogenic
method of enqiry advocated by Harre and Secord (1972) provides a strong link between these complementary approaches
to conversation. In viewing social behaviour as lawfully
mediated by experienced meaning, precision of meaning in
the ethogenic approach corresponds to accuracy of measurement familiar to the physical sciences. Empirical verification of meaning is achieved by the self-monitoring of a
social episode and the negotiation of accounts between
participants. The process of negotiation parallels therapeutic conversation, in which the increasing authenticity
of accounts corresponds to the growth of client insight.
Personal construct theory provides a sound theoretical
base and a systematic technique for operationalising this
process, and a modified Repgrid procedure for negotiating
social constructions is presented as a workshop activity.
This activity exhibits role-making processes by staging
a semi-active role-playing Senario, following which participants attempt to formulate and negotiate constructions
based on the behavioural elements elicited during role-
playing. Such a procedure offers a means for analysing
the role/rule models persons construct and bring to bear
on everyday social situations.

Reference

1. Harre R. and Secord, P.F. (1972). *The explanation of social behav-*

iour, Basil Blackwell, Oxford.

27. ANALYSIS OF PERSONAL CONSTRUCTS IN PERSON PERCEPTION

SEYMOUR ROSENBERG, SAM KINGSLEY AND MICHAEL GARA

Rutgers University, New Brunswick, New Jersey, U.S.A.

Methodology

This session was a workshop-discussion to review and update the new methodological approaches for obtaining and analyzing interpersonal constructs described by S. Rosenberg in New Approaches to the Analysis of Personal Constructs in Person Perception. *(Nebraska Symposium on Motivation*, Vol. **23**, 1977). This session included (1) *data-gathering* aspects such as the use of various free-response methods as well as a completely naturalistic approach (e.g. analysis of a writer's novels) and (2) *data-analysis* aspects such as clustering and multidimensional scaling. The session also included some critical comparisons among the various extant methods.

The inspiration for this session came from the interests expressed by a number of people who attended the Nebraska meetings for a detailed discussion of methodoloy - interests which could not be adequately met at Nebraska, given the Symposium format.

Research Progress

Three separate research studies were presented in this session.

(1) The Dimensions of Personality Perception by Seymour Rosenberg The adequacy of the EPA system (evaluation, potency and activity) as a scheme for the dimensions of personality perception was tested with personality descriptions from a free-response method and from a provided list of traits. In the free-response method, each subject described himself and a number of people known to him using the terms of his own choice. In the provided list of traits, each subject used a set of common traits to describe himself and a number of people known to him. The results show that E is the only strong dimension underlying personality perception for most of the subjects; P and A exist only in a few subject's perceptions. Orthogonality was not found on an individual level, and seemed to be produced from the aggregation of data across different individuals. An alternative model is proposed in which a general evaluation dimension underlies personality perception and in which content properties, not independent

of evaluation, add dimensionality to personality perception. Major content properties vary across individuals.
The results of this study show that this flexible model
may adequately represent the content and structure of personality perception and may incorporate individual differences simultaneously.

(2) The Structure of Self-Descriptions by Sam Kingsley
Implicit self theory is the name we have given to the
structure and content of self-conceptions. An individual's
self-concept is assumed to consist of a set of multiple
selves; each self can be identified by the way an individual perceives himself vis-a-vis another person (or group
of persons) that he knows. To obtain a subject's self-
conception as a set of multiple selves, he is asked to report the feelings elicited in him by each of a large number of people that he knows. These feelings can be viewed
as the elements in the structure of self-conception, particularly since trait terms are explicitly included. The
subjects in this study were seventeen college students.
For each subject, a multi-dimensional configuration of the
feeling terms was constructed from the co-occurrence patterns of the terms. Evaluation was shown to be a dominant
feature of the structure of self-descriptions, though each
subject emphasized different content aspects of general
evaluation, for example, maturity, psychological stability,
interpersonal integrity.

*(3) The Identification of Superordinate and Prototypical
People in Personality Impressions by Mike Gara* Kelly proposed that human beings embrace ordinal relationships
among constructs. This research explores the possibility
of using this same notion to model the relationship among
people (elements). The use of this model allows for the
identification of both superordinate and subordinate or
prototypical people in 15 free response protocols. Superordinate people were found to be well known individuals
in a subject's life, the construction of which provides
him or her with a diverse repertoire of constructs with
which to anticipate person events. Subordinate people are
prototypes, distilled portions of constructs provided by
the superordinates. Such people tend to be known to the
subject only by reputation and are often mythical in nature,
although there are marked individual differences in the
kinds of people that a subject uses in either a superordinate or prototypical fashion. There was some evidence for
a typology of subjects in this respect.

28. A PERSONAL CONSTRUCT THEORY OF DEPRESSION

DOROTHY ROWE

St. John's Hospital, Lincoln

That language structures reality rather than reality structures language has been stated by philosophers and linguists from Vico to Kant, through von Humboldt to Ernst Cassirer and George Steiner, through C.S. Pierce and Dewey to George Kelly. It can be argued that a person's behaviour is the outcome of his individual language, which is the fusion of sentences, feelings and images and by which he creates his world.

The experience of depression may be of immense feelings of guilt, anger and despair, but the overwhelming feeling is that of isolation. The depressed person finds himself alone, separated from all human contact and in a world which has taken on a hostile appearance. Gone are any memories of a happy past and lost are any hopes of a happy future. Each depressed person can describe his experience in an image, and all these images have one common feature - the person sees himself as imprisoned. His image may be of being in a pit or in a black tunnel or under a bell jar, but, whatever it is, he is in inescapable isolation.

In personal construct theory terms, depression can be defined as 'that experience which accompanies the selection from the set of possible states of a person's language structure that particular state or system of propositions whereby the person sees himself as being cut off from and as choosing to be cut off from interaction with others, both people in his external reality (e.g. wife, friends) and figures in his internal reality (e.g. his God, happy memories or his dead mother, his good self, his success-ful future).'

Reference

1. Rowe, D. (1978). *The Experience of Depression*, John Wiley (in press).

29. DIALECTICAL FEATURES OF KELLYIAN THEORIZING

JOSEPH F. RYCHLAK

Purdue University, U.S.A.

As a former student of George Kelly's at the Ohio State University, Dr. Rychlak was greatly impressed by the para-llels between the Philosophy of Constructive Alternativism and the historic use of dialectical conceptions and reason-ings in human affairs. Although others have also noted this similarity, Dr. Rychlak is one of the few people who has carried on a continuing discussion with George Kelly on this very topic.

Dr. Rychlak believes that a proper theory of personality demands some form of dialectical phrasing if it is
to capture true humanity, and it is hoped that interested
participants might wish to discuss this topic in the light
of Kellyian theory. Although other theories, including the
Freudian and Jungian formulations, are readily conceptualised in light of dialectics, there is no better example
of a dialectical theory than Kelly's formulation. Dr.
Rychlak fears that there is a tendency today on the part
of some interpreters of Kelly to distort the true spirit
of his theory by turning it into a mediational conception
along the lines of what is today called 'cognitive psychology'. This psychology is in reality a continuation of
the mechanistic, efficient-cause theories of our past,
theories which George Kelly rejected and actively opposed.

Hence, it is hoped that an open-ended discussion will
follow a beginning statement by Dr. Rychlak, which will
build on this central comparison and lead thereby to a
deeper understanding among the participants of the psychology of personal constructs, dialectics, and above all,
the human image.

30. THEORIES OF SOCIAL RELATIONSHIPS AND PERSONAL CONSTRUCT THEORY

MONICA SHAW AND ROBERT HEYMAN

Newcastle upon Tyne Polytechnic

There have been few attempts to develop general theories
of social relationships in Social Psychology. We start
from the assumption that theories which are available such
as social exchange theory and role theory, take little
account of the actor's own view of relationships. We would
view these 'theories' as possible interpretive frameworks
which the actor may employ in making sense of relationships. This position is consistent with personal construct
theory, except that we argue that the range of possible
alternative ways of construing relationships is extremely
limited. We propose four constructs of relationships,
namely exchange, reciprocity, egocentrism and altercen-
trism and discuss their implications for issues in relationships such as rule-making, control and conflict.

31. TOWARDS A REFLEXIVE AND CONSTRUCTIVE SOCIAL PSYCHOLOGY

PETER STRINGER

University of Surrey, U.K.

Is personal construct theory unduly, or even hopelessly,

individualistic? The rep grid and the therapist-client
context of much of the work with the theory have done
nothing to help. How far does the sociality corollary re-
dress the balance?

Are we reflexive enough? We treat the psychologist and
the layperson as individuals with common processes. How
often do we treat them, *as a dyad in relation*, as having
processes in common with any other two persons?

If construing-in-relation were to be our subject matter,
what is the difference between studying a psychologist-
layperson relation and studying a relation between two
laypersons? Does the psychologist's role irretrievably
distance him, in reflexive terms, from the latter kind of
relation, which presumably is his ultimate interest?

Some people seem to be grappling with similar issues -
cf. Toch's peer interviews, Mair's conversational model,
Harre and Secord's negotiation of accounts, and the Repop-
ort's collaborative interviewing and interactive research.
Do they go far enough?

Someone somewhere is waiting to hear from us - we hope.
There appear to be two ways of addressing him. We can act
as transducers of the relations of others, the psychologist as faithful reporter who belies his own part in the
enterprise. Or we can operate ourselves, by constructing
inquisitive relations with others. We can tell not only
what we and others discover and invent, but also what our
relation was in the process. Is the psychologist as con-
structor of relations, through example, a possibility?

32. INTERPERSONAL ATTRACTION AND SIMILARITY IN PERSONAL CONSTRUCTS

ROELF J. TAKENS

Free University, Amsterdam, Holland

Empirical data suggest the importance of similarity in
the areas of values, opinions and attitudes in (dyadic)
relationships with respect to interpersonal attraction.
It seems that we like those people most whom we perceive
as similar to ourselves, because in that way there is a
big chance that our percepts and concepts are given social
validation, which will induce a rewarding social relationship.

This reasoning fits well in Kelly's personal construct
theory: consensual validation for one's view of 'the world'
and of interpersonal events is presumably best achieved
by associating with those who construct their world in a
similar way.

Kelly's commonality corollary and, to some extent, his
sociality corollary too, lay the foundation of our research with the repertory grid, in which we hypothesized

that people who like one another construct their world
in the same way much more than people who dislike each
other. In other words: their (use of) personal constructs
are much more akin.

For this we analysed the grids of some samples of students who liked each other versus students who did not
(in this case the other person was said to be disliked).
All of these students were in their final year, so they
knew each other already for several years.

Our results were that we could not differentiate between attractive and non-attractive dyads by means of a
content-analysis of construct-similarities. Neither was
it possible to make such a differentiation on the basis
of a comparison of the *structure* of the constructs involved when the participants were asked to rate themselves
on *each other's* construct-contrast pairs.

On the other hand we found a very significant relationship between liking for another person and *perceived similarity*. This finding concurs with most research findings
nowadays.

33. HOW TO DEAL WITH MANIPULATIVE BEHAVIOUR/HOW TO LIVE WITH A PSYCHOPATH. A PERSPECTIVE BASED ON PERSONAL CONSTRUCT THEORY AND ASSERTIVENESS TRAINING

FINN TSCHUDI AND SIGRID SANDSBERG

University of Oslo, Norway

The workshop is an extension of the perspective provided in *Honest and loaded questions. A personal construct
theory view of symptoms and therapy*. (1977), *In: New Perspectives in Personal Construct Theory*. Academic Press.

A common problem in interpersonal relations is evasive-
ness, deviously going about one's aims, what we generally
have called 'posing loaded questions'. When deviousness
is combined with eliciting and playing on the other person's guilt feelings, this is a pattern which often (especially in Scandinavian psychiatric literature) is called
'psychopathy'. Such manipulative behaviour may be regarded
as a violation of the other's personal rights. A tentative
definition of manipulative behaviour might be: imposing
one's own structure on the other, not permitting the
other to elaborate his/her own construct system. (This
may be carried out in different modes of consciousness.)
We apply a Kellyian perspective in understanding and dealing with such behaviour.

Some recent advances in 'assertiveness training' (see
especially M.J. Smith (1975) *When I say no I feel guilty*.
Bantam) offer techniques to withstand manipulative behaviour and to promote honest questions. 'Loosening' and

'tightening' are particularly useful in clarifying assertiveness techniques as 'fogging', 'negative inquiry', 'negative assertion' and 'broken record'.

We use the concept of 'manipulation' in a restricted
manner, focussing on hostile behaviour in close relationships, where the participants cannot easily leave the
field. Perhaps the ultimate aim of the transaction is a
quest for growth and intimacy?

Emphasizing the mutuality of the interaction, it may
often be difficult to decide who is manipulating whom.
This implies reciprocity; generally the quality of the
interaction is *created* by generic processes and does not
simply unfold according to a predetermined script. There
is an *emergent quality* to most interactions. On the other
hand the interaction *may* have stagnated in a Hegelian
master - slave relation.

The process point of view underlines the need for techniques which give *both* participants in the interaction the
possibility of elaborating the relationship.

If manipulation means imposing one's own construct system on the other (treating the other as a thing), one
alternative is to invite to a *dialogue:* trying to understand the other's construct system and at the same time
clarifying one's own. This suggests a dialectic process,
as for instance role taking, uncritical acceptance, using
the invitational mood and loosening and tightening. The
assertiveness techniques we are discussing may be regarded
as further explorations of these avenues.

The notion of 'the personal scientist'* is fundamental
in our discussion. Our aim is to promote techniques which
enable us to collaborate as personal scientists: understanding each other's hypotheses, offering alternatives,
and - when the contradictions are outlined and the aims
clarified - to negotiate workable compromises.

*Kelly's term 'man - the scientist' is now regarded as a sexist term
and we suggest that it no longer be used.

34. THE REPERTORY GRID IN RESEARCH ON THE PSYCHOLOGICAL THERAPIES

DAVID WINTER

Enfield District Hospital, Middlesex

The repertory grid fulfils the need for an instrument
sensitive to those aspects of selection, process, and outcome in the psychological therapies which are both personally relevant to the client and relevant to the areas of
therapeutic focus. Results are presented from a study by
Winter and Trippett, and from ongoing research, on the usefulness of serial grid assessments in exploring such issues.

In the former study, after inspection of their initial grid, individualised predictions in grid terms of positive outcome were made for each client in a psychotherapy group, and significantly more of these predictions were confirmed than general predictions applied to each client. Also, consensus grids suggested that the typical client was initially limited in his construing by his ideal self construct but during therapy developed an actual self construct independent of the latter. The validity of inferences drawn from a statistical abstraction such as the consensus grid far removed from the raw data, is considered.

Serial assessments using grids and independent measures are at present being carried out on clients clinically assigned to group psychotherapy or behaviour therapy. These samples are differentiated by aspects of the content of their construct systems, which also correlate with measures predictive of therapeutic response. Rather than the client being a passive victim of a disease process, the content of his construing appears to actively determine the symptoms which he selects and the meaningfulness to him, and his consequent response to, different types of treatment.

Individualised predictions are proving no more successful than less laboriously and more arbitrarily derived predictions of reduction in extremity of those construct correlations and element distances which reach the 5% significance level. The issue of grid interpretation and prediction, and the desirability or otherwise of developing a general rationale for making such predictions, is discussed.

35. SOCIAL SKILLS AND SUPERORDINATE CONSTRUCTS

GREGORY C.D. YOUNG

University of Oxford, U.K.

It is argued, contrary to Kelly's Sociality Corollary, that a person may participate in a social process involving another person without accurately construing the construction process of that other. It is proposed that individuals do not need/require an accurate empathic understanding of each other to be socially competent.

The thesis of this paper is that an individual's understanding and resultant application of social skills functions as a superordinate construct cluster which subsumes and consequently integrates the rest of an individual's construct system. It is asserted that this construct cluster may initially serve to organise information; a filter which selectively perceives, by means of differentiating pertinent from non-pertinent information, an interpretation that is valued above other possibly competing conceptions.

Such a superordinate structure may be diplomatic in its function since incompatible interpretations of experiences may then be reconciled by subsuming them beneath a superordinate organisation offering higher, more abstracted similarities. On the other hand, it also allows the possibility of greater selectivity of information such that our perceptions may become over-selective; at which point the resultant interpretations become too narrow and confined to be capable of representing accurately the intended meaning of another.

It is proposed that this conceptualisation may explain recent results which suggest that social incompetence can cause or exacerbate some mental disorders. Without an integrative structure, such as a social skills orientated superordinate network, the processing and subsequent interpretations of information may become inhibited and possibly distorted, consequently affecting future relationships existing between constructs, and hence, an individual's perception of the world and himself.

36. IDENTITY DEVELOPMENT AND ETHNICITY: EXTENSIONS OF PERSONAL CONSTRUCT THEORY

PETER WEINREICH

University of Bristol, U.K.

Identity development is viewed as a socio-psychological process in which a person's changing construal of self depends on his attempts to (*a*) resolve his identification conflicts with significant others, and (*b*) integrate any new identifications he forms in changing social situations. Extensions of personal construct theory include a definition of a person's conflict in identification with another and an empirical procedure for establishing the magnitude of, and the dispersion of, his identification conflicts with several significant others. Empirical work with adolescents of Caribbean, Asian and native white parentage establishes the importance of ethnic identification conflicts in their self-concept developments. Changing identifications and reorganization of value systems over time are illustrated in certain case studies. These show that the routes to self-concept change involve sometimes complex changes in identifications across ethnic boundaries.

AUTHOR INDEX

SUBJECT INDEX